Politics, Policy, Pedagogy:
Education in Aotearoa/New Zealand

Politics, Policy, Pedagogy: Education in Aotearoa/New Zealand

Edited by
James Marshall,
Eve Coxon,
Kuni Jenkins,
Alison Jones

©2000 James Marshall, Eve Coxon, Kuni Jenkins and Alison Jones
©2000 Dunmore Press Ltd

First Published in 2000
by
Dunmore Press Limited
P.O. Box 5115
Palmerston North
New Zealand
http://www.dunmore.co.nz

Australian Supplier:
Federation Press
P.O.Box 45
Annandale 2038 NSW
Australia
Ph: (02) 9552-2200
Fax: (02) 9552-1681

ISBN 0 8 86469 379 6

Text: Times 10.5/12.6
Printer: The Dunmore Printing Company Ltd
                  Palmerston North
Cover design: Murray Lock Graphics

Contents

Preface

This book has been written by a group of colleagues who, in the main, teach at the University of Auckland's School of Education. We were concerned to produce a text for Year One students of education interested in issues of cultural and policy studies. Two earlier texts, *Myths and Realities,* first published in 1990 and revised in 1995, and *The Politics of Learning and Teaching in Aotearoa/New Zealand,* published in 1994, were dated and no longer met our needs. The former had been written mainly for liberal arts students pursuing a B.A. degree and the latter for pre-service teachers pursuing a B.Ed. degree. There is only one conjoint paper now in the area of cultural and policy studies for those degrees.

The policy orientation of this book was adopted to meet those conjoint interests and needs. At the same time we have taken the opportunity to bring the content into the twenty-first century. This is a particularly challenging time for education as we enter what has been called the knowledge economy, and we have attempted to introduce readers to these new challenges.

We wish to thank Lauren Massey for permission to use some earlier material adapted from *The Politics of Learning and Teaching in Aotearoa/ New Zealand.*

James Marshall
The University of Auckland

Politics, Policy, Pedagogy: an Introduction

James Marshall, Eve Coxon, Kuni Jenkins and Alison Jones

Apart from the stylistic effect, we have chosen the title *Politics, Policy, Pedagogy* to emphasise that whatever happens in education is influenced by pedagogy – Paulo Freire's famous book reflects this fact in its title, *Pedagogy of the Oppressed* (Freire, 1972). And what happens in pedagogy, teaching styles, curriculum, and so on, is the outcome of certain policies adopted by schools or educational institutions or governmental bureaucracies. Freire also reminds us that education can never be neutral, for it is an inherently political activity. So politics, policy and pedagogy are closely intertwined, and we attempt to show how, through consideration of a number of issues and questions related to the practice and structure of education in Aotearoa/New Zealand. At a time when the world is becoming a global village connected by electronic communication, we also look at the 'bright new future' that we are offered in the twenty-first century. The first chapter sets the theoretical historical scene in New Zealand, providing a backdrop to the more detailed discussions of contemporary issues and policies which follow.

The structures of New Zealand's educational system, at all levels, were changed quite dramatically by the fourth Labour Government (between 1984 and 1990), and by the National administration between 1990 and 1999. The new Labour administration seems intent to change, if not undo, some of those structural changes. But at the time of the changes the educational sectors, institutions, unions and associations, at all levels, did not seem able to obtain 'seats' at the agenda tables, especially when *policy* began to be implemented. In general they were not well prepared and were not ready to respond to these proposals and subsequent changes. Yet international experience of similar structural changes and changed beliefs about the purposes of education indicated what we might have expected.

This book is written on the assumption that a better understanding by *all* New Zealanders of the social, historical, ethical and political parameters that structure the conditions under which policy in education is formulated and developed will improve the quality of policy making and educational practice. Teachers, students and lay people alike should be in a better position to help set the educational agendas, and should not let themselves become the mere instrumental implementers of agendas set elsewhere.

Even though 'pedagogy' is in the title, this is not a book about *how* to teach, *what* to teach, *whom* to teach, or how to maintain discipline, though it may challenge many of our ideas about these matters. It is, however, designed to expose and clarify our *presuppositions,* or our deeper underlying and often unarticulated beliefs, on such matters. As examples, why did open-plan classrooms become the accepted mode of teaching in junior classes? Why do we test for reading performance at about age six? Why do some children receive transition, or 'work', education? Why was corporal punishment abolished in New Zealand schooling? The standard, almost given, answers to all of these questions claim that it is to do with better pedagogy, and teaching of an appropriate content for the individual learner, in a more caring and humane atmosphere. Yet once those answers are challenged, or slightly different questions asked, issues are raised about control and power and exclusion of minority groups.

Some other answers that might surface would be that open-plan classrooms presuppose middle-class forms of control which favour children from that class (Bourdieu and Passeron, 1977); that certain views about citizenship presuppose a necessary standard of functional literacy (Lankshear, 1988); that transition education is for failures who will need to be integrated into working life (Korndorffer, 1987); and that corporal punishment was not abolished on humane grounds but only when a majority of teachers were convinced that other forms of social control were possible in schools (Marshall and Marshall, 1997). When we start to get answers like these to our questions, then we can start to ask further questions about the ethnicity, class and gender of those who do not benefit from such arrangements.

As well as these sorts of ongoing questions about how the benefits of education are distributed, there are questions about issues which have recently hit headlines and which demand answers beyond the usual simple responses. Why the interest in boys' school achievement now, when boys have always 'lagged behind' girls in some areas of education? Why has touching kids become 'inappropriate' in the primary classroom, when it has in the past been considered crucial to good and caring teaching? Are male role models now necessary in the primary classroom, when they have not been there in the past? Like the previous ones, these questions are about what counts as 'good practice' which reflects political and social factors rather than some essential truth about what is best.

This book is written to raise critical and theoretical questions about the assumptions which legitimate issues in New Zealand education. At the outset it must be emphasised that it is not intended as a criticism of what New Zealand teachers generally do. New Zealand teachers are recognised internationally as being very, very good in what they do in institutional settings in regards to learning and teaching. We accept this point, but our intention is to pursue questions about the 'why' of what teachers do.

A theoretical assumption (borrowed from critical theory – see, for example, Gibson, 1986) which underpins the chapters of this book is that there is nothing 'natural' about any of the things we do in the name of schooling, or about unequal social relations and the beliefs and practices which maintain and reproduce them. We consider that critical thinking is crucially important to our discussion of the politics of education in Aotearoa/ New Zealand. Schooling (institutionalised learning and teaching) is an everyday experience – a 'given' – and the learning and teaching practices associated with it are accepted by many as natural, common-sense ways of doing things. There are, however, many issues to do with learning and teaching processes in our educational institutions which should be of concern to all professional educators, and as educational researchers and theorists we seek to identify the complexities of some of these.

Education Policy [1]

While there are introductions to the study of education for first-year students and interested lay people, there is no introductory book on New Zealand education with an explicit interest in the area of *policy studies*. Since the mid-1980s there has been an almost overwhelming amount of governmental policy directed at changing (or 'reforming') education. However, little at an introductory level has been written, either to look at those changes, or to explore the development of the underlying policy, in terms of that emerging area of studies which has come to be called *policy studies*. This book is designed, in part, to begin to fill that gap. (At more advanced levels see Marshall and Peters, 1999; Peters and Marshall, 1996; Middleton, Codd and Jones, 1990.)

But what is policy? What is an educational policy? How does a policy differ from a slogan? If a stated electoral promise is that we are going to

[1] *This section has been written by James Marshall*

improve the education facilities for pre-school children, is that to be understood as being a slogan – mere rhetoric – or a promise to provide such policies? If the latter, then would the demand that all pre-school institutions have qualified personnel count as part of a policy to improve the education of pre-schoolers? What would count against such a promise? Perhaps a refusal to pay equal salaries for qualifications across the pre-school and primary/secondary sectors might count as policy which did not promote such a promise. So how do we know what counts as a policy which promotes such a general aim, and what counts against it? Do we need some general criteria to distinguish good policies for stated aims, and, of course, bad policies? If so, we need to know how to read and understand a policy document. But more importantly, what is a policy document? This question presupposes a more fundamental question – what is a policy?

What is Policy?

This is a difficult question to answer because 'policy' refers to a wide and complex 'space' of plans, documents and practices. These, in turn, range from the complex and often unfathomable concerns, plans and workings of the state to the more tangible area of the concerns, plans and workings of such entities as local residents' associations. Education policy spans this wide and diverse range from that of the state to that of the local school. At the level of state concerns, there are general moral and political positions which governments are concerned to pursue and, indeed, often commit themselves to pursue if elected. Policy is usually directed at perceived issues or problems or new ventures, all of which depend upon knowledge or data. But the collection of information, and its classification and recording, require some theories as to *how* to collect and *what* it is important to collect. How we subsume data under wider general theories presupposes the general areas of science and the social sciences, including sociology, welfare, criminology, psychology, anthropology, politics and education (obviously not an exhaustive list). But in order to present policy briefly, and to a wide readership, often these deeper theoretical principles, concepts and prescriptions need to be assumed, or to be suppressed (because of political reasons, for example). Shifts can occur then at both the theoretical and the linguistic level. This requires an informed critical reading to ascertain what theories underlie a policy document or practice, and whether in translating from theoretical concepts to more accessible terminology something has been lost or hidden, or whether multiple readings and multiple responses can or will occur. Such questions arise as: has the absence of theory been because of further concerns about its political acceptability? Just what does devolution of responsibility mean? Is my language (and thereby culture) being devalued? We are talking, then, about forms of understanding which require some form of *critical analysis* of policy.

The question of what is policy is difficult to answer! However, in an introductory text to policy we must try to map out the terrain of policy and demarcate it from other close areas such as evaluation and the development of programmes, even if we later want to talk and work across any such boundaries. In linguistic terms we must attempt some form of *definition*, though that may be difficult if not impossible in some cases. In spite of such difficulties, let us now turn to mapping out a terrain to which we can apply the term 'policy'.

Fortunately Bruce Haynes (1997) has provided a readily accessible book that provides a number of answers to our question. As a start we might say that a policy is a set of interrelated decisions taken by an authority. This set of decisions concerns the selection of goals, or ends, and the means of achieving them in a specified situation.

What we should note in this definition are:
- the notion of a decision to select (and state?) goals (ends) and means of achieving them;
- the notion of policy as reflecting the *intentions* of certain people;
- the difference for policy between my setting personal *rules, values and philosophies,* and authorities setting policies;
- the necessary 'presence' of authorities.

Policy has been said, then, to be concerned with setting goals, but goals for what? Usually these goals are associated with a problem or an area of concern. Further important questions arise:

- *How* is the problem defined?
- *Who* defined the problem?

The Well-defined Problem

Policy analysis must look for a well-defined problem. Defining the problem is both an interpretative and an inherently politically loaded activity. In most 'problem' areas there are serious incompatibilities between rival accounts or interpretations of what *constitutes* the problem to which policy is to be directed. Discrepencies between these accounts of the problem may in some cases be unresolvable, especially when the recipient population is posed with a definition of the problem by bureaucratic and centralised-thinking technocrats. Briefly the definition of the problem must itself be located in the social and historical context. Otherwise any goal and policy will be just a means to *that* bureaucratically defined end or goal (see further Peters and Marshall, 1996: 140-143).

Policy and Practice

So far in moving towards an account or definition of 'policy' we have identified the notions of a document which states the intentions of policy makers, that they must (?) be authorities, and that a policy should give some directions for its implementation. But what of hidden or covert policies of governments, or aspects of policies which are intended but not explicitly or clearly stated? They may not be stated in public documents or even stated at all. Here we can recount the covert policies of governments and police in South Africa against freedom fighters, and the policies of torture and murder in Chile against opponents of the Pinochet regime. In New Zealand there is clearly a set of policies relating to the Security Intelligence Service which are not in public documents, or which seem contrary to what is stated in public documents. How can we identify these covert policies?

Obviously we have to identify the *practices* of those authorities. This raises a conjoint issue about the evaluation of policies. Governments in New Zealand have originated much policy but have been very tardy in evaluating the outcomes of their policies, particularly social policy. For years, at least since the famous statement in 1939 by the Minister of Education Peter Fraser on the aim of education as promoting equality of opportunity, we have collected little or no data on the outcomes of such policy initiatives.

Since the huge changes in governmental administration in the mid-1980s, we have become much more conscious of the effects of government actions, even if the reporting methods and discourse of 'measured outputs' may leave much to be desired. One can only measure quantitatively that which can be measured quantitatively. Thereby a large number of parameters and areas are ignored, particularly in general wellbeing and educational matters. And, of course,where evaluation runs counter to established policy or overt or hidden policy it may be suppressed or attacked.

Finally, human endeavours are meaningful: they have an end or a purpose. This is the case for education also. Unfortunately, much recent talk in education has replaced talk about what our goals in education really are – the ENDS – with talk about the MEANS of achieving such ends. Ends and means have become disconnected in our talk on education, and need to be reconnected. So to talk about policy we must talk about the ends of certain types of human endeavour. For an important book that tries to reverse this trend see Blake *et al.* (1998).

The reader is recommended to read Haynes (1997) on additional aspects or categories for understanding types of policy.

The Demise of Localism

There has been a major international shift in how educational policy is to be conceived and articulated in policy documents. At one time education policy was conceived, articulated, and resided in local domains – policies were localised, domestic and in the domains of nation states. Within such entities there were the concerns of localised ethnic/cultural groups, particularly those of indigenous peoples (Heyneman, 1990: 467).

Since the 1960s we have learned that there are also universal issues and dilemmas in the field of education, characteristics which transcend country categories. These are said to be 'genuinely international issues', as of much concern in OECD countries as in developing countries. Arguably some of these do not transcend national, ethnic or cultural boundaries. If they do so, this may be only because these 'universal' issues had to be formulated in accordance with certain rules, and they had to be transmitted and learned in a certain technocratic and universal manner so as to make those issues universal, and to make universal judgements possible. In other words there are universal 'definitions', which reside in a context of universalism, and which are assumed both to be meaningful and to be applicable universally. Whether they are the definitions of significant and important educational issues for particular local endeavours is, of course, another matter.

Furthermore, it is not at all obvious that definitions of other major issues such as selection, subject matter, quality, equity, and the status of teachers can be universalised beyond 'local' and particular social, cultural and ethnic contexts. They can be extended only when assumptions about universalising those definitions are made in advance. Thus education is no longer conceived as particular, if not idiosyncratic, to a domestic domain, for it has now been turned into a strategic factor in the efficiency of national economic policies.

Jean-François Lyotard (1984) talks here of 'performativity', or the subsumption of education to the efficient functioning of the social system. According to Lyotard, education is no longer concerned with the pursuit of ideals such as personal autonomy, emancipation, or leadership, but, instead, with the means, techniques or skills that both contribute to the efficient operation of the state in the world market and to the maintenance of an internal cohesion and legitimation of the state. However this requires individuals of a certain kind – perhaps *easily governable* individuals. It also requires particular roles for individuals and the state, and a particular relationship between the state and individuals which ensures not only the security and economic wellbeing and power of the state, but also the welfare and wellbeing of the population.

How to Understand Policy Documents

When we see a statement of policy, such as an official document produced by a state agency (e.g. Ministry of Education), we normally expect it to be a statement of the intentions of that agency, of what they wish to introduce or change within a particular area of their responsibility. But is that statement neutral, concerned to improve education overall, for all people in New Zealand, or is it also a weighted political document? Thus, if decisions are taken to increase subsidies for private schooling whilst at the same time providing scholarships or subsidies for less well-advantaged students to attend such schools, do we interpret this as improving education overall, or is it also, or merely, a policy for directing resources to a particular sector of the nation? No doubt such decisions could be defended as improving the best schools by improving the quality of their students, at the same time as promoting equality of opportunity by providing access to such quality schools. However, it might be asked, why is there a quality gap between state and private schools? Why is this gap, apparently, being maintained, if not increased? Why are resources not directed instead at reducing such a gap, by allocating scarce resources to improving state schools?

If we wish to know the likely outcomes of such policies and/or the intentions of legislators, what this example illustrates is that we need some way of reading or understanding policy documents, so that these issues can be exposed or brought to the surface. Is the policy in the example above a humanitarian gesture by well-meaning bureaucrats and politicians, to improve the lot of children from economically disadvantaged social circumstances? Or is it a more cynical move, to attract voters who already send their children to private schools? What are the effects of diverting these resources, or of moving children from one set of social and cultural practices to a culture which may be very different? As a start to reading these documents we need, then, a *critical* 'nose'.

Reading Policy

We are fortunate that, in New Zealand, John Codd (1988) has provided a schema or method for understanding education policy documents. Initially we will look at his views. His concern is that the orthodox liberal view of the state's function as a neutral provider of opportunities for social mobility, and as acting in 'the public interest', has been called in question by both neo-Marxist and neo-liberal criticisms of education. Both ideologies criticise the state for producing policy which serves a political purpose, 'constructing particular meanings and signs that work to mask social conflict and foster commitment to the notion of a universal public interest' (Codd, 1988: 21). Under a cry of 'what we all want', the effects of these policies and documents are the production and maintenance of consent, but from policy documents (the official discourse of the state) which are inherently contradictory.

Codd discusses some of the ways in which such documents can be understood. First he discusses what he calls the technical-empiricist approach to policy making – possibly the most common way of interpreting the situation (ibid.). Here policy analysis is interpreted as a *means* to an end – the analysis of the reports on information relevant to the issue provided by researchers, the production of the document by the policy makers, and the interpretation and implementation of the policy by policy providers. The end – the policy document – can be seen as a vehicle of communication between these three poles of policy. The outcome, from this point of view, is to understand the policy document as a statement of the courses of action which the policy makers *intend.*

Unfortunately, as many people will have taken part in the production of the text of the policy document, it is not obvious that the text can be taken as evidence of the intentions of the state. All that we have as evidence for any such intentions is the text itself. Therefore, as we cannot ask the writers, to gain any idea of what those intentions might be, we have to know something about the context in which the text was written. More simply, to ascertain my intentions when I say to a group gossiping on the corner that I am going to the shop, something needs to be known about the context. Am I the owner, and late to open my shop? Do I go each morning to purchase a newspaper? Do I need cigarettes? Or do I have a list in my hand, written by my partner? There are different possible answers here to a question concerning my intentions. Some possibilities for my intentions are to assume my responsibilities to customers; to protect my commercial interests; to do the crossword or to read the sports results; to appease my craving for nicotine; to appease my garrulous, demanding partner, etc. In order to be certain of what my intentions are, we need to know the contexts and which of these aspects are true at this time.

Thus, even in a very simple instance, we cannot be sure about the intentions of a stated 'policy' concerning actions (mundane as it is). If it is difficult to be clear about the intentions in a simple example like this, then it may be extremely difficult in a complex case like the state and its education policy.

Rather than searching for the intentions of authors, suppose that we take the text and examine the differing *effects* upon its readers. In the shop example above, the effects may be as follows: one person may interpret my remark as exhibiting my social and civic responsibilities, and decide to support me for council. A second, of Marxist persuasion, may mutter darkly some anti-capitalist slogan. Another well-meaning individual may tell me the football score (even though I want to know more about the match), whilst another, an inveterate smoker and a scrounger, may walk with me in the hope of a free cigarette. Finally, the local Anglican lay preacher may see, yet again, my loving and caring behaviour! All of these are possible effects upon the listeners of what has been said. These effects are very different. There are issues in this example to do with improving information, meeting needs, offering services, balancing the books, and caring for others. Any one of these responses could also be part of a response to an education policy document!

Codd's point is that education policy documents have been *constructed* in a particular social and historical context. In order to understand such documents, we need to understand that context. The method of anchoring the text into its social and historical context is referred to by Codd as *deconstructing the text* (Codd, 1988: 27-30).

The Book

In Chapter 1 Judith Simon provides an historical underpinning of the evolution of educational policies in Aotearoa/New Zealand. This is not a blow-by-blow account of what happened, but a critical historical investigation of the myths that we have generated and maintained in New Zealand about our education system. She is particularly concerned about the myth of equality. She deals with this vast topic by dividing it into three workable sections. These are: the events leading up to the 1877 Education Act and the Secondary Schooling Act of 1903; the development of schooling for Maori; and the events of the twentieth century in education in relation to the education of Maori and the promotion of racial harmony.

In the next chapter, 'Gender Matters in Schooling in Aotearoa/New Zealand', Alison Jones addresses what are considered the most popular contemporary questions on the terrain of gender and schooling in Aotearoa/New Zealand. The issue which has gained most educational and media attention in the late 1990s has been the education of boys. Why is it that such attention and anxiety is generated at this particular time? Is it because boys' advocates have recognised the significance of being disadvantaged, and are now required to engage in a 'politics of vulnerability' in order to get attention and resources? Is it because boys are responding to the shifting, globalising labour market and on-going mechanisation in ways which render irrelevant schooling as we know it? It may be that boys are a barometer of the disjunction between a schooling system which has essentially remained unchanged for decades, and the new requirements of a technologically and globally based market economy.

On the other hand, girls' and boys' school achievement, when measured by grades, is not significantly different. The major differences in achievement are those between social class and ethnic groups, where Maori and Pacific Islands and working class people still gain far less than a fair share of educational resources and credentials in Aotearoa/New Zealand. If gender differentials are relatively insignificant, why then does gender remain an issue in schooling?

In Chapter 3 Roger Dale outlines the importance of the promise of education to provide equality of opportunity for people's futures, determined on the basis of their achievement rather than on the basis of their ascribed status, such as gender, age or ethnicity. The chapter's particular focus is on the relationship between social class and educational achievement. Fundamentally it shows that working class children and students underachieve in comparison with their middle class counterparts. The evidence, both from New Zealand and internationally, clearly shows that not only are working class children less successful in the education system, but that for any given level of qualification, working class students are less successful in the labour market. The remainder of the chapter examines some explanations for this relationship. It considers both arguments that see it as a result of 'working class failure' (which have historically received most attention) and those that see it as a result of 'middle class success'. It approaches these explanations through a threefold breakdown of how class works – through class-related dispositions and resources, and through the different power of different classes. Its conclusions are broadly pessimistic: that the gap between working class and middle class children in capacity to benefit from schooling is already large before they reach school; that school processes and practices are more akin to those that middle class children are used to; and that middle class parents are better able to access the benefits of education for their children. Overall, the problem is seen as *systemic* rather than the 'fault' of any group or groups within the system. In light of this it is suggested that the education system might be seen as successful in limiting the worst effects of class differences in schools, as much as unsuccessful in not eliminating them.

The 'Maori Education Policy' chapter, by Kuni Jenkins and Alison Jones, focuses on the Ministry of Education's bold new statement of purpose on their web page (www.minedu.govt.nz/web/doc): *Te Ihi, Te Mana, Te Mātauranga: Empowering Education.* This slogan, in its balanced use of Maori and Pakeha language and concepts, looks at first glance as though it marks the truly bicultural intent in New Zealand education policy. However, with a closer look, it becomes clear that this slogan contains within it a tension which lies at the heart of contemporary education policy for Maori in Aotearoa/New Zealand. The Maori text, with its reference to Maori power, knowledge and status, reflects a strong sense of place and standing, and existing power for Maori in education. But the Pakeha phrasing suggests that Maori are yet *to be made* powerful, or *to become* powerful. The tension between Maori and Pakeha understandings of education are played out in a range of policy texts and practices. While there is a desire on all sides to 'reduce disparity' between Maori and Pakeha in the education system, Maori interpretations of what counts as disparity, and how it might be reduced, often do not match those of Pakeha. Ultimately, Pakeha still maintain firm control – even within a 'devolved' system – of Maori education.

The concerns expressed by Eve Coxon and Diane Mara in Chapter 5 on Pacific Nations' education are with educational issues pertaining to both education in Pacific countries and to Pacific peoples in Aotearoa/ New Zealand. In order to provide a critical analysis of education policy in both arenas, this chapter is presented in two parts. The first part focuses on the ongoing educational relationships between New Zealand, as one of the larger and more powerful states within the South Pacific, and the small states of the region. In order to demonstrate the shifts in New Zealand's education policy for Pacific countries, New Zealand's historical location in the region during the periods of colonialism and decolonisation is outlined. The post-colonial period is then discussed with particular attention to how New Zealand's economic restructuring and education policy redirection over the past 10-15 years has impacted on the small island countries of the Pacific. The second part of the chapter traces developments in education over the past thirty years or so for New Zealand-based Pacific Nations peoples. It argues that an understanding of the political, social and economic context of Pacific communities, as a significant minority population within Aotearoa/New Zealand, requires the employment of the sociological concept of 'marginalisation'. This concept is used to describe how structures and policies operate to exclude the interests of minorities and to confine them to a subordinate position. The chapter critically analyses present education policy directions, in terms of whether or not they ensure equity of access, treatment and outcome in educational provision for Pacific peoples.

In the final chapter James Marshall looks at the allegedly 'Bright Futures and the Knowledge Economy', in relation to education. In late 1999, the New Zealand Government launched what it called The Bright Future Package which was an attempt by government to coordinate the education, research, business and government sectors. James Marshall argues that none of this is particularly new, as many of the changes required for what has been called the knowledge economy and the knowledge society have already been introduced in New Zealand education. There were the changes to the national curriculum in 1993, the first official document on technology and education in 1995, and a series of restructurings of education dating back to 1988 at least. Marshall looks at neo-liberalism, knowledge, information and skills, technology and education, vocationalism, new managerialism and the possible effects of globalisation. His final question concerns the future, and whether it will be bright or just different.

References

Blake, N., Smeyers, P., Smith, R. and Standish, P. (1998), *Thinking Again: Education after Postmodernism,* London & New York: Routledge.

Bourdieu, Pierre and Passeron, Jean-Claude (1977), *Reproduction in Education, Society and Culture,* transl. Richard Nice, London & Beverley Hills: Sage

Codd, John A. (1988), 'The Construction and Deconstruction of Educational Policy Documents', *Journal of Educational Policy,* 3(3), pp. 235–247. Reprinted in J. Marshall and M. Peters (eds) (1999), *Education Policy,* Cheltenham: Edward Elgar.

Freire, P. (1972), *Pedagogy of the Oppressed,* Harmondsworth: Penguin.

Gibson, R. (1986), *Critical Theory and Education,* London: Hodder and Stoughton.

Haynes, B. (1997), *Education Policy*, Wentworth Falls, NSW: Social Science Press.

Heyneman, S. P. (1990), 'The World Economic Crisis and the Quality of Education', *Journal of Educational Finance,* 15 (4), pp. 456–469.

Korndorffer, Wanda (ed.) (1987), *Transition: Perspectives on School to Work in New Zealand,* Palmerston North: Dunmore Press.

Lankshear, C.J. with Lawler, M. (1998), *Literacy, Schooling and Revolution,* London: Falmer Press.

Lyotard, J-F. (1984), *The Postmodern Condition: A Report on Knowledge,* Minnesota: University of Minnesota Press.

Marshall, James D. and Marshall, Dominique James (1997), *Discipline and Punishment in New Zealand Education,* Palmerston North: Dunmore Press.

Marshall, J. D. and Peters, M. A. (eds) (1999), *Education Policy,* Cheltenham: Edward Elgar.

Middleton,S., Codd, J. and Jones, A. (eds) (1990), *New Zealand Education Policy Today: Critical Perspectives*, Palmerston North: Dunmore Press.

Peters, M. A. and Marshall, J. D. (1996), *Individualism and Community: Education and Social Policy in the Postmodern Condition,* London: Falmer Press.

Chapter 1

Education Policy Change: Historical Perspectives

Judith Simon

The Beginnings of Public Schooling in New Zealand

New Zealand has had a national system of education since 1877. Reflecting on this state education system, a British educational commentator (Bird, 1930) asserted that the development of New Zealand society and, hence, its education system, had been guided by two principal ideals: egalitarianism and racial harmony. In this chapter we shall be looking at the way the policies underlying the New Zealand education system have developed, and considering the extent to which those claims are justified.

This section is concerned with events leading up to the Education Act of 1877 and the Secondary Schools Act 1903, and the extent to which these Acts and their outcomes supported egalitarianism. The following section looks at the development of schooling for Maori in the nineteenth and early twentieth centuries, and considers how it exemplifies the ideal of racial harmony. The final section examines public schooling in New Zealand throughout the twentieth century in relation to both egalitarianism and racial harmony. To begin with, however, we need to examine the notion of egalitarianism itself.

Egalitarianism

The *Concise Oxford Dictionary* (1990) defines egalitarianism as 'relating to the principle of equal rights and opportunities for all'. This definition accords with the following explanation of democracy offered by T. B. Bottomore (1964: 129):

> It implies that there should be a substantial degree of equality among

men [and women], both in the sense that all adult members of a society ought to have, as far as possible, an equal influence upon those
decisions which affect important aspects of the life of the society,
and in the sense that inequalities of wealth, of social rank, or of education and access to knowledge, should not be so considerable as to
result in the permanent subordination of some groups to others in any
of the various spheres of social life, or to create great inequalities in
the actual exercise of political rights.

An egalitarian society, therefore, would not have significant class
differences, nor would it have significant inequalities in relation to gender
or ethnicity, as all such social groups would enjoy equal rights and
opportunities. An egalitarian education system, therefore, could be taken
to be one that promoted equal rights and opportunities for all members in
the society in general. It is important to recognise, however, that the
concepts of 'equality' and 'egalitarianism' are open to a number of different
interpretations. In New Zealand education the term 'equality' has been
used variously to mean 'equality of access' to education, 'equality of
treatment' and 'equality of opportunity' and 'equality of outcomes' (see
McKenzie, 1975; Braithwaite, 1982).

The ideal of egalitarianism was nurtured in New Zealand in the early
years of European settlement. Most settlers in the nineteenth century came
from Great Britain – a rigidly class-based society. At that time, members
of the lower classes in Great Britain had fewer rights and opportunities
than members of the middle and upper classes. For example, because voting
rights were tied to ownership of property, those who were too poor to own
property had no votes. Thus privilege was *inherited* by those born into the
middle and upper classes.

Most of the immigrants from Great Britain to New Zealand in the
nineteenth century were from the upper working classes and the lower
middle classes – referred to by Wakefield as 'the anxious classes' (Sinclair,
1988: 101). They were ambitious and enterprising people, emigrating in
search of material advancement. Most of them had experienced class
oppression in their homeland and were seeking to escape from it here.
New Zealand was seen as a brave new world; a land where equal
opportunities were available to all regardless of class background and
where, for those prepared to work hard, there were no barriers to success.

Yet the reality of New Zealand society contradicted these perceptions.

While many perceived it as a classless egalitarian society, the politics and economy of New Zealand from the 1850s to the 1890s were, in fact, dominated by a small élite class of landowners, merchants and other influential people (Simpson, 1984: 19-27). Nevertheless, egalitarianism was held up by many as the ideal by which the development of the society should be guided and, without doubt, this perspective played a significant part in the establishing of the national education system.

The 1877 Education Act laid the foundation of the New Zealand education system as we know it today. It provided, for the first time in New Zealand, *a national* system of education at the primary school level that was *funded* by the state and *controlled* by the state. This, however, occurred thirty-seven years after the signing of the Treaty of Waitangi and, as we know, settlers had been arriving in large numbers throughout those years. What had happened during that period as far as schooling was concerned? Had there been schools? And if so, who had funded and controlled them?

The Early Schools for Settlers' Children

Schools were started almost as soon as the first settlers arrived. From 1840 through to 1853 schools were established and run by churches and by individuals on a private enterprise basis. Fees up to one shilling a week were charged in most cases.

The types of schooling provided at that time, as one would expect, were modelled on the English and Scottish systems of the period – often with very little modification (UNESCO, 1972: 10). The first school in Auckland opened in 1843. It was a Roman Catholic school but was not restricted to Catholic children – indeed, non-Catholics had also contributed towards setting it up. The subjects taught were 'all the branches of the common good education', together with needlework for the girls (Mackey, 1967: 44-45).

Until 1870, however, no more than half of New Zealand children aged between five and fifteen went to school. There were no compulsory attendance laws. This was a matter of concern for a number of members of society who believed strongly that elementary schooling should be available to all children, and even compulsory. One such campaigner for universal education was Alfred Domett. In 1849 he was advocating universal schooling largely on the grounds that it would assist in developing the moral character of the child and, in doing so, would help to prevent crime. Thus we see that schooling was perceived by some, not so much as a means of increasing the life-chances of the child, but as a means of social control. Support for such social control of youth grew stronger in the latter years of the century, as changing social conditions produced destitute and neglected children who roamed the streets, engendering moral panic through their activities (see Shuker, 1987a).

Social control was also one of the major objectives behind moves leading to the establishment of universal education in Britain in 1870. (For discussions on the different arguments associated with the establishment of universal schooling in Britain, see Simon, 1974; Silver, 1983.) Settlers in New Zealand during the late 1860s had access to newspapers from Britain which reported extensively on the debates raging there on the idea of universal schooling, so they were familiar with the various arguments promoted. New settlers arriving during this period were a further source of information on these issues. These factors all had a strong influence on the situation in New Zealand. Egalitarianism, therefore, was not the only guiding principle behind the drive to establish universal schooling in New Zealand.

The Provincial Schools

For the first twelve years after the signing of the Treaty of Waitangi New Zealand, as a Crown Colony, was politically controlled by Great Britain. In 1852, however, the Constitution Act heralded the beginning of self-government. The country was divided into six provinces, each with its own provincial council. As it became clear that the churches did not have sufficient resources to continue running the schools, these provincial councils gradually took responsibility for education within their own areas (McGeorge and Snook, 1981: 7). Consequently the systems of schooling developed differently in the various provinces, these differences being related, to a large extent, to the ways schools had developed in those settlements before the provinces were set up. While in some cases funds were allocated to the church schools, there was also a general move towards the establishment of publicly funded schools controlled by the provincial councils through education boards and local committees (ibid.: 8).

Mackey (1967: 62) observes that opinions concerning education during the provincial period became more widespread and more diverse than during the Crown Colony period, with more people having the opportunity to express their views because of the existence of popular assemblies. Debates focused largely upon the control of schooling, the funding of schooling and the place of religious instruction within schooling.

The Nelson province has generally been credited with setting up the most efficient system. It was to become a model not only for the other provinces but also eventually for state educational legislation (Mackey, 1967: 92- 93). The Nelson Provincial Council developed a system of local taxes for education, taking over some of the existing schools and making grants to denominational schools. This meant that the fees could be kept very low, making the schools available to most children. Any religious instruction in these schools was required to be 'free from all controversial character and imparted at such hours that parents objecting [might] be able to withdraw their children from the school at the time when it is given'. By this means Nelson effected a compromise between the factions debating the issue of religious instruction in schools, namely the secularists and the supporters of religious education (Campbell, 1941: 29 – 33; Mackey, 1967: 92-98).

Both Otago and Canterbury had been settled under religious auspices; the former by the Presbyterians and the latter by Anglicans. In both cases provisions were made for large endowments for religious and educational purposes (Campbell, 1941: 33). Thus schools had been set up and run in Otago mainly by the Presbyterian church, and in Canterbury largely by the Anglican church (Mackey, 1967: 107-118). Otago developed an efficient provincial system largely funded through first, an annual poll tax on adult males, and then through rates. Fees, however, were still charged and, although low, they served to exclude the poorest children from access to schooling. A distinctive feature of the Otago system, reflecting its Scottish heritage, was the provision also of a high school. While the first Education Ordinance (1956) under the Otago Provincial Council decreed that secular instruction should be available to children of all religious denominations, tensions developed in Otago as the Presbyterian church resisted efforts to loosen its hold on the system (Mackey, 1967: 118-130; Campbell, 1941: 33-44). In Canterbury the provincial government made grants directly to the heads of the Anglican, Wesleyan and Presbyterian churches, leaving it to them to organise and control schooling as they saw fit. Later, however, as a result of disputes between secularists and supporters of religious schooling, funding was withdrawn from the private denominational schools and provided only for public schools (Campbell, 1941: 39-41).

The South Island provinces, it can be seen, developed reasonably effective systems of public schooling. Progress in the North Island, however, was much slower. This was mainly for economic reasons, with the North Island provincial governments suffering frequent financial difficulties. As late as 1872 neither Wellington nor Auckland had set up a single common school (Campbell, 1941: 42).

In Wellington schools had been run by a number of churches, but they had charged very high fees and by doing so had kept their clientele very exclusive. Only the well-off could afford schooling for their children. Under the first Education Act of the Wellington Provincial Council, schooling became militantly secular. The council refused to make grants to the church schools and it was intended that the public schools would be funded from a special rate. The Act, however, was largely inoperative within the city of Wellington and the private and church schools continued to provide most of the schooling there throughout the provincial period. It was not until the beginning of the 1870s that Wellington began to make much progress in building up a public education system.

In Auckland province, the situation was different again. There was very little money available from provincial taxes since most of that money had been used in the Land Wars against the Maori. The schools were run almost entirely by the churches until 1869, when an Act was passed to provide secular schooling for all children. (It was unable to take immediate effect, however, because of financial difficulties.) There was general agreement during this period until 1872 that education in Auckland was in a lamentable state, with thousands of children going without schooling (Mackey, 1967: 101-107).

Efforts to Develop a National System – The Education Act, 1877

By the 1870s it was becoming evident that, overall, the way in which schooling was organised throughout the country was producing gross inequalities. While the prosperity then reigning in the southern provinces enabled them to develop and maintain effective public-funded education systems, the situation in the northern provinces was markedly different. Auckland, for instance, after a decade of the Land Wars together with stagnation in land sales, was almost in a state of bankruptcy (Mackey, 1967: 105). Furthermore, statistics gathered in 1869 revealed that substantial numbers of children, even in the prosperous areas, were not receiving schooling of any kind (McKenzie, 1969: 26). Overall, public dissatisfaction with the quality and quantity of the education services available was beginning to grow, leading to demands from a number of sources for a national system of education (ibid.: 25). As J.D.S. McKenzie (1969: 250) observes, New Zealand by 1870 was beginning to think as a nation, and there was growing support for the principle that education facilities should be available to all children in the land.

Events overseas also had a bearing on the thinking of the public. Inevitably the debates in Britain on universal schooling had an influence on views here. Politicians and others calling for universal schooling, however, were not necessarily in agreement with one another on the roles that schooling should perform within society. Some who were concerned about the growing numbers of urchins who were beginning to roam the streets, perceived schooling as a means of social control (McKenzie, 1975: 93). Others were motivated by the belief that it was the right of every citizen to be educated – 'that whatever capabilities he may have in him [*sic*] however small, may have some fair chance of development' (ibid.). Some (mostly from the impoverished provinces) claimed that state-funding schooling would be an equaliser, in that it would provide the same opportunities for children from the poorer areas of the country to gain access to schooling as were provided for children from the wealthier areas (McKenzie, 1969: 26). A major reason, therefore, for demands for universal education and, eventually, the 1977 Act, was concern to bring about equal access to schooling for all children (see McKenzie, 1975: 93-94).

These ideas about equality in 1877 had been shaped by perceptions of what had been promoting inequalities beforehand. Some children, for a number of reasons, had been given the opportunity to go to school while others had not. Hence access to schooling was seen as the solution. To facilitate this, the 1877 Act contained a clause to make schooling *compulsory*. This idea had not been supported by all communities. Nevertheless, as McKenzie (1975: 93) observes, the claim that 'in the interests of equality of enjoyment of individual right, parental discretion should be foregone and attendance at school enforced upon all children of legislatively defined school age' became one of the moral imperatives underpinning the Act. (It is important to remember, however, that compulsory schooling was also sought for other reasons, particularly that of social control.)

Richard Harker (1985: 57-60) has analysed the parliamentary debates leading up to the 1877 Act and identified four major arguments presented in favour of universal education. These were (1) social control; (2) the production of a discerning electorate; (3) the enhancement of productivity; and (4) individual rights to education. As he points out, while arguments (2) and (4) reflect humanitarian and egalitarian ideals, the others can be seen to be concerned with economics and law and order. Harker asserts that universal education became a reality *only* because all four arguments happened to point in the same direction.

Under the Act, the Department of Education was set up to centralise control of schooling, but some control and influence were still to remain in the various regions through the establishment of education boards. A third and minor level of control was to be with the local school committees. Through the Department of Education, grants from the consolidated fund were to be made to the education boards and the school committees, calculated on the average attendance in the school. This was intended to be a fairer system than that which had operated previously. Schools could be provided in areas that previously had been unable to afford them, and school fees were abolished. Seemingly, therefore, no child was to be denied access to schooling on the grounds of poverty (see Mackey, 1967: 180-81; Cumming and Cumming, 1978: 97-102). Together the new measures might be seen as actively supporting egalitarianism and the belief that education was the *right* of all citizens, not a privilege.

There were some other complicating factors, however, that had not been resolved. In taking over the control of the schools, the state was taking control away from the churches. This, in turn, raised a number of questions concerning the role of the churches in relation to the schools. If church schools were to be supported, would this involve all churches – or just some churches? (There was strong opposition in some quarters to state aid for Catholic schools.) Debates also raged on whether there should be religious teaching in state schools. An examination by Davis (cited in McGeorge and Snook, 1981: 8) of the debates and divisions of 1877, discerned three separate groups: (1) secularists opposed to both religious instruction in state schools and aid to denominational schools; (2) those who supported the Catholic case for state aid but were opposed to religious instruction in state schools; (3) those who wanted religious instruction in state schools but were opposed to aid for Catholic schools. Eventually the perceived solution to these problems was to have no religious teaching in the schools funded by the state, and not to give state aid to church schools. Hence the decision was made that New Zealand state schools should be *secular* (see Dakin, 1986; Mackey, 1967: 153-177).

It is clear that the Act was expected, amongst other things, to overcome particular inequalities in the society by making available to all children 'equality of enjoyment of individual right' to schooling (see McKenzie, 1975: 93). The Act set out to provide, first, elementary schooling (i.e. schooling at the primary level) that was free for all children aged between five and fifteen, secular and (in general) compulsory for all children aged between seven and thirteen. Second, it seemingly set out to provide impartial control of schooling. With the state in control, it was assumed there would be no privilege of one locality over another, nor of one religion over another. The state was perceived as a neutral body which would distribute funds, and hence opportunities, impartially.

A year later further regulations were enacted to establish a national standards syllabus, intended to ensure that all children would have access to the same body of knowledge (McKenzie, 1975: 94; see also Dennis, 1979, for an examination of the standards that had prevailed in the provinces). In order to be promoted from one standard to the next, pupils were required to pass an examination, supervised by an inspector, in reading, spelling and dictation, writing, composition, arithmetic and, at Standard VI level, geography and drawing. The guidelines for teachers on the 'standards' were very specific; for example the Standard II prescription for spelling was 'Words of one or two syllables, including words containing silent letters or other peculiarities, and easy words of three syllables' (Department of Education, 1900: 11). Arithmetic prescribed for Standard II was:

> Numeration and notation of not more than six figures; addition of not more than six lines with six figures in a line; short multiplication, and multiplication by factors not greater than twelve; subtraction; division by numbers not exceeding 12, by the method of long division,

and by the method of short division; multiplication tables to 12 times 12; relative values and chief aliquot parts of the ton, hundred-weight, quarter, stone and pound; relative lengths of the mile, furlong, chain and rod. Mental arithmetic adapted to this stage of progress.

Did the 1877 Act Promote 'Equality'?

We need to look now at the outcomes to see whether the Act really did promote 'equality' in the society – whether it helped to develop a more egalitarian society.

In the first place the Act was concerned only with elementary – or primary – schooling. Thus it set out to provide equal opportunities for all children to have access to a *basic* education only. There were secondary schools operating at this time but, like the former primary schools, they charged fees. The Act did nothing to change the way in which they operated. Students who wanted a secondary education still had to pay fees, and this, of course, helped to maintain the class differences that the Act was expected to overcome.

Rather than do away with fees for secondary schools at this time, the state provided scholarships for children of unusual attainment and ability to carry on their education at any school approved by the Board (NZPD, 1877: 37). As the Minister of Justice who had drawn up the Education Bill explained:

> It is especially provided that reasonable district fees should be paid, because special provision is made for children of special attainments obtaining assistance by means of scholarships. It is not intended to encourage children whose vocation is that of honest labour to waste in the higher schools time which might be devoted to learning a trade...
>
> (ibid.)

At the same time, however, the Act did not prevent anyone whose family *could* pay the fees from attending secondary school – no matter how lacking in attainment and ability they might be. Thus, the supposedly neutral state was sanctioning access of the already privileged groups to secondary schooling, while placing restrictions on the access to it of those who lacked these privileges. This could only serve to reinforce class differences.

Such anomalies became the subject of fierce debate – especially as the secondary schools were largely endowed through public funds. Premier Richard Seddon was one of those who attacked the inequities of the system, stating:

> I have seen schools where there were children of eight, ten and eleven who could not pass Standard Three ... . But these schools are endowed with public funds... . If I had the power I would turn out every pupil who could not pass Standard Six... . The highest education must be brought within the reach of all so that all the brightest intellects may be highly educated for the benefit of the whole country.
>
> (cited in McLaren, 1987: 79)

While this argument undoubtedly reflects an attempt to make the education system more egalitarian, its reliance on the Standards examination system meant that it could still perpetuate inequalities. This system led to the situation where teachers placed primary emphasis on gaining high pass rates. As a result, students were encouraged to learn by rote for the exams. Inspectors reported on cases where pupils were able to recite the definition of an island, but were unable to identify an island on a map (McKenzie, 1975: 96). Furthermore, education boards could be seen to be encouraging such outcomes. Kay Matthews (1988: 35) explains that the Hawke's Bay Education Board 'offered a bonus to teachers if their pupils did well in the Standard Examinations' and observes:

> It is not surprising, therefore, that teachers actively discouraged those pupils likely to fail from attending examinations. 'Percentage of passes' became the only aim worth pursuing when professional reputation and bonus depended on them.

The Secondary Schools Act, 1903

In 1903 the Secondary Schools Act of the Seddon government provided for free places in secondary schools for all children who completed their primary schooling with a Certificate of Proficiency. This seemingly set out to overcome the earlier inequalities. However, there were differences in the *types* of secondary schooling provided. Provisions had been made in 1900 for manual, technical and commercial education in schools. 1905 heralded the establishment of the first technical high school, and by 1910 technical high schools had been established by law in all the main centres (see McKenzie, 1992; McKenzie, Lee and Lee, 1990). These moves inevitably helped the education system to continue to operate as a social filter, with middle class children mostly being channelled into academic education and working class children mostly being encouraged into manual and trade-type education.

These moves reflected the ideology of meritocracy which had begun to rise over the past twenty or so years. Sometimes referred to as the 'meritocratic myth', this ideology can be represented by the equation ABILITY + EFFORT = MERIT. John Codd (1985: 43-44) explains how expansions in the tertiary sector of the labour market at this time – including public and private sectors, commerce, transport and communications – had led to a great deal of social mobility, with the resulting competition for social status representing a threat to the established middle and upper classes. Schooling thus became a site of struggle between, on the one hand those demanding social equality and, on the other, those demanding social selectivity. Pressure was therefore placed on schools to distribute educational qualifications through a system of credentialling that would be accepted as fair to all sectors of society (ibid.). The ideology of meritocracy, in this context, was to assume an important role: that of concealing the contradictions embodied in a *selective* education system that was offering to extend opportunities and rewards across social boundaries in order to produce a more egalitarian society. The central goal of education under meritocracy was to make the curriculum and its associated credentials available to *all*, in such a way that differences in achievement and reward would be perceived as the outcomes of differences in the abilities and efforts of individuals. An important development which assisted these selection processes and, seemingly, validated their outcomes, was that of the group intelligence test (ibid.). Thus, in order to provide equality of opportunity to all on the basis of merit, schools were expected to select and group children on the basis of presumed differences in ability, and then reward them differentially in terms of their achievement (ibid.; see also Openshaw, Lee and Lee, 1993; McKenzie, 1987; Shuker, 1987b).

There were also differences in the schooling opportunities provided for boys and girls. Ruth Fry (1985: 47) points out that girls were not encouraged to learn mathematics, the reason offered being that they lacked the innate ability to cope with the subject. Indeed, she says, it was argued by some that 'too much mental exertion on mathematics would be mentally and physically debilitating and possibly de-sexing' (see also Fry, 1988: 33; O'Neill, 1992: 83-86). On similar grounds girls were also denied opportunities to learn related subjects such as geometrical drawing and physical science. Dr Truby King, the founder of the Plunket Society, was a strong opponent of higher education for women, claiming that excessive schoolwork was damaging to the mental health of girls. He asserted that brain work sapped from girls the strength they should be storing for motherhood (Fry, 1988: 35). On the other hand, as Margaret Tennent (1977: 146) notes, it was assumed that the education of girls in the housewifely arts would provide:

> ...an economical and seductively simple solution to such wide-ranging problems as wife-desertion, poverty, child-neglect and juvenile delinquency by making the wholesome charms of the home more compelling than the suspect attractions of the urban street or bar!

Fry (1985: 47) observes, however, that another reason why girls were not given opportunities in the area of the physical sciences was economic. Funding to girls' schools was either very small or non-existent. Hence subjects such as chemistry and physics, which required equipment, were discouraged. When science was eventually introduced as a compulsory curriculum subject for girls, it was in the form of home science. The prescription was for 'elementary science related to the home and domestic hygiene'. The focus, therefore was on preparing girls for domestic roles in society rather than on increasing their life-chances (ibid.: 50-51).

Fry (1988: 39) also points out that from 1919, girls taking home science for Matriculation were permitted to take arithmetic rather than full mathematics. (The option was also available to boys taking agriculture but was used by them less often.) While at the time this was perceived as a form of affirmative action, the outcome was that in some girls' schools arithmetic *only* was offered. The practice, observes Fry (ibid.), 'which was to persist till 1943':

...hardened the attitude that girls were less able in mathematics and would have less use for the subject. It contributed to the vicious circle which produced a limited number of women qualified to teach the subject. At the same time it meant that there were two levels of Matriculation, a pass with mathematics being considered superior.

Thus we see that while the Education Act of 1877 and the Secondary Schools Act of 1903 may have been intended to promote equality in terms of access to schooling, the processes of schooling nevertheless helped to perpetuate inequalities related to gender and social class.

European-Style Schooling for Maori – The First Century

It is often assumed that the Education Act of 1877 signalled the beginning of state involvement in education in New Zealand. In fact, the state had begun a system of schooling for Maori children ten years before that, with the Native Schools Act in 1867. However, even *this* was not the beginning of state involvement in schooling in New Zealand. Twenty years earlier, in 1847, the Governor had begun giving subsidies to the schools run by the missionaries for Maori children. An important question we need to ask is: Why did the government make provisions for the schooling of Maori during this period?

Many who know something about the early Maori schools might respond to this question by saying that schooling was provided for Maori in order to assimilate them into European culture. This is quite true, but by itself is an inadequate explanation. It simply leads to another question: why did the government want to assimilate Maori into European culture? To answer this we need to consider what the notion of assimilation involves, and examine some of the implications it has as a social policy.

Assimilation

The notion of assimilation as a social policy developed out of nineteenth-century European beliefs about race and civilisation. Most Europeans of this time perceived the races of the world in hierarchical terms ranging from inferior to superior, from savage races through to civilised races. The British in particular perceived themselves as representing the pinnacle of civilisation.

The missionaries in New Zealand were predominantly British and perceived civilisation and Christianity as closely bound up with each other. Hence they set out to 'civilise' the Maori, to prepare them to receive the Christian gospel. Civilising the Maori involved persuading them to give up their customs, habits, values and language, and take on those of the European – in other words, assimilating them into European culture. During the early missionary period the missionaries did not seek full assimilation of the Maori. They did not attempt to teach them the English language but instead chose to learn the Maori language themselves. Statesmen were also anxious to assimilate the Maori into European culture. At the time of the Treaty of Waitangi (1840), and in the early years of colonisation, this concern, to a large extent, reflected a humanitarian but paternalistic desire to protect the Maori from the disasters that other 'native' peoples had suffered through contact with colonists (see Ward, 1974: 36). So convinced were these statesmen of the superiority of their own way of life that they genuinely believed they were bestowing benefits upon Maori by 'civilising' them. At the same time, however, statesmen were concerned to establish British law in the country. Assimilating Maori was one means of getting Maori to accept that law. Because British law was used to facilitate European acquisition of Maori land, the policy of assimilation also served the colonists' interests. While the establishment of British law and the policy of assimilation were represented as benefiting Maori in those early years, in later years they were to be more openly employed to support settlers' interests. Both the missionaries and the government saw schooling as the primary means of assimilating or 'civilising' the Maori.

The Mission Schools for Maori

The first mission school in New Zealand was opened in 1816 at Rangihoua. After failing to generate much interest amongst Maori, it closed within two years. Maori interest in schooling, however, began to develop in the 1820s. By the early 1830s a growing enthusiasm for reading and writing became apparent.

To a large extent the interest of Maori in schooling arose from their admiration for European technology. They wanted to have access not only to that technology but, more importantly, to the knowledge and thinking that produced it (Jackson, 1975: 31). In other words, they wanted access to Pakeha wisdom. While stressing the superiority of European culture in their teachings, the missionaries linked European skills and technology to Christianity. As explained by Judith Binney (1969: 152): 'One approach was to make the Maoris realise that Christian society was the result of God's favour; that the material prosperity of the Europeans was directly connected to their religion'. It is not surprising therefore that in their search for Pakeha wisdom, the Maori turned to the missions. After all, as Jackson (1975: 31) observes, 'they had the book'.

The mission schools during this period all used the Maori language as the medium of instruction. By 1827 the Gospels had been translated into Maori, and by 1830 the missionaries had their own printing press and thus were able to produce printed materials in greater quantities. The curriculum for the schools around Paihia at this time consisted of reading, writing, arithmetic and catechism, and in the girls' schools, sewing and housekeeping skills were included.

With enthusiasm for literacy developing amongst Maori, their trade with Europeans, which a few years earlier had centred on clothing, became concentrated on books and printed matter. Slates and pencils were also in demand (Jackson, 1975: 33). Yate (1835: 231) recorded that Maori were prepared to receive books as wages or in exchange for other goods. Morley (1900: 47) reported on an occasion when five bushels of potatoes had been offered for one copy of a 117-page book of scriptural readings. While conversion to Christianity increased during this period, conversions were surpassed by the spread of literacy and the demand for books (Jackson, 1975: 33).

There are a number of contemporary accounts of the ease with which Maori acquired the skills of literacy and numeracy. Brown, an early trader, claimed for example that Maori were able to master the skills of literacy within a fortnight (Brown, 1845: 98). Although his claim may have been exaggerated it nevertheless indicates that, by European standards, Maori aptitude in acquiring the skills of literacy was remarkable. This claim is supported by Bishop Pompallier who wrote (1888: 47):

> They easily learn to read and write without the necessity of constant teaching. It is only necessary to give them a few leaflets of easy reading, and to write some characters on bits of slate to enable

them to read and write their own language within three months.

The Wesleyan missionary, Turton, further claimed that while the ability of the Maori to learn to read was equal to that of the Europeans, their perseverance in mastering the skills was much greater (Parr, 1961: 439).

In their enthusiasm for literacy, Maori were soon teaching each other and setting up their own village schools (Angas, 1847, II: 10-11). Brown (1845: 98) made the following observation:

> If one native in a tribe can read and write, he will not be long in teaching the others. The desire to obtain this information engrosses their whole thoughts and they will continue for days with their slates in their hands...

Jackson (1975: 33) gives some indication of the extent of the spread of literacy during this period:

> The spread of books (and with them literacy) by direct and indirect diffusion meant that a large number of Maori people were soon literate in their own language. Markham (in March 1834) estimated that there were 'not less than Ten Thousand people in the island that can read, write and do sums in the Northern end of the island.' More impressive still are the figures available for book production in New Zealand. From 1835 to 1840 William Colenso printed about 3,500,000 pages of religious material and in 1840 produced over 2,000,000 more. In 1841 the newly-established British and Foreign Bible Society printed 20,000 New Testaments; in 1843 and again in 1845 other lots of 20,000 were turned off the press. This meant that by 1845 there was at least one Maori Testament for every two Maori people in New Zealand.

Particularly significant about the Maori in this period is the remarkable facility and perseverance they demonstrated, as a previously non-literate people, in acquiring the skills of literacy and numeracy. More important, however, is the fact that this enthusiasm for gaining these new skills and knowledge arose from Maori's own perception of them as of relevance and value to their lives. They sought these skills in order to enhance their traditional way of life.

Claims regarding the extent of Maori literacy during this period are contested, however, by D. F. McKenzie (1985: 15) who argues that 'early missionaries and recent historians alike misread the evidence'. This came about, he says, largely because the missionaries 'reported what they knew their London committee wished to hear' (ibid.: 16). McKenzie claims that most Maori responses to print did not constitute reading but rather 'oral repetition from memory ... masquarad[ing] as reading' (ibid.: 17). He challenges also the reports of the quantities of material printed, and points out that the quantity should not be taken as an indicator of literacy since many Maori sought books because they perceived them to possess a mystical quality. While the assertion regarding the missionaries' reports may be true, the fact is that many reports about Maori interest in and aptitude for literacy came from traders and travellers such as Brown and Angas, who had no reason to support the missionaries. Whilst it seems clear that Maori did seek books for their mystical quality, as McKenzie claims, this does not negate the fact that many Maori also sought books for more utilitarian reasons. Jackson (1975: 34) points out that there were two parallel modes in the Maori use of books and printed material; the mystical and the pragmatic, with the latter dominant. Jackson also points out that from 1840, literacy as a mode of communication was immensely important to the Maori. He cites ample evidence of the use of literacy in communications of Maori with European, and Maori with Maori, to show that its pragmatic use was extensive (ibid.: 38-44). The research of Sinclair (1991: 34) also demonstrates that literacy amongst Maori was widespread by the 1850s.

However, the introduction of the skills of literacy was also to bring profound changes to Maori culture and social structure. Jackson shows how a focus on literacy, the Bible and European values during the 1830s served to marginalise Maori traditional culture and knowledge (Jackson, 1975: 37). He observes that although Maori had refocused their attention on this knowledge by 1850, it was never fully regained. The work of Kuni Jenkins (1991) also demonstrates graphically how in the processes of gaining the skills of literacy, Maori were subjected to and influenced by European values, especially the missionaries' beliefs about the inferiority of Maori culture. Jackson also notes that significant changes to the traditional status system of Maori came about when ex-slaves and commoners who had learnt to read and write were seen to command 'the secrets and sources of European knowledge and religion'. By standing outside the traditional status system, he explains, such people implied direct challenge to Maori codes of tapu and mana (1975: 37). It can be argued, nevertheless, that while literacy clearly had profound effects upon Maori social life, Maori themselves were largely in control of these changes at this stage.

Maori interest in and enthusiasm for literacy began to wane in the mid-1840s. While there are a number of reasons for this, one major cause was Maori frustration with the missionary policy of teaching – and printing – only in the Maori language, thus restricting reading material almost entirely to the Scriptures. Of great significance was the fact that by this stage the Treaty of Waitangi had been signed, and a steady migration of British settlers who were anxiously seeking land had begun. Maori needed to be able to deal with both the settlers and government administrators. They realised that to do this they needed to learn English. The knowledge and skills they sought were not to be found in the Gospels written in Maori.

The missionaries responded to this declining interest in their village day-schools by setting up larger boarding schools called 'central institutions'. It was hoped that moving the Maori children away from their parents would hasten the assimilation process. The teaching of English was included in the curriculum of these schools. A number of Maori responded with enthusiasm to this new move, and provided land and money for establishing these schools.

Government Funding of the Mission Schools

Government funding of the mission schools began with the Education Ordinance of 1847 and was continued through the Native Schools Act of 1858. In seeking to understand why the government provided this support for the schools, we need to look more closely at the wider social relations prevailing at that time.

The government's funding of the schools was part of its native policy, and a major concern of government native policy at this time was acquiring Maori land (Oliver, 1988: 4). Maori, to a large extent, had been willing to sell land during the first few years of colonisation but became reluctant to do so as more and more settlers poured in and the demand for their lands increased. By the 1850s Maori began to explore ideas of inter-tribal unity as a means of resisting the pressure to part with their lands. In the Waikato this led to the establishment of the Kingitanga (King Movement). At about the same time, New Zealand gained 'responsible government' which meant that it was no longer a Crown Colony and was self-governing. Thus, by the 1860s 'native policy' was being driven largely by the demands of the settlers and the land-speculators (ibid.). Mounting tensions between Maori and settlers eventually culminated in wars throughout the 1860s.

While war proved to be one effective means of separating Maori from their land, another means that proved to be even more effective was the *law* (Kelsey, 1984). In 1862 and 1865 Native Land Acts were passed. These represented the first stages of the government's efforts to put an end to Maori communal ownership of land. They made way for the individualisation of the titles to Maori land and the setting up of a Native Land Court to make it easier for Europeans to purchase Maori land. In 1863 legislation was passed to allow the government to confiscate huge tracts of 'rebel' Maori land. In selecting the land for confiscation, however, the government paid more attention to fertility and strategic location than to the owners' part in rebellion (Sorrenson, 1987: 185). As Sinclair (1991: 20) explains:

> The fact is that the government took whatever land it had occupied and wanted. It was the most ruthless act in New Zealand's European history, and the source of bitterness to the present day.

As a result, by the end of the century, Maori were both politically and economically marginalised. They were reduced to four per cent of the population and Pakeha were in full control of the country (Department of Statistics, 1988: 50).

It is clear then that the period in which the government made provisions for the schooling of Maori was a period of crisis in Maori – Pakeha relations – a period when Maori and Pakeha were locked in a struggle for sovereignty and control of resources. If we look more closely at some of the conditions the schools were required to meet in order to get funding, we see that the government was using the schools to support its own and the settlers' interests in this struggle. These intentions are made even more apparent when we examine the reports of the inspectors of the schools.

Government subsidies were given to the boarding schools of the Anglican, Roman Catholic and Wesleyan missions on condition that the schools teach English, provide industrial training as well as religious training, and be subject to government inspection annually. Boarding schools were favoured over day schools because they removed Maori children from the influence of their families and villages. This, together with the requirement that English be taught, can be seen as intended to hasten the assimilation of Maori to Pakeha cultural customs. Barrington (1966: 1-2) states that Governor Sir George Grey believed assimilation would be more speedily achieved by removing Maori children from 'the demoralizing influence of the villages'.

We also see from the inspectors' reports that this assimilation aim was clearly intended to facilitate the establishment of British law. Hugh Carleton, in one report, spoke of schools 'aiming at a double object, the civilization of the race and the quieting of the country' (AJHR, 1862, E-4: 17). George Clarke, a missionary who was also Civil Commissioner for the Bay of Islands stated that 'schools will give the government an immense moral influence in the country such as is not attained in any other way' (AJHR, 1863, E-9: 18). Carleton also suggested that prizes should be given to Maori students for the best examination in the book *Ko Nga Ture* – a précis of English law, compiled by order of the government 'for the use of the Native race' (AJHR, 1858, E-1: 77). Later he suggested that prizes should be given also for proficiency in the English tongue, adding that 'as a further inducement to exertion, hopes of employment in the Government service might be held out' (AJHR, 1862, E-4: 16). A very clear indication that the assimilation agenda was intended to support and facilitate European access to Maori land can be found in the report of Henry Taylor, in 1862. Taylor asserted that the 'most serious impediment to progress' in 'carrying out the work of civilization' within the schools was the Maori custom of communal ownership of property. He complained in his report that 'tribal rights destroy personal ownership' and that 'few attempts had been made by the Natives to individualize property'. He then argued for the ideas of individual ownership to be developed within the classroom (AJHR, 1862, E-4: 35). This report was made in the same year as the Native Land Act, intended to encourage Maori to individualise the titles to land holdings in order to make it easier for Europeans to purchase them.

From these reports it is clear that, at a time when the government and Maori were locked in a power struggle, government aid to the mission schools was directed towards the establishment of British law in order to strengthen the power of the government, to facilitate alienation of Maori land, and to secure social control.

A number of the mission schools, however, had been established by endowments of land and money from Maori themselves. It is unthinkable that Maori would have knowingly provided for schools to support this government agenda. There is a need for further research into the views of Maori at this period, but the evidence that is available indicates that Maori expectations in regard to schooling were very different from those of the government.

Some insight into what Maori wanted from schooling is provided by the statements of Maori chiefs who endowed the mission school run by Archdeacon Octavius Hadfield at Otaki. At a meeting with commissioners enquiring into the schools in 1858, Tamihana Te Rauparaha explained that he and other Maori had donated the land for the school – 700-800 acres – as well as providing money for it – £389 18s 11d in total. He added that he had told the Archdeacon at the time that there should be a 'really good English master to take charge of the school'. He had stressed that 'the master is the main thing'. He also expressed some dissatisfaction with the way the school was being run. Chiefs Matene Te Whiwhi and Hukiki are also recorded as expressing similar sentiments at the meeting (AJHR, 1858, E-1: 4-5).

Both Tamihana Te Rauparaha and his cousin Matene Te Whiwhi were involved during this period with attempts to establish kotahitanga – inter-tribal unity – to combat the threat posed by European demands for land. We can assume therefore that the reason they wanted their children to gain European knowledge and fluency in English was to help them deal with such threats. A similar outlook can be seen amongst Maori such as Wiremu Tamihana who were behind the establishment of the Kingitanga (AJHR, 1862, E-4: 5). Ward (1974: viii) contends that this view was widely shared by Maori at that time. On the surface then, the intentions of the government in regard to schooling appear to be similar to those of the Maori. Yet when we look more closely, we see that they are essentially different. Maori embraced schooling as a means to maintain their sovereignty and enhance their life-chances. The government, on the other hand, sought, through schooling, to gain control over Maori and their resources. Maori wanted to *extend* their existing body of knowledge. The government, with its assimilation policy, intended to *replace* Maori culture with that of the European. This raises a further question: did the government, in setting out to 'civilise' the Maori, intend them to learn enough of European culture to compete on equal terms with Pakeha, in government and in control over resources?

The missionaries had included industrial training in their schools as a means of training Maori in the skills needed to enable the missions to be self-supporting (Barrington and Beaglehole, 1974: 3). Grey, in stipulating industrial training as one of the conditions for the provision of government funding to the mission schools, saw it as a necessary requirement for the 'children of an almost barbarous race or ... the children of hardy colonists, who had a ... country to create' (dispatch from Governor Grey to Colonial Office, London, 1847).

However, the industrial training in the schools became a cause of much dissatisfaction for Maori parents. A report on Otaki school in the mid-1850s indicates that the pupils aged between 8 and 15 spent only two-and-a-half hours daily in lessons and up to eight hours in hard labour on the land (AJHR, 1858, E-1: 54-55). Both school inspectors and missionaries recorded strong resistance from Maori parents to such regimes. Paora Tuhaere of Orakei expressed his indignation to W. Rolleston that Maori children 'were set to work as servants' (AJHR, 1867, A-3: 1), and the Reverend J. Whiteley spoke of Maori parents complaining in words such as: 'We thought you took our children from us to give them schooling but instead you are making slaves of them' (ibid.). Henry Taylor, the government school inspector, however, contended that Maori had been entering schools with the mistaken impression 'that they came only to learn and not to work' (AJHR, 1862, E-4: 38). Carleton, in a school report of the same year, asserted: 'It will scarcely be maintained that education consists only of book learning' (ibid.: 15).

From all the reports it seems abundantly clear that intellectual development was given a low priority by both government and missionaries in the native school policy of this time. Instead, the assimilation agenda and industrial training were treated as the major concerns. It seems apparent from this that the government intended the schools to prepare Maori for labouring class status. This view is supported by the following statement from Henry Taylor (AJHR, 1862, E-4: 38):

> I do not advocate for the Natives under present circumstances a refined education or high mental culture; it would be inconsistent

> if we take account of the position they are likely to hold for many
> years to come in the social scale, and inappropriate if we remember
> that they are better calculated by nature to get their living by manual
> than by mental labour.

We can see from this that the government was not just concerned with replacing Maori traditional knowledge and culture with that of the European. It was concerned also to limit the amount and type of European knowledge to which Maori were to be given access. In rationalising this limited curriculum, Taylor was employing the racist claim that Maori were suited 'by nature' to manual work.

Thus, while Maori were seeking through schooling to enhance their life chances, the government, was setting out to control and limit those life chances. It seems apparent, however, that Maori eventually became disillusioned with the mission schools. By the mid-1860s they had abandoned them. The government, seeking a more effective vehicle for its assimilation policy, then began working towards setting up its own schools.

The 'Native Schools' System

Under the Native Schools Act of 1867, the government set up a system of secular village day-schools referred to simply as 'Native Schools'. They were controlled by the Department of Native Affairs until 1879 when they were taken over by the newly established Department of Education. They continued to operate under this Department as a separate system parallel to that of the public schools until 1969.

When the Maori Schools Bill was debated in Parliament, some politicians appeared to support it out of genuine concern for Maori interests. However, it won support largely on economic grounds in relation to social control. Hugh Carleton asserted that 'things had now come to pass that it was necessary either to exterminate the Natives or civilise them' and opted to support the Bill to avoid the cost of further wars. (By this stage the major wars over land had been fought in Taranaki and the Waikato.) Major Heaphy VC stated that 'any expenditure in this direction would be true economy, as the more the Natives were educated the less would be the future expenditure in police and gaols' (NZPD, 1867: 863).

Under the Act, members of a Maori community who wanted schooling for their children were required to form a committee and formally request a school. They were also required, initially, to supply the land, and pay half the cost of the building and a quarter of the teacher's salary. An amendment to the Act in 1871 relaxed the financial conditions somewhat, allowing for extra land to be provided in lieu of money. A number of Maori communities responded positively to the move and by 1879, 57 Native Schools had been established. These were mainly in the far north and eastern parts of the North Island, amongst communities that had not been directly affected by the recent wars. There was, though, strong resistance to government-funded schools in Taranaki and the Waikato.

In 1879 the control of the Native Schools was transferred from the Native Department to the Department of Education. The Department of Education had been established under the 1877 Education Act which provided for state-controlled schooling throughout New Zealand. Although there were two parallel systems operating, no official restrictions on racial grounds were placed on either Maori or Pakeha children attending schools of either system. McKenzie (1982: 5) points out, however, that there was scope under the 1877 Education Act for teachers to refuse children entry to public schools on such grounds as want of cleanliness, gross misconduct or incorrigible disobedience. Furthermore it was intended that each Native School would be integrated into the public schools system as soon as the children in it were Europeanised. The policy that the schools should not be racially segregated might be seen to have stemmed from the humanitarian idealism evident at the time of the Treaty (Ward, 1974: 211). McKenzie (1982: 12) points out, however, that parliamentarians supported the idea of an integrated system primarily because they believed (incorrectly as it turned out) that it would be cheaper to run.

The Department of Education appointed its first inspector of Native Schools, James Pope, in 1880. In the same year Pope helped prepare the Native Schools Code which set out the ways in which the schools were to operate. As explained by Pope (AJHR, E-2: 16); the role of the Native Schools was:

> ...to bring to an untutored but intelligent and high-spirited people into line with our civilisation and by placing in Maori settlements European school buildings and European families to serve as teachers, especially as exemplars of a new and more desirable mode of life.

This clearly spells out that the assimilation policy was to continue to have priority in the schooling of Maori. Under the Native Schools Code it was made clear that all teaching was to be conducted in the English language. Teachers were instructed to teach Maori children to read, write, and speak the English language, to 'further instruct them in the rudiments of arithmetic and geography, and generally, endeavour to give them such culture as may fit them to become good citizens' (AJHR, 1880, H1F:1). Under Pope's regime provisions were made for some Maori to be spoken in the junior classes – until the children were fluent in English. However, from the time his successor William Bird took office in 1903, the Maori language was forbidden at school. This was because the department was following a new method of teaching English – the direct method – based upon the understanding that a second language would be learnt more quickly and effectively if the first language was not used at all (see Simon, 1998: 74-86).

There is no doubt that many Maori were anxious for their children to learn English, and gave their support to the idea of teaching being conducted only in English. During the 1870s a number of prominent Maori took petitions to Parliament calling for emphasis on English-language teaching in schools (see Barrington, 1966: 3). As expressed by one group of petitioners, the hopes and intentions behind such requests were that Maori would become 'acquainted with the means by which the Europeans [had] become great' and consequently would not hold 'a poor position in the future of the colony' (ibid.). This affirms that Maori at this stage perceived schooling largely as a means to their survival and success in a Pakeha-dominated society. While we have this evidence that Maori were anxious to learn English, we have no evidence that they ever sought to undermine or destroy the Maori language. Furthermore, it is highly unlikely that in promoting an emphasis on the English language they ever conceived the possibility that this could place the Maori language at risk. Clearly what they wanted was that their children would become bilingual. This further highlights the distinction between government intentions and Maori aspirations in relation to schooling.

The curriculum in the Native Schools reflects some of the ideas used to support universal education during that period. It did not aim to extend the pupils intellectually, but rather it sought to train them to be law-abiding citizens and to provide them with sufficient schooling for mainly labouring class roles within the society (see Shuker, 1987b: 44). Provisions were made, however, for a system of scholarships to enable clever Maori children to gain further schooling at the denominational boarding schools. The idea was to develop an educated Maori-élite who would eventually return to their villages and spread the gospel of assimilation – thus helping to further Pakeha interests (AJHR, 1881, E-7: 1-11).

Space does not permit a detailed discussion here on secondary schooling for Maori. Mention should be made, however, of Te Aute College where the principal, John Thornton, adopted a policy of coaching his most promising students for the matriculation examination of the University of New Zealand. This produced, in the last decade of the nineteenth century, the first wave of Maori university graduates, beginning with Apirana Ngata and including Te Rangi Hiroa (Peter Buck), Maui Pomare, Rewiti Kohere and Tutere Wirepa. Work by John Barrington (1988; 1992) provide valuable insights into the agenda of the Department of Education in regard to the secondary schooling of Maori pupils at the beginning of the twentieth century (see also Simon, 1993).

When Pope took office the Maori population was in a critical state, struggling with severe epidemics of European diseases against which they had no immunity. Pope addressed himself to these issues, and under his guidance the Native Schools became centres for spreading European ideas on health and hygiene into Maori communities and for fulfilling a paternalistic role generally. Whilst this may have benefited the physical health of Maori, it also promoted the idea that European knowledge was the only valid knowledge on health. This not only reinforced the notion of the superiority of European knowledge in general over that of the Maori, but at the same time cultivated Maori dependence upon Europeans as the bearers of that knowledge. Thus it served to increase Pakeha power and control over Maori (see Simon, 1998: 120-130).

While schooling for Pakeha became compulsory in 1877, it was not made compulsory for Maori until 1894. Nevertheless, during the latter part of that century Maori increasingly came to perceive schooling as their one means of surviving in the Pakeha-dominated world, and the number of Native Schools increased. By 1907 there were 97 Native Schools and this number grew to 166 by 1955 (Barrington, 1971: 26). At the same time, however, Maori children were also attending public schools. In many cases, particularly in the early years, they suffered a great deal of racial discrimination there and were given little or no support in their attempts to learn English (see McKenzie, 1982). Nevertheless, by 1909 the number of Maori children attending public schools was exceeding the number in the Native Schools.

Although the Native Schools had many shortcomings, Maori children were probably better off within them than they were in the public schools. Within the Native Schools they at least experienced the security of a predominantly Maori community, and the fact that their fellow pupils were mostly their siblings and cousins provided them with some support in coping with the culturally alien school programme. Furthermore, some of the Pakeha teachers in the Native Schools were sensitive to Maori values and thinking, and developed good relationships with their communities and pupils, which facilitated effective learning. The geographic isolation of the Native Schools also helped the Maori communities to resist the assimilation policy and to continue to keep their cultural practices alive – at least during the first thirty years or so of the next century.

Overall, however, by the beginning of the twentieth century the assimilation policy had proved highly destructive to Maori society. While Maori support for schooling arose from the desire to gain access to Pakeha wisdom and fluency in English, the cost of gaining this knowledge was high. Schools promoted the Pakeha way of life while simultaneously denigrating the Maori way of life. Thus, in practice, the assimilation policy disempowered Maori by increasing their dependence upon Pakeha. It also demoralised Maori by disparaging the language and the traditions of their ancestors. Although Maori resisted, to a large extent, the pressure to give up their cultural practices, they were unable to avoid being affected by European racial ideas of superiority and inferiority. This is particularly significant when viewed with the suffering increasingly experienced through the workings of the Native Land Court. By 1892 Maori were left with less than one-sixth of their land (and that was mainly bush-clad and in remote areas). Forced into a precarious subsistence life, they were scarcely able to grow enough crops for themselves, and had to depend for their survival upon work as seasonal labourers for European farmers and public works (Sorrenson, 1987: 192). They were, as Sorrenson explains, 'in danger of becoming, as they had always feared they would become, hewers of wood and drawers of water for the Pakeha'.

Summary

Maori had sought Pakeha-style schooling during the early missionary period in the hope of expanding their horizons and gaining 'Pakeha wisdom' that would enable them to fulfil mainly traditional goals. Following the Treaty of Waitangi and the rapid influx of settlers, knowledge was sought as a means of combating the threat that the settlers represented to their sovereignty and resources. In the latter years of the century they were seeking schooling as a means of surviving and succeeding within a Pakeha-dominated world. For a minority of Maori (mostly those who had retained their lands), schooling *did* fulfil these hopes. For the majority of Maori, however, that promise was never realised. Schooling served instead to reinforce their subordinate status in their own land. It was a means of furthering Pakeha economic and political interests. By the early years of the twentieth century, many Maori had retreated into a state of despondency and a pattern of underachievement in schooling was becoming entrenched. This was a remarkable contrast to the enthusiasm and competence that had characterised the Maori response to schooling a century earlier.

Schooling in the Twentieth Century

In this chapter we have been looking at the New Zealand education system in an effort to see the part it has played in relation to the development and maintenance of inequalities within our society. So far we have looked at schooling provided for non-Maori and for Maori throughout the nineteenth and early twentieth centuries.

In the first section we saw that in the period leading up to the 1877 Education Act, although egalitarian ideals were expressed, other concerns, particularly those of economics and social control, also played a significant part in the decisions to establish universal schooling. We saw also that through the education Acts and policies of the time, schooling continued to reproduce the existing inequalities within the society, particularly those of class and gender. In the second section we saw how schooling for Maori supported other measures taken by the state in its efforts to alienate Maori from their lands and prepare them for working class status. The picture was hardly one of 'racial harmony'.

To note, however, that social control and economic concerns played a significant part in the establishing of universal schooling is not to deny that a genuine concern for egalitarianism was also involved. What we have to recognise is that different groups within the society were competing to have their concerns addressed through the education system. In the case of the 1877 Education Act, as Richard Harker (1985: 57-60) has pointed out, the reason that those seeking universal schooling from egalitarian motives were able to achieve their goal was because universal schooling was also being sought at that time by the other groups concerned with social control and economics. Thus the interests of these different groups appeared to be in harmony, when in fact they were in conflict. Similarly the interests of Maori supporting the mission schools appeared to be in harmony with those of the state in its subsidising of those schools, when in fact they were in conflict.

These situations help us to see that the education system can and does function as a site of struggle or contestation for different groups within the society. When one group wins out in the contest it is because at that time it has sufficient power to do so.

C. E. Beeby (1986: xviii), in writing about educational 'myths', claims that the prevailing myth during the early years of the New Zealand education system was that of survival of the fittest. This claim might seem to be at variance with the claim that a spirit of egalitarianism prevailed at that time. In fact it highlights the point made above, that different discourses co-exist and compete within a society at any one time. As we saw, it was the survival of the fittest myth which eventually won in the contest at that time. Beeby speaks, however, as if these myths eventually die or come to be replaced. It is probably more accurate to perceive the situation as one where one discourse may gain ascendancy over other competing discourses at a particular period, and lose its influence at another time, retaining nevertheless the potential to become dominant again in the future. This will become clearer as we proceed through the chapter.

This section will survey the development of public schooling in New Zealand throughout the twentieth century, starting from the time of the election of the first Labour Government in 1935. This occurred at a time when New Zealand was in the grips of a severe depression. Almost all members of the society suffered. By 1933 three-quarters of the adult male population was registered as unemployed (King, 1987: 287). Maori were in the worst position. They were the first to be laid off, and it is estimated that they represented 40 per cent of the unemployed. When the Labour Government was swept to power, it was widely believed that it would be striving to create a more egalitarian society.

1937 saw the abolition of the Proficiency Examination which children had been required to pass in order to gain entry to secondary schools. Then in 1939 the Minister of Education, Peter Fraser, presented his government's policy on education in the now famous statement (AJHR, 1939: 2-3):

> The government's objective, broadly expressed, is that every person whatever his level of academic ability, whether he be rich or poor, whether he live in town or country, has a right, as a citizen, to a free education of the kind for which he is best fitted and to the fullest extent of his powers. So far is this from being a mere pious platitude that the full acceptance of the principle will involve the reorientation of the education system.

This could surely be regarded as the founding charter of New Zealand's modern education policy. Beeby (1986: xxii) describes it as heralding a new myth of equal opportunity. In fact we can also recognise it as an expression of the earlier egalitarian credo – now prevailing more strongly than previously. This is particularly evident in the final statement, which indicates that the system would be changed to ensure that equality of opportunity would be provided. We need now to look at some of the ways in which the system did change under the Labour Government, and the effects of those changes.

Abolition of the Proficiency Examination in 1937 had certainly made way for more children to attend secondary schools. Shuker (1987b: 61) points out that in 1937, 65 per cent of primary school leavers went on to secondary schools. For some children, however, particularly rural children, having this right made little immediate difference to their lives, simply because there were no secondary schools near their homes. Maori, especially, were mostly living in isolated rural communities far from the towns where the secondary schools were located.

Fraser's statement, while it appears to aim at the fulfilment of the individual, poses some important questions: if each individual were to be given the kind of education for which he or she was best fitted, who was to decide what that kind of education was – the individual or the state? And on what basis could such decisions be made? In fact it was the state, as we shall see, that largely came to control such decisions through the schools, particularly through the institution of IQ and aptitude tests, examinations and entrance qualifications. State control of such decisions is evident especially in the type of secondary schooling that was eventually provided for Maori.

The first Native District High School was opened in 1941, seemingly as an effort to make equality of opportunity a reality. However, as the Senior Inspector of Native Schools, T.A. Fletcher, explained at that time, the core curriculum of the new schools was to be (AJHR, 1941, E-3: 3):

> ... homemaking in the widest sense, including building construction and all its features, furniture making, metal work and home management, including cookery, home decorating, and infant welfare for the girls. The aim is to teach the skills and develop the tastes that make the house not merely a place of habitation but a home in the best sense of the word.

We can see that this is a continuation of earlier policies to limit Maori education to mainly manual and domestic training, and to put pressure on Maori to adopt European values and customs. No School Certificate courses were included in these schools until Maori parents themselves demanded them in 1945 (Barrington, 1992: 70). (The School Certificate examination had been introduced in 1935 and added to the existing university Matriculation exam. School Certificate in those days examined technical subjects and Matriculation examined academic subjects. School Certificate as a general examination at Form 5 level was not introduced until 1945.)

Thus we can see that the provision of equality of *access* to schooling for Maori did not provide them with equality of *opportunity* with all other children, that is, those attending the grammar schools. Rather the policies and provisions could serve only to widen the gulf between Pakeha and Maori in terms of economic and political power. This could hardly be regarded as a recipe for racial harmony.

Nevertheless, it is true to say that under the Labour Government, greater educational opportunities than ever before were created. Dr Beeby was appointed Director of Education, and under his direction the Department of Education adopted what has come to be referred to as a 'liberal-progressive' approach to education, and expanded both its administration and professional influence over secondary schools (see Shuker, 1987b: 62).

The Thomas Report

In 1944 a report on the post-primary curriculum was published (see Shuker, 1987b: 160-163; Openshaw, Lee and Lee, 1993: 169-176). Known as the Thomas Report, this supported the Labour Government's philosophy in that it set out 'to ensure, as far as possible, that all post-primary pupils, irrespective of their varying abilities and their varying occupational ambitions, receive a generous and well-balanced education' (Shuker, 1987b: 160). Following publication of the report, the school leaving age was raised to fifteen and a new School Certificate examination, separate from University Entrance, was introduced together with accrediting for University Entrance. New regulations in 1945 set down a core curriculum that was compulsory for all schools to follow until the end of the fourth form. This involved core studies in English, social studies, general science, mathematics, music, art and craft and physical education. This core curriculum was intended to ensure that each school provided what the Thomas Committee considered to be a 'generous and well-balanced education' (ibid.).

The importance the Labour Government placed on education was evident in its high expenditure on it, even throughout the war years. In its efforts to make secondary schooling more accessible to all children, it was remarkably successful overall. However, while the public responded eagerly to these opportunities, it did so primarily in order to gain academic credentials for the job market. This meant that the object of fulfilling the needs of the individual was mostly overridden by the desire for credentials, and this inevitably continued to be the most powerful influence on the curriculum (see Shuker, 1987b: 119-130). Thus the system was still strongly competitive in the way it operated. Meritocratic ideas were still prevailing (still survival of the fittest). While schooling gave the appearance of providing equality of opportunity, it continued largely to reproduce the existing structures – and hence the inequalities.

The Currie Report

In 1962, towards the end of Beeby's tenure as Director of Education, a Commission on Education (chaired by Sir George Currie) was set up to examine and report on the education system. Invoking the credo of equality of opportunity, the Currie Report expressed confidence in the existing education system. In general it accepted Fraser's 1939 statement and asserted that the fundamental structures and values of the existing system should be maintained. It stated (Department of Education, 1962: 11-12):

> Nothing that has been said or written in evidence before the Commission has given any grounds for believing that there is in the community any large body of sentiment opposed to the ideas expressed by Mr Fraser, nor in the 22 years that have passed since he made it has there been any movement – social or political – which would suggest any retreat from this viewpoint. Rather it might be claimed that the influence of the second World War and its aftermath have strengthened this sentiment as one of the dominant democratic ideas of the New Zealand community.

The report thus gave support to, first, the claim that equality of opportunity was the central aspiration of New Zealand education and of the community as a whole; second, the belief that the system was progressing towards that principle; and third, the notion that state activity was benevolent and should be employed to encourage further progress of this system (see McCulloch, 1990: 38-43; Scott, 1996).

We can see from this that the report, in fact, was remarkably complacent in its assumptions that there was a general consensus in public opinion regarding education. It acknowledged, however, the existence of some inequalities in the society, and identified four groups with 'special needs': (1) rural communities; (2) new urban dormitory suburbs; (3) the physically and intellectually handicapped; and (4) the Maori people (Department of Education, 1962: 14-16).

It is doubtful, in fact, whether concern for the Maori would have been mentioned at all had not a report on the Department of Maori Affairs – the Hunn Report – been published a year earlier (see Hunn, 1961). The Hunn Report demonstrated statistically that in relation to the rest of the society, Maori were severely disadvantaged in the areas of housing, health and employment and education. Taking cognisance of this, the Currie Commission felt the need to add a further chapter on Maori education to its report. At the same time, however, it did not question the direction the education system was heading. In general it seemed very satisfied with it. The major recommendation it made in relation to Maori was that the Native Schools system (by then called Maori Schools system) should be abolished and the Maori schools transferred to board control – that is, that they become public schools. The reason given for this move was a 'concern regarding race relations'. The report (Department of Education, 1962: 401-402) further explains this:

> From the angle of world politics ... this country is drawn, perhaps unwillingly, into considering its solution of inter-racial problems in the light of what is being attempted and achieved in the world outside New Zealand. Happenings in Asia and Africa do not leave us unmoved. There is a feeling in this country, in the minds of both Maori and Pakeha, that if other races are with such energy setting about the task of assimilating and adapting to their needs the European economic, political and social structure, the New Zealand Maori should certainly not lag behind.

There is an irony in the recommendation. While the Native Schools system, as we saw in the previous section, had been set up by the government in 1867 as a means of implementing the assimilation policy, many of the Native Schools themselves had, over the years, come to be accepted as valued features of Maori communities. While undoubtedly still fulfilling a paternalistic role, they were at least focusing on perceived needs of Maori children. Furthermore, there is evidence revealing that not all teachers in the Native Schools adhered to the departmental edicts to limit Maori opportunities through the curriculum and to forbid the Maori language (see Simon, 1998). In contrast to the Maori schools, many of the education board schools at the time treated Maori children with indifference or hostility if they did not fit in with the Pakeha-oriented system. McKenzie (1982) demonstrates this in regard to Maori in board schools during the nineteenth century; many of the conditions he describes continued well into the twentieth century. Few, if any, board schools attempted to cater for the specific needs of Maori pupils before the 1960s and, even after that period, Maori needs were widely ignored. While there were considerable variations across the Native Schools it would probably be true to say that, by and large, they served the Maori children better than the board schools. The Currie Commission, however, in the name of egalitarianism, resolved that the Native Schools system should be disbanded and, as a result, it ceased to exist in 1969.

By this time, however, Maori were living largely in urban areas, having migrated throughout the 1950s and 1960s into the cities. Here they took on mainly working class jobs. We can see that the type of schooling they had received over several generations had prepared them for such roles. In the 1960s and 1970s Pacific Islands peoples began migrating here in search of work. In many of the Pacific Islands, schooling had been controlled and managed by the New Zealand Education Department, with policies similar to those applied to Maori. It is not surprising therefore, that most of the Pacific migrants also took on working class jobs.

With the large numbers of Maori and Pacific Island children in urban schools, the inequalities in regard to ethnicity became much more visible and Maori themselves became far more vocal in protesting about the education system. The department's main response to this was the development of 'taha Maori' programmes for schools and policies of 'multicultural education'. This latter was also an acknowledgement of the Pacific Islands presence in the schools. During these years New Zealand schooling was also subjected to a well developed left-wing critique, which highlighted the extent to which the system assisted the reproduction of inequalities relating to gender and class as well as those of ethnicity (see, for example, Walker, 1973; Nash, 1983; Codd, Harker and Nash, 1985; Smith, L., 1986; Smith, G., 1986; Jones, 1991; Simon, 1986). All these factors called into question the claimed commitment of the Department of Education to equality of opportunity, and served generally to undermine confidence in the system.

When the fourth Labour Government came to power, its first Minister of Education, Russell Marshall, initiated a review of the school in which the views of the general public were sought (see Department of Education, 1987). More than 21,000 submissions were received by the Review Committee. Although the review was never acted upon formally, the published findings served to highlight the diversity of views and demands of the community in regard to the education system. These included calls from the radical left – including many Maori and their supporters – calling for bicultural and bilingual schooling; liberal calls for more extensive multicultural programmes to provide equality of opportunity; and from a neo-conservative – or new-right – group that was rapidly gaining strength, demands for a back to basics education (see quotes in the margins of both the draft and final versions of *The Curriculum Review* for examples of all these viewpoints). This last mentioned group had in recent years become increasingly vocal in its criticism of the liberal-progressive orientation of the education system, as is evident in the following submission to the Curriculum Review committee (1987: 67):

> This entire series is attempting to foist on parents your preconceptions of what you want to include; our opinions will of course be totally ignored. Most of us don't want your 'multi-cultural' garbage – we want our children to be taught basics.

Calls for back-to-basics education came from interest groups such as the Employers Federation. Reflecting growing trends in the US and in Britain, they argued for a 'return' to a system based on meritocracy providing credentials for the marketplace. (The word 'return' is placed in quotation marks since, as we have seen, the system had never really abandoned this stance.) This new-right group tended to equate equality of opportunity with a lowering of standards. Its views received support from Treasury when it published a report on education to brief the incoming government in 1987. Treasury challenged the perception of the education system as a public good and argued that, instead, it should be understood as a commodity of the marketplace (Grace, 1990).

The diversity of views and demands evident at this time demonstrates clearly how the education system functions as a site of struggle or contestation for different interest groups within the society.

The Picot Report

Shortly after *The Curriculum Review* was published in 1987, the Prime Minister, David Lange, relieved Russell Marshall of his position as Minister of Education and assumed the position himself. One of his first actions in that role was to set up a taskforce to review education administration. The report of this taskforce, the Picot Report, was published in 1988. This report can be seen as an effort to reconcile the conflicting views in society in regard to education. It recommended that, instead of being tinkered with, the existing system should be radically restructured. It recommended reducing the amount of central control and shifting greater decision-making power to local school Boards of Trustees. The government's education policy, based on these recommendations, was set out in *Tomorrow's Schools*. We can see that the Picot Report differed from the Currie Report in several respects. In particular it moved away from the belief that the state was the most appropriate authority to control education. It claimed, furthermore, that the administrative reforms it recommended would benefit society and the economy in general as well as the most deprived groups.

In other ways, however, it represented a continuation of the previous policies. It was still retaining a concern with equality, but now this was expressed not in terms of equality of opportunity but in terms of equity – or equality of results/outcomes. Following Picot, equity objectives were expected to underpin all activities in schools. This is spelt out in the *Charter Framework* (Ministry of Education, 1990: 5):

> The board of trustees will ensure that the school's policies and practices seek to achieve equitable outcomes for students of both sexes, for rural and urban students, for all students irrespective of their religious, ethnic, cultural, social, family and class backgrounds, and irrespective of their ability and disability.

Equity therefore was to be the guiding principle of the education system. However, there was also to be an emphasis on efficiency and standards. Together these emphases can be seen as efforts to reconcile both the radical-left and the new-right views.

One educationist observes that this focus on equity could be understood as a new educational myth, open to two different interpretations. On the one hand it could be perceived as a device which would shape the development of schooling through the 1990s and into the twenty-first century. On the other hand it could be interpreted simply as a means of concealing the inadequacies of schooling and the persistence of inequalities (Jones *et al.*, 1990: 48). The developments in education over the next few years should reveal to us which view is the more accurate interpretation.

Conclusion

Through this brief overview of the history of European-style schooling in New Zealand we have seen that the education system has always been a site of contestation and struggle for different interest groups within the society, with each seeking to shape the system according to its own set of values and concerns. While conflicting educational 'myths' or discourses are seen to co-exist at all times, some of them, together with the groups who share them, gain ascendancy at particular periods of time and influence the direction of the education system. We have seen that while the ideals and discourses of egalitarianism and 'racial harmony' have played significant roles in the shaping of New Zealand education policy, both the policies and the practices within the schools have continued, in varying degrees, to reproduce social inequalities.

References

AJHR - Appendices to the Journals of the House of Representatives.

Angas, G. F. (1847), *Savage Life and Scenes in Australian and New Zealand,* London: Smith, Elder and Co.

Barrington, J. M. (1966), 'Maori Scholastic Achievement: A Historical Review of Policies and Provisions', *New Zealand Journal of Educational Studies,* 1(1), 1-14.

Barrington, J. M. (1971), 'Maori Attitudes to Pakeha Institutions after the Wars: A Note on the Establishment of Schools', *New Zealand Journal of Educational Studies,* 6(1), 24-28.

Barrington, J. (1988), 'Learning the Dignity of Labour': Secondary Education Policy for Maoris', *New Zealand Journal of Educational Studies,* 20 (2), 151-164.

Barrington, J. (1992), 'The School Curiculum: Occupation and Race', in G. McCulloch (ed.), *The School Curriculum in New Zealand: History, Theory Policy and Practice,* Palmerston North: Dunmore Press.

Barrington, J. M. and Beaglehole, T. H. (1974), *Maori Schools in a Changing Society,* Wellington: NZCER.

Beeby, C. E. (1986), 'Introduction', in W. L. Renwick, *Moving Targets: Six Essays on Educational Policy,* Wellington: NZCER.

Binney, J. (1969), 'Christianity and the Maoris to 1840: A Comment', *New Zealand Journal of History,* 3 (2), 143-165.

Bird, W.W. (1930), 'A Review of the Native School System', *Te Wananga,* Vol II, No 2, 1-26.

Blond's Encyclopedia of Education (ed. Edward Blishen) (1969), London: Blond Educational.

Bottomore, T. B. (1964), *Elites and Society,* London: Pelican.

Braithwaite, E. (1982), 'Education and Equality', *Access,* 1(1), 33-50.

Brown, W. (1845), *New Zealand and its Aborigines,* London: Smith Elder and Co.

Campbell, A. E. (1941), *Educating New Zealand,* Wellington: Department of Internal Affairs of New Zealand.

Codd, J. (1985), 'The TOSCA Controversy: Political and Ethical Issues', *Delta,* 36, 39-52.

Codd, J., Harker, R and Nash, R (eds) (1985), *Political Issues in New Zealand Education,* Palmerston North: Dunmore Press.

Concise Oxford Dictionary (edited by R.E.Allen) (1990) (8th Edition), Oxford: Clarenden Press.

Cumming, I. and Cumming, A. (1978), *History of State Education in New Zealand 1840-1975,* Wellington: Pitman.

Dakin, J. C. (1986), 'Contemporary Public Opinion and the Secular Provision of the Education Act, 1977', *New Zealand Journal of Educational Studies,* 21 (2), 189-194.

Dennis, W. H. S. (1979), 'Curriculum Copying: New Light on the Development of 'Standards' in New Zealand During the 1870s', *New Zealand Journal of Educational Studies,* 14 (1), 3-22.

Department of Education (1900), *The Standards,* Wellington: Government Printer.

Department of Education (1944), *The Report of the Consultative Committee on Post-Primary Education* (The Thomas Report), Wellington: Government Printer.

Department of Education (1962), *Report of the Commission on Education* (Currie Report), Wellington: Government Printer.

Department of Education (1987), *The Curriculum Review: Report of the Committee to Review the Curriculum for Schools,* Wellington: Government Printer.

Department of Statistics (1988), *The April Report, Vol. I New Zealand Today*, Wellington: The Royal Commission on Social Policy.

Fry, Ruth (1985), *It's Different for Daughters: A History of the Curriculum for Girls in New Zealand Schools, 1900-1975*, Wellington: NZCER.

Fry, Ruth (1988), 'The Curriculum and Girls' Secondary Schooling 1880-1925', in S. Middleton (ed.), *Women and Education in Aotearoa*, Wellington: Allen and Unwin.

Grace, G. (1990), 'Labour and Education: The Crisis and Settlements of Education Policy', in M. Holland and J. Boston (eds), *The Fourth Labour Government: Politics and Policy in New Zealand* (2nd Edition), Auckland: Oxford University Press.

Harker, R. (1985), 'Schooling and Cultural Production', in J. Codd, R. Harker and R. Nash (eds), *Political Issues in New Zealand Education*, Palmerston North: Dunmore Press.

Hunn, J. K. (1961), *Report on the Department of Maori Affairs*, Wellington: Government Printer.

Jackson, M. D. (1975), 'Literacy, Communications and Social Change: A Study of the Meaning and Effect of Literacy in Early Nineteenth Century Maori Society', in I. H. Kawharu (ed.), *Conflict and Compromise: Essays on the Maori Since Colonisation*, Wellington: A.H. and A.W.Reed.

Jenkins, K. (1991), 'Te Ihi, Te Mana, Te Wehi O Te Ao Tuhi: Early Maori Literacy', Unpublished MA thesis, The University of Auckland.

Jones, A. (1991), *'At School I've Got a Chance...': Pacific Islands and Pakeha Girls at School*, Palmerston North: Dunmore Press.

Jones, A., McCulloch, G., Marshall, J., Smith L. and Smith G. (1990), *Myths and Realities: Schooling in New Zealand*, Palmerston North: Dunmore Press.

Kelsey, J. (1984), 'Legal Imperialism and the Colonization of Aotearoa', in P. Spoonley *et al.* (eds), *Tauiwi: Racism and Ethnicity in New Zealand*, Palmerston North: Dunmore Press.

King, M. (1987), 'Between Two Worlds', in W. H. Oliver (ed.), *The Oxford History of New Zealand*, Auckland: Oxford University Press.

McCulloch, G. (1986), *Education in the Forming of New Zealand Society: Needs and Opportunities for Study*, Monograph No 2, NZARE.

McCulloch, G. (1990), 'Historical Perspectives on New Zealand Schooling', in Alison Jones *et al.*, *Myths and Realities: Schooling in New Zealand*, Palmerston North: Dunmore Press.

McCulloch, G. (ed.) (1992), *The School Curriculum in New Zealand: History, Theory, Policy and Practice*, Palmerston North: Dunmore Press.

McGeorge, C. and Snook, I. (1981), *Church, State, and New Zealand Education*, Wellington: Price Milburn.

McKenzie, D. (1975), 'The Changing Concept of Equality in New Zealand Education', *New Zealand Journal of Educational Studies*, 10 (2), 93-94.

McKenzie, D. (1984), 'Ideology in the History of New Zealand Education', *New Zealand Journal of Educational Studies*, 19(1), 2-9.

McKenzie, D. (1987), 'The Growth of School Credentialling in New Zealand, 1978-1900', in R. Openshaw and D. McKenzie (eds), *Reinterpreting the Educational Past: Essays in the History of New Zealand Education*, Wellington: NZCER.

McKenzie, D. (1992), 'The Technical Curriculum: Second Class Knowledge?', in G. McCulloch (ed.), *The School Curriculum in New Zealand: History, Theory, Policy and Practice*, Palmerston North: Dunmore Press.

McKenzie, D. F. (1985), *Oral Culture, Literacy and Print in Early New Zealand: The Treaty of Waitangi*, Wellington: Victoria University Press.

McKenzie, D., Lee, G. and Lee, H. (1990), *The Transformation of the New Zealand Technical High School*, Delta Research Monograph 10, Palmerston North: Massey University.

McKenzie, J. D. S. (1969), 'The First Legislation on National Education', *New Zealand Journal of Educational Studies*, 4(1), 24-40.

McKenzie, J. D. S. (1982), 'More than a Show of Justice? The Enrolment of Maoris in European Schools prior to 1900', *New Zealand Journal of Educational Studies*, 17 (1): 1-20.

Mackey, J. (1967), *The Making of a State Education System*, London: Geoffrey Chapman.

McLaren, I. (1987), 'The Politics of Secondary Education in Victorian New Zealand', in R. Openshaw and D. McKenzie (eds), *Reinterpreting the Educational Past: Essays in the History of New Zealand Education*, Wellington: NZCER.

Matthews, K. (1988), *Behind Every School: The History of Hawke's Bay Education Board*, Napier: Hawke's Bay Education Board.

Ministry of Education (1990), *The Charter Framework*, Wellington: Ministry of Education.

Morley, W. (1900), *History of Methodism in New Zealand*, Wellington: McKee and Co.

Nash, R. (1983), *Schools Can't Make Jobs*, Palmerston North: Dunmore Press. NZPD - New Zealand Parliamentary Debates.

Oliver, W. H. (1988), 'Social Policy in New Zealand: An Historical Overview', in *The April Report*, Vol 1. Wellington: Royal Commission on Social Policy.

O'Neill, A.-M. (1992), 'The Gendered Curriculum: Homemakers and Breadwinners', in G. McCulloch (ed.), *The School Curriculum in New Zealand: History, Theory, Policy and Practice*, Palmerston North: Dunmore Press.

Openshaw, R., Lee, G. and Lee, H. (1993), *Challenging the Myths: Rethinking New Zealand's Educational History*, Palmerston North: Dunmore Press.

Openshaw, R. and McKenzie, D. (eds) (1987), *Reinterpreting the Educational Past: Essays in the History of New Zealand Education*, Wellington: NZCER.

Parr, C. J. (1961), 'A Missionary Library: Printed Attempts to Instruct the Maori, 1815-1845', *Journal of the Polynesian Society*, 70 (3), 429-450.

Pompallier, J. F. B. (1888), *The Early History of the Catholic Church in Oceania*, Auckland: H. Brett.

Scott, D. (1996), 'The Currie Commission and Report on Education in New Zealand, 1960-1962', Unpublished PhD thesis, The University of Auckland.

Shuker, R. (1987a), 'Moral Panics and Social Control: Juvenile Delinquency in Late 19th Century New Zealand', in R. Openshaw and D. McKenzie (eds), *Reinterpreting the Educational Past: Essays in the History of New Zealand Education*, Wellington: NZCER.

Shuker, R. (1987b), *The One Best System? A Revisionist History of Schooling in New Zealand*, Palmerston North: Dunmore Press.

Silver, H. (1983), *Education as History*, London: Methuen.

Simon, B. (1974), *The Two Nations and the Educational Structure, 1780-1870*, London: Lawrence and Wishart.

Simon, J. A. (1986), *Ideology in the Schooling of Maori Children*, Delta Monograph No 7, Pamerston North: Massey University.

Simon, J. A. (1993), 'Secondary Schooling for Maori: The Control of Access to Knowledge', in G. H. Smith and M. Hohepa (eds), *Creating Space in Institutional Settings for Maori*, Research Unit for Maori Education: The University of Auckland.

Simon, J. (ed.) (1998), *Nga Kura Maori: The Native Schools System, 1867-1969*, Auckland: Auckland University Press.

Simpson, T. (1984), *A Vision Betrayed: The Decline of Democracy in New Zealand*, Auckland: Hodder and Stoughton.

Sinclair, K. (1988), *A History of New Zealand*, Auckland: Penguin.

Sinclair, K. (1991), *Kinds of Peace: Maori People After the Wars, 1870-85*, Auckland: Auckland University Press.

Smith, G. H. (1986), 'Taha Maori: A Pakeha Privilege', *Delta*, 37, 11-23.

Smith, L. T. (1986), 'Seeing Through the Magic: Maori Strategies of Resistance', *Delta*, 37, 3-8.

Sorrenson, M. P. K. (1987) (1981), 'Maori and Pakeha', in W. H. Oliver (ed.), *The Oxford History of New Zealand*, Auckland: Oxford University Press.

Tennent, M. (1977), 'Natural Directions: The New Zealand Movement for Sexual Differentiation in Education During the Early Twentieth Century', *New Zealand Journal of Educational Studies*, 12(2), 142-153.

The Treasury (1987), *Government Management: Brief to the Incoming Government 1987, Vol. 1 & Vol. II*. Wellington: Government Printer.

UNESCO, National Commission of (1972), *Compulsory Education in New Zealand*, Paris: UNESCO.

Walker, R. J. (1973), 'Biculturalism in Education', in D. H. Bray and C. G. N. Hill (eds), *Polynesian and Pakeha in New Zealand Education, Vol I: The Sharing of Two Cultures*, Auckland: Heinemann.

Ward, A. (1974), *A Show of Justice: Racial 'Amalgamation' in Nineteenth Century New Zealand*, Auckland: Auckland University Press/ O U P.

Yate, W. (1835), *An Account of New Zealand and of the Formation and Progress of the Church Missionary Society in the Northern Island* (2nd edition), London: Seeley and Burnside.

Chapter 2

Gender Matters in Schooling in Aotearoa/New Zealand

Alison Jones

"Some of the women teachers seem to favour the girls and ignore the boys. The girls and the teachers say things like 'typical males' sort of thing."

"Some girls are keen on using the computers, but they don't get a look in, unless the teachers kick the boys off. The girls seem less assertive in getting control of the keyboards. They annoy me because they stand back and let the boys in"

"The tuakana-teina thing means that the kids do sometimes look out for each other, but the boys tend to chuck their fists around a bit."

"Girls do better, and there are a group of girls who tend to tell the boys what to do. They think they're the teacher!"

"The boys are bullies and give cheek and hassle us girls. They don't listen to us, and they put us down and make fun of us when we say things in the class. I wish we didn't have boys in our class."

These comments, by teachers and students in Auckland schools, speak of boys and girls as separate and opposing groups. Girls and boys are attributed with different characteristics and behaviours (girls tend to be less assertive, the bullies tend to be boys, girls do better). While studies indicate that many of these gender stereotypes do describe the behaviours of many boys and girls, simple stories of difference do not begin to tell of the complexities of gender which face teachers and students in New Zealand schools and classrooms.

Before we address the question of how gender 'matters' in education, let us attempt to get clearer about gender. 'Gender' is used in a frustratingly wide range of ways, and it is a term which seems to get more complicated the closer you look. Gender is often thought to be 'whether you are male or female' (i.e. your sex). But gender is primarily about *social relationships*, not just biology. It is a term which refers to the ways women and men experience and enact the categories 'women' and 'men', and their culturally associated ideas of femininity and masculinity.

The *meanings* of 'feminine' and 'masculine' obviously differ across societies and cultures, and change historically. So while there might be general agreement on what biologically counts as a male or female within any one society or across societies (and some babies' bodies are surgically modified to conform to one or other biological sex norm), there might be disagreement about what boys and girls 'are like' and 'ought to be'. In some places, a girl might be disciplined if she shouts too loudly or acts violently, because she is not behaving properly (like a girl). Boys doing the same things might just be 'normal' – 'boys will be boys'. In some settings, girls are expected to serve men, because that is how (proper) 'girls' behave. When a boy is very gentle he may be criticised as effeminate or sissy, because he is not behaving like a boy. In Samoa, such boys may be seen not as odd but as taking a natural social position as a fa'afafine (which is neither a boy *nor* a girl).

In other words, what counts as a proper 'girl' or 'boy' will depend on the dominant cultural norms and beliefs about gender in any particular society or part of it. Children and adults are constantly and subtly disciplined to conform to the dominant social ideals of masculinity and femininity, whether via disapproval or approval, or through seductive popular images. Certainly none of us can escape gender; ideas about how we are to be women and men are deeply embedded in all the beliefs, behaviours and social interactions which form our everyday lives. For each of us, regardless of our ethnicity, social class, work, geographical location, dis/ability and sexuality, our gender is an essential part of our identity. To get a sense of how fundamental gender might be, consider how disconcerted we become when we cannot identify the sex of a child or adult, or when we discover what we thought was a boy is really a girl, or vice versa. We often find ourselves unable to be confident about how to behave towards someone until we know if they are male or female.

The Ministry of Women's Affairs' (1996: 7) definition of gender reminds us that gender is not just about identifying boys and girls, women and men; it is also a *political* term: '[gender is] more than biological differences between men and women. It includes the way those differences, whether real or perceived, have been valued, used and relied on to classify women and men and to assign roles and expectations to them.' That is, gender is about the *social implications* of our biological differences, about the *value* linked to maleness and femaleness respectively.

Some say that gender refers to 'the socially imposed dichotomy of masculine and feminine roles and character traits' (Kramarae *et al.*, 1985). Others argue that gender is 'a structure of political power masquerading as a system of natural difference' (Dimen, 1992). These commentators are suggesting several things about gender as a political category. One is that, while gender differences might be seen as 'natural', naturalness is *learnt*, and gender and gender differences are largely a product of the ways we are brought up, or socialised, into the rules and ideals of our cultures. Another point is that gender is invariably understood as a *dualism* or a dichotomy – that is, women and men are seen to be 'opposites' (as well as naturally going together). And most importantly, these commentators suggest that gender differences are marked by patterns of social privilege, inequality and power.

When we understand gender in these terms, it becomes evident why it might matter in teaching and learning. First, if gender is largely *learnt*, then all our education, whether at home, at school, on the street or in front of a screen, can be seen to 'teach' gender – what is masculine and what is feminine, what 'men' are like, and what 'women' are like. And, if we learn our gender, it can be *shaped* and altered through educational processes. Hence, gender in education matters because it is not irrelevant to teaching and learning – in school, as well as elsewhere. It is worth noting, as an aside, that it is possible to assert that gender is both learned *and* biologically based. While our genes and evolutionary history may shape our gender (women's and men's genetic differences may be expressed in some social differences), it is our social and cultural environments which determine how we can experience, and how we shape the expression of, those biological tendencies.

Second, if gender is not just about social difference but also about inequality and power differences, it is clearly relevant to education. New Zealanders place high value on social equality and equal opportunities. If inequalities are played out in schools, and gender groups get unequal treatment or do not get the same benefits from education, then gender matters in schooling. As importantly, schools are seen by New Zealanders as offering the conditions necessary for breaking into cycles of gender inequality which may characterise families and other aspects of the society. When schooling is seen as a key to moving towards a more gender equitable society, then gender matters in school, because schooling should lead the way in gender fairness and equality.

Some say that gender matters because girls (and women) are penalised on the grounds of their gender. Girls, they say, are disadvantaged in school and elsewhere: "Girls might do relatively well at school, but they often don't have a lot of confidence in what they do, so what good is that achievement?", or "Boys still take up most of the space and time in schools, and they dominate the computers, the playground and teachers' attention", or "Men still earn more than women, even though women tend to get the higher grades in education", and "Men continue to get most of the top jobs in education".

Others agree that gender is an issue in schooling but, they say, the real concern is boys – their achievement, their behaviour, and the lack of male teachers: "Boys are falling behind girls in schools, and something must be done about it", or "Many boys are switched off by school, because there are too many women teachers", or "We need to teach boys how to be less violent and to like reading", or "We need more Maori men teaching our mokopuna to give them good male role models".

For many New Zealanders, though, gender in schools is not, or should not be, an issue. Some teachers and parents say: "I don't think about children as boys and girls. They are just kids to me – all with different needs and personalities". In a similar vein, others say: "Our tamariki are children, not male and female", or "We should not treat boys and girls differently in the classroom. We are all basically the same – human beings. Gender is irrelevant".

Many others would say gender does not matter because gender differences are relatively insignificant. They point to New Zealand research which indicates that gender is the least influential variable in achievement differences in schooling (Alton-Lee and Praat, 2000: 25; Nash and Harker, 1997a). Gender is irrelevant, they insist, because one's ethnicity and social class are the factors that make the difference. The very small differences in achievement between girls and boys are well-overshadowed by differences between ethnic and class groups. This is an important point, and one I address further below.

In this chapter, I take the position that gender *does* matter in education – but I refuse any argument which puts boys and girls into a competition over who is most disadvantaged. Rather, I am critical of this framing of gender questions (despite its continuing ubiquity in the New Zealand literature). I consider ways of understanding the many and complex gender issues which daily confront teachers and students in New Zealand classrooms, including the disjunctions and contradictions in the interplay of gender and power.

Gender Matters in School

Feminist scholars, researchers and teachers have been foremost in drawing attention to gender as an issue in New Zealand schools, pointing out the ways schooling has tended to privilege male perspectives and, they argue, to disadvantage girls and women (see for instance, Jones *et al.* 1995, Middleton and Jones 1992, Jones and Middleton 1996). Recently, educationists concerned about boys have joined feminists in focusing on gender as a pressing issue in schools. Boys' apparently slipping achievement relative to girls' in New Zealand schools, and concerns about some detrimental effects of New Zealand ideals of masculinity, have been added to the discussions about gender and male power in education.

These two main sets of concerns about gender seem to be in serious tension. How can males be *both* 'dominant' *and* 'underachieving' in schools? Can girls be *both* disadvantaged *and* often do better than boys? Rather than seeking one right answer to these questions, in this chapter I embrace the contradictions they suggest, and approach gender as a shifting network of power relationships rather than a linear and hierarchical one where males or females are invariably 'on top'. Within a feminist tradition, I would argue that this shifting network of power relations nevertheless occurs on the wider terrain of patriarchy (characterised by the assumption of male-as-norm). Gender difference, I would argue, cannot be seen as working on neutral territory.

Gender Matters 1:
Schooling for equality: opportunities for girls and boys

Prior to the late 1970s in New Zealand, gender equality was not generally considered to be an important issue. Until that time, conservative views of gender determined the ways curriculum, teaching and school discipline were understood. It was assumed that women and men had different, distinct social roles: men as breadwinners, leaders and protectors of their families; women primarily as mothers, wives and nurturers (see Ryan, 1988). Social stability and individual well-being was considered to rest on the maintenance of these 'naturally' different gender activities, and so schooling reflected the wider traditional beliefs. Girls studied cooking and sewing, boys did metal work. Boys got caned, girls did not. Girls who avoided 'hard' sciences were seen as merely expressing their natural femininity; boys who got into fights were merely 'being boys'. Textbooks for new readers in the early 1970s still contained illustrated sentences such as "Girls like to play with the baby" and "Boys like play-fighting".

Due to the increasing economic necessity for paid work for both women and men, the increasing relative availability of positions for women in the labour market, and the now-widespread feminist ideology asserting women's rights to fulfilling and independent lives, conservative gender ideas in education diminished in popularity throughout the 1970s. It was the feminist activism in the 1970s and 1980s which managed to ensure at last the inclusion of gender in the discourses of equal opportunity which had formed the proud centrepiece of New Zealand education policy since the 1930s. Since the 1980s, liberal notions of equality of opportunity in the education of girls and boys have come increasingly to predominate, as the language of 'fairness and equality' for boys and girls in the education system has become widely accepted (Middleton and May 1997; Middleton 1985, 1988a; May 1992). This was evident particularly in the policy documents produced to guide the administrative and curriculum reforms in the education system in the 1980s and 1990s.

The contemporary liberal views on gender and education have their roots in a classical liberalism whose basic elements, applied to gender, look something like this:

1. All men and women share a unique human essence – a 'potential' or ability – which individuals can develop through intellectual or physical work.

2. This essence is expressed differently in different individuals, but is basically independent of social context – one's gender, class or ethnicity.

3. A good society is one which allows maximum opportunity for *all*

individuals, regardless of their gender (or ethnicity or class), to develop and exercise their abilities.

This recipe for a good society is in sharp contrast with a gender-conservative one which is based on the idea that what is most significant about women's and men's abilities is not their similarity (ensured by their shared humanness) but their difference.

Liberal arguments for equality are based on the beliefs that women and men as groups have the *same* range of potential, and that all individuals ought to have the *same* opportunities to develop their potential. This demand for equality is justified partly on the grounds of fairness and partly for economic reasons (Jones *et al.*, 1995: 118ff). Because gender equality, however justified, is now a dominant cultural value in New Zealand, it is generally expected that education policy and practice will ensure that gender does not confer an advantage or disadvantage. Boys and girls are expected, in an ideal, gender-egalitarian society, to take a comparable range of subject choices, to get the same amounts of attention from their teachers, and to get similar quantities of enjoyment and satisfaction from their schooling experience, as well as to be suspended at similar rates, and to achieve a similar range of grades.

This idea may sound attractive in theory. However, the achievement of ideals of gender equality usually requires practices which do *not* enact equality and sameness. *Equity* is the term which draws attention to these complexities, and which has been used since 1989 in New Zealand educational policy aimed at gender equality (see Jones *et al.*, 1990: 121ff). Equity is the application of a particular notion of fairness: positive discrimination. In schools, it involves the provision, not of equal resources, but of *unequal* resources and attention to groups of students so that fairer outcomes can be achieved. Gender examples include forms of positive discrimination such as maths and science classes especially for girls, English classes for boys only, girls-only and boys-only time on the school computers, inviting Maori or Tongan male sporting heroes to promote reading in the school, or special attempts to hire and promote women rather than men at higher levels of the education decision-making hierarchy.

Current Gender Policy and New Zealand Schools

There was little critical policy development in the 1990s with regard to gender and schooling in New Zealand (Alton-Lee and Praat, 2000: 55), unlike the situation in Australia where there has been extensive Government support for policy and practice initiatives for 'understanding the process of the construction of gender', curriculum teaching and learning, violence and school culture, and post-school pathways (MCEETYA, 1995). The Girls and Women section of the New Zealand Ministry of Education was disestablished in 1992 and no other infrastructure to resource gender and education policy issues has been put in place.

Principles of gender equality are evident, however, in the National Education Guidelines established in 1990 to provide the framework for the delivery of formal schooling in New Zealand. Amongst other things, the Guidelines aim for 'Equality of educational opportunity for all New Zealanders, by identifying and removing barriers to achievement'. The Curriculum Framework section of the Guidelines aims at a 'gender inclusive curriculum' which 'acknowledges and includes the educational needs of girls equally with those of boys, both in its content, and in the language, methods and approaches, and practices of teaching' (Ministry of Education, 1993: 1).

Alton-Lee and Praat (2000: 55) point out that although the New Zealand Curriculum Framework gives boys and girls equal weight in its language, boys are usually positioned within the default/main/normal/invisible category of 'all students', but not as boys. For example, the 'Science in the New Zealand Curriculum' statement alerts teachers to attend to 'Science for all', 'Girls and science', 'Maori and science', and 'Students with special needs and interests'. Boys do feature as a 'tagged' group in the English curriculum statement, where their poor average achievement has caused concern.

However, despite the liberal policy rhetoric (which is now more than a decade old), some maintain that girls and boys continue to get an unequal deal from schooling. Girls, they say, still get less attention from their teachers, females continue to be more negatively and less frequently found in textbook illustrations, girls continue to be subject to boys' harassment and violence, and often have less confidence in their abilities than they should. Females are also paid one-sixth less than their male peers when they move into employment, despite doing as well, if not better, educationally than males. Others argue that liberal educational policies of equity have not benefited boys, who are increasingly switched off school, have lower literacy rates than their female peers, don't have male role models in the classroom, more often require remedial help, are more often expelled, leave school with fewer qualifications, have higher unemployment rates than women, are more likely to commit suicide, and do not do as well as girls in terms of school grades.

Gender Matters 2:
The importance of being disadvantaged

Researchers and writers who focus on gender use the language of *disadvantage* to characterise boys' and girls' school experience. Disadvantage has been a popular term since the 1980s to call attention to groups of children – usually girls, Maori, Pacific Islands, rural or disabled (Department of Education, 1987: 10) – considered at risk of not getting the advantages offered by the best New Zealand schooling. Most of these children were seen as being disadvantaged by sexism, racism, poverty, geographical location or discrimination – set-backs which the school could at least try to alleviate with good equity policies and practices. Equity policies which sought to protect and resource the disadvantaged were implemented in schools.

As a result, 'disadvantage' has developed a reputation as a powerful weapon in the struggle for resources and attention in education. Inevitably, in this environment, a politics of vulnerability has developed in which ability to demonstrate disadvantage confers a moral entitlement to resources and support. Boys (particularly Pakeha boys) have been seen by some as missing out on the 'privileges' of disadvantage. Boys' advocates have engaged in a political struggle to ensure boys take a place alongside (or even instead of) girls in the ranks of the educationally disadvantaged. Some, such as Fergusson and Horwood (1997: 84) who researched over 1,000 children born in Christchurch, insist that 'the traditional educational disadvantage shown by females has largely disappeared and has been replaced by an emerging male disadvantage'.

While disadvantage may give access to a moral high ground and its potential entitlements, it also may have unwelcome consequences. Now that *all* groups are effectively 'disadvantaged' the term is, unsurprisingly, losing its value. Moreover, some have argued that disadvantage is a term which can unwittingly contribute to the very factors it seeks to alleviate:

once a group is 'disadvantaged', its members are seen – and see themselves – as lacking something, as victims and in need of rescue (Jones and Jacka, 1995). Women and girls have historically been dogged by such negative and 'disempowering' descriptions; disadvantage has been a troublesome addition to the list of girls' descriptors. It may also become troublesome for boys; not the least because boys-as-disadvantaged could come to see themselves as victims, and blame women and girls (especially women teachers) for leaving/dumping them in their new, vulnerable status which was once the preserve of women.

Sexism and Disadvantage

Boys' attempts to enter the terrain of disadvantage, however necessary, further draw attention to the complexities of the territory. Disadvantage associated with girls is usually understood as an aspect of *sexism*, which has been defined as those beliefs and practices which limit particularly girls' and women's opportunities, practices and beliefs through stereotypic notions of gender difference which involve inferiority being associated with 'female' attributes (Department of Education, 1989: 11).

Some feminists have resisted any tendency to use the term 'sexism' to refer to practices which disadvantage men or boys, arguing that while individual or small groups of men might be discriminated against on the basis of gender, the predominant social power relations continue to favour men as a group. They assert that 'discrimination' or 'prejudice' may be more appropriate terms. Sexism, they maintain, refers to ideas and gendered practices, which are sanctioned and made meaningful within the overarching power relations of a patriarchy (in which women are secondary), and which contribute to its maintenance. One paradox of this sort of view is that sexism may in fact *benefit* individual women in the short term, while relying on wider ideas about women which may *not benefit* them in an overall, structural sense. For instance, a woman may get favoured treatment from the car mechanic because he believes she needs gallant assistance. Or, as in a recent tragic situation in the Bay of Plenty, the only female in a group of men and boys on a sinking boat was given the one lifejacket, because she was 'a girl'. She was saved and the rest drowned. Both sets of generous actions in these stories enact a conservative gender assumption that women are 'weak' and 'need special protection'. Clearly, sexism is not a simple theoretical idea, which we can simply be 'against' or 'for'. Gender discrimination has layers of complexity, and may be contradictory in its effects – at individual, social and historical levels.

Some have pointed out that patriarchal social relations not only disadvantage women, but also detrimentally affect many men in so far as a patriarchal society may selectively reward 'machismo' masculinities (which can have negative effects, including violence, car smashes, and accidents of all kinds) and punish other, nurturing, masculine behaviours. Women, they insist, are not the only possible victims of sexism. Gay boys at school, for instance, are ridiculed and bullied because they are not 'real men' (Quinlivan and Town, 1999). All boys can be seen as victims of sexism according to this argument, in so far as they are 'disciplined' to conform to dominant ideals of maleness.

Discussion about how sexism might work draws attention to the idea that we cannot simply see gender differences in education as having equal effects for boys/men and girls/women. Take, for instance, the case where a female school teacher had consensual sex with a sixteen-year-old male pupil. Her shamefaced and regretful admission was accepted with some sympathy by the public. If she had been male and the pupil female, the public response would probably have been quite negative. The discrepancy between these responses can be seen as an example of sexism in action; *not* so much because the male teacher would have been discriminated against (as he certainly would have been), as because male and female sexuality is seen in such different ways. The male pupil was seen as 'lucky', while the putative female student would have been seen as a victim. The female teacher was not seen as predatory because it is assumed women tend not to know their sexual selves; their sexual desires are not as 'serious' as men's are.

Gender Matters 3:
Gender differences in school

When we hear about 'gender differences in school' we do not usually think of sex. Rather, most public concern is with *achievement outcomes*, and the belief that girls and boys ought to do equally well at school. This latter belief is a relatively new one. Prior to the late 1970s it was generally accepted in New Zealand that girls would be better at some things (social relationships, languages, and activities that involve small body movements, for instance), and boys would do better at subjects involving logic or 'hard' sciences, or hard physical work. As I have already mentioned, post-1970s it has become a fashionable cultural assumption that boys and girls as groups can and should achieve equally in most things, particularly educationally.

While gender equality is a 'politically correct' view which many of us articulate, it is often not reflected in our common sense assumptions about girls and boys. This discrepancy is not surprising. Indeed, no-one is free from it. We do not, after all, live 'outside' a patriarchy, even if we resist its effects. While there has not been equivalent work done in New Zealand, Walkerdine (1989), a British educational researcher, has made interesting remarks about common assumptions regarding boys' and girls' ability and attainment, particularly in mathematics. Walkerdine suggests that girls' success in maths is seen by teachers and girls themselves as a result of 'hard work' rather than cleverness in maths, while boys' success is considered a result of maths aptitude. On the other hand, boys' failure is seen as evidence of 'mucking around', while girls' failure signals their lack of ability.

The underlying assumption is that boys' failure needs to be explained, as does girls' success. We unconsciously do not expect girls to do well at maths and science, Walkerdine suggests, because it offends our deeply held traditional notions of femininity, or woman-as-not-intellectually-able. When girls do well it is 'explained' through their effort (to overcome their natural inability in these areas). Boys, on the other hand, are simply lazy if they fail – otherwise their natural ability would show itself. These same assumptions may be at work in current worries about boys 'falling behind' girls in school grades. Girls' school achievement has not been seen as cause for public celebration or congratulation. Instead, the improvement in achievement patterns for some girls (which are the result of changed economic and cultural practices and beliefs) has largely produced anxiety: about boys' relative (and unnatural) 'failure'.

Walkerdine's work fits with the findings of New Zealand maths researcher Jenny Young-Loveridge (1992) who noted that the primary schoolgirls in her study tended to be pessimistic about their maths ability, and the boys tended to be optimistic – even when they had little objective ground for that optimism. Boys tend to assume they can do it; girls are more likely to assume they can't, even when they can. And when girls achieve particularly well in science or maths it is still likely to be seen as odd, exceptional and noteworthy.

It is clear that cultural assumptions about gender difference are contradictory. On the one hand there is a social agreement that boys and girls can and should do equally well at school, and on the other there are ingrained assumptions about different 'normal' masculine and feminine aptitudes. Nevertheless, the current debates about gender in education are based on the social ideal of sameness and equality, and in particular how that ideal is *not* achieved in areas such as the following.

Curriculum Choice and Attitudes

It is believed that in order to ensure equal access to careers and employment, girls and boys 'should' choose the same range of secondary school subjects: equal participation patterns are considered to be a measure of gender equality. Although gender differences in participation rates in school subjects have been reducing over the last decade, there are still some fairly marked differences: more boys still tend to choose physics, girls tend more often to choose English, languages and biology. For instance, in 1998 while 30 per cent of Year 12 boys took physics, only 14 per cent of Year 12 girls opted for this subject. In comparison, 21 per cent of Year 12 boys chose biology in contrast to 33 per cent of Year 12 girls (Ministry of Education, 1998: 76). Maori and Pacific Islands girls and boys tend particularly to avoid maths and 'hard' sciences in the senior years. Not surprisingly, pupil attitudes to school subjects reflect these patterns of choice. Local studies (Flockton and Crooks, 1996; Martin, 1996; Garden, 1997) present a bleak picture of girls' and Maori and Pacific Islands students' enjoyment of school science and maths. While girls seem to enjoy these subjects in primary school, their attitudes and confidence tend to deteriorate in the late primary and early secondary years (see also Praat, 1999).

In the English curriculum, more boys than girls tend to have a negative attitude to reading, and Pakeha and Maori boys read fewer books (Flockton and Crooks, 1996; Wagemaker, 1993). Fathers are much less likely than mothers to discuss reading with their children across all ethnic groups. And if you are from a wealthier ('professional') family you are more likely to discuss reading at home (Bardsley, 1991). One qualitative study of fifth form boys' attitudes to English (Stephens, 1996) suggested that for some boys, English was a feminine subject and, as such, to be avoided like the plague. There is certainly anecdotal evidence that homophobia as well as sexism plays a part in New Zealand boys' anxiety about reading, when boys associate particularly fiction-reading with 'girl' and 'poof' behaviour. Yet despite many boys' negative view of reading, about three quarters of the fiction texts used for school study are by male authors who, according to one researcher, 'tend to portray males in a stronger physical and emotional light than the females' (Burnett, 1998: 3).

Grade Achievement

Concern about boys in school has coalesced in particular around their lower grade achievement levels in school examinations, compared with their female peers (called 'boys' underachievement'). The 1999 Education Review Office (ERO) report on boys' achievement states unequivocally that 'Girls currently outperform boys at school against most measures of achievement' (p.3). The report provides figures of aggregated 1998 School Certificate results, showing that girls gained more A and B grades, while boys gained more D and E grades. Girls' results were better within each ethnic group (although Pacific Islands girls and boys tend pass school certificate at a similar rate). The average size of the 'gender gap', the report says, is 5.84 per cent. It is worth mentioning right away that such summary statements can be misleading. Because girls usually do a lot better than boys in English, it is deceptive to gather together results for 'all papers'. Aggregating English results with all the others may hide the fact that differences are not great in other subjects or may favour boys.

Other statistics give a less clear account; different data sources seem to tell different stories. Data from School Certificate examination results indicate that girls do get slightly better grades than boys in most school subjects, including science. But according to international standardised studies of science and maths achievement, there is no significant difference between New Zealand boys and girls at the primary level, and boys tend to score better than girls at the secondary level (for a detailed analysis of gender and maths and science achievement patterns, see Alton-Lee and Praat, 2000; Praat, 1999).

The same disparity between results of international measures of achievement levels and local assessments is evident in English. International studies show that New Zealand girls do much better than boys at age 10, but that there are no significant gender differences at age 14 (Alton-Lee and Praat, 2000: 150). Local examinations and assessments indicate that while there are no significant gender differences at school entry, girls of all ethnic groups do better than their male peers in senior secondary school English examinations (Lauder *et al.*, 1995).

Some insight into the discrepancy between international tests and local assessments in English might be found in Fergusson, Lloyd and Horwood's (1991) study of teacher ratings of primary student reading and writing performance. They maintain that the teachers in their study tended to rate girls' performances more highly, over and above the gender differences the authors found in standardised tests of the children's reading and writing competence. Fergusson and his colleagues conclude that teachers' assessments of competence may be influenced by other factors such as the student's demeanour and diligence, influences which tend to mitigate against boys. McDonald (1994: 90) suggests an alternative explanation. She maintains that 'standardised tests are biased against girls and do not give them full credit for their academic performance'.

It should be remembered that, aside from some English results, the mean differences between boys and girls in school achievement are very small. Mean gender differences are the smallest of group differences; that is, students from low socio-economic groups and Maori and Pacific Islands boys and girls fare far worse than their higher socio-economic and Pakeha peers in all academic subjects, regardless of gender. Nash and Harker's (1997a) analysis of School Certificate results by social class and ethnicity revealed that differences in English scores between students from professional families, and those from unemployed, unskilled or semi-skilled families, to be almost *three times* greater than gender differences within social-class bands.

Another point to be made is that, contrary to the media headlines, there has not been a 'sudden slide' in boys' achievement. New Zealand school inspectors' reports from the last century onwards indicated that girls have always done better than boys in English, and that girls tended to progress more quickly than boys through the primary school (McGeorge, 1987). Public concern about boys arose in the late 1990s not because of boys' abrupt decline in achievement, but when some girls' increasing improvement in secondary school maths and science (and other subjects) finally came to public attention, and female unemployment levels dropped below those of men. Men and boys were no longer unproblematically 'on top' in terms of grade achievements in the subjects which have been seen as a measure of intelligence.

Why is there sudden interest in boys now? There are several possible answers. One is that, as I suggested above, contrary to the gender equality assumption currently in vogue, we subconsciously expect boys to do better than girls, particularly in the 'logic' subjects (science, physics and maths). When they do not, we are concerned that there is something 'wrong'. Another answer refers to the changing employment patterns for men and women resulting from the reduction in low-skilled manual work opportunities, particularly for working-class men in New Zealand, due to mechanisation and globalisation, and the apparently increasing opportunities in service fields for women. Girls have had plenty to encourage them to improve their poorer performance in maths and science and other subjects: a shifting labour market which offers more opportunities for women, and changing social expectations regarding women's financial autonomy and independence.

Changes in the job-market translate into a certain anxiety for young men in the traditional education system, and the possibility that they perceive schooling as less relevant to their work opportunities. Jane Gilbert (1998: 13) has suggested that boys and girls often make intuitively well-informed decisions about their educational choices and behaviour. She says that some boys may not be disadvantaging themselves if they don't 'keep up' with girls. They may 'slack off' in school because they have perceived that school grade achievement is becoming less critical to financially rewarding work opportunities for them. Gilbert suggests that information technology, and financial and investment sectors, which are attractive to some boys, are distinguished by their valuing of risk-taking, 'creative', 'innovative' or 'breaking set' behaviours (behaviours associated with competitiveness and aggression, and therefore with masculinity). When risk-taking and entrepreneurial creativity, as well as information technology skills, are those which are likely to lead to well-paying jobs for some, then the need to strive for improved grades at school is seen as irrelevant. Gilbert suggests that it is boys in particular who are responding to the new work opportunities in ways which downplay academic achievement.

Boys' Domination of Airspace and Teacher Attention

The use of space offers a highly visible marker of gender difference and inequality. Studies of the gendered use of space tend to show consistently that men take up more room when they sit and stand, that men's sports still take up more space (not only in terms of square metres on the paddock but more centimetres in the newspapers and sound-bytes on the television), and that men still tend to dominate mixed conversation and airspace generally. In terms of schooling, many studies have highlighted boys' verbal space-taking in classroom lessons. When Karen Newton (1992) observed 'morning talk' sessions in an Auckland primary school, she noted how the sessions were often constructed around the interests and experiences of boys. She found that such topics as the boys' sports games and their toys (such as remote-controlled cars), were most often the focus of the presentations, making it difficult for girls to interrupt the agenda of 'male topics' and begin talking about their interests and concerns.

When she studied co-educational science classes in a Wellington secondary school, Scott (1992:38) noted that 'boys dominated the classroom interactions and practical work. In every observation it was found that boys more than girls called out, raised their hands and called the teacher over'. In the experimental girls-only class, according to Scott, the students considered their class to be less inhibited and livelier than the co-ed group, and the girls reported feeling more confident.

Alton-Lee and Nuthall (1991), studying in detail teacher–pupil interaction in a New Zealand primary classroom science unit on 'weather', found that teachers initiated more responses in boys (60 per cent of responses) than in girls (40 per cent). They argued that such bias has the effect of focusing the content of the curriculum more on the interests of boys and their experiences. Girls and boys might learn in this sort of setting that science knowledge is 'boys' knowledge' and that what boys think is more important than what girls think. One study of Maori immersion classes suggested girls and boys gained equitable attention there, though in bilingual classes the old pattern of male domination of airspace seemed evident (Carkeek, Davies and Irwin, 1994).

Why the concern about teacher attention patterns? If girls do reasonably well in school with less teacher attention, does attention from the teacher matter? Surely if girls are doing okay, then their relative silence is not a problem? There are several possible answers to these questions. If we measure school success in terms of grades, perhaps teacher attention patterns do not matter; there may be little relation between pupil–teacher talk and achievement levels.

But if schooling is about more than grades, and also about developing a sense of how and whether we are skilled and competent, how to express our interests, or about gaining a sense of ourselves as valued and authoritative individuals, then the answer has to be that teacher attention patterns *do* matter. When they get less attention from teachers, girls (and boys) may be learning that girls' interests, perspectives and knowledge do not matter as much as boys' do. When girls stand aside to let boys speak more, to have more physical space, or to take over the keyboard or whatever, they re-enact the idea that girls are not as competent and their needs are fewer and less important than boys'. (Girls who resist standing aside, though, risk being ridiculed as 'bossy' and 'pushy' because they are refusing to be good 'girls'.)

Of course, the fact that boys gain more teacher attention does not mean necessarily that the attention is 'a good thing'. Studies note that although boys gain more teacher attention, much of that attention is negative; that is, boys tend to disrupt and 'misbehave' more than girls, and therefore the teacher ends up interacting with them. So 'more teacher attention' may point to problems and negative outcomes for boys. Boys' attention-getting 'off-task' behaviour may signal their inability or unwillingness to engage with the required school work. In addition, disruptive boys can have very negative effects on male peers who are distracted into behaviours which don't contribute to good 'achievement outcomes' for boys.

Teachers who believe that their public verbal interactions are significant to children and young people have devised strategies for regulating their own gendered attention patterns by, for instance, asking boys and girls to speak in turn, having boys or girls only classes or groups, drawing attention to gender inequality in classroom interactions, focusing strongly on verbal positive reinforcement for boys rather than reprimand, monitoring their own tendencies to overlook the less assertive girls (and boys) in the class, and considering ways positively to foster boys' schoolwork-based independence. That is on their good days, anyway! Some New Zealand researchers suggest that all students need training in group techniques which facilitate exploratory talk from boys and girls (Gilbert and McCormish, 1990).

The Construction of Curriculum Subjects

It is generally accepted that all knowledge, including school knowledge, is necessarily a shared *interpretation* of the world. Inevitably, what is generally accepted as valuable knowledge (curriculum) in education is a reflection of the interpretations, interests and experiences of those who produce that knowledge, and those who are in a position to be able to determine the curriculum. Some educationists have pointed out that what counts as science, social studies, maths and so on is often based around male, and Western (or Pakeha), interests and experiences. Speed and acceleration in science books may be explained using examples and images of, say, racing cars; force may be illustrated with pictures of men using hammers or axes. Generic diagrams of the human digestive or muscle systems are often portrayed in the 'neutral', default male body (Bell, 1988).

Not only might the curriculum be shaped by what interests boys/men, but information and knowledge may also be shaped by traditional conservative notions of femininity and masculinity. This means that gender stereotypes may not be explicitly taught, but may be implicitly assumed as part of the 'hidden curriculum' (i.e. knowledge that is learnt, but not explicitly or intentionally taught). For instance, Gilbert (1996: 42) gives an amusing account of the ways cultural assumptions about feminine 'passivity' and male 'action' are interwoven in accounts of fertilisation. The standard account in New Zealand biology textbooks, she says, gives a story of the sperm which is one of 'a noble struggle, it is a thrilling self-congratulatory narrative'. The entrepreneurial sperm are seen as energetically penetrating the impassive, blob-like egg. Gilbert draws attention to other scientific representations where the sperm has a weak tail, and rather than being entered by the sperm, the egg 'actively envelops the sperm'. This different scientific account does not assume that a traditional gendered narrative needs to shape our understanding of fertilisation biology.

The hidden curriculum of female inferiority is also 'taught' when the generic male stands in as the subject of human activity. Most of us are aware of the problems with referring to all human beings as 'he'. And we are familiar with the still-common practice of calling all animals 'he', including hens and cows. We may not even notice when a vet on a children's television programme asks the proud owner of a fat black chook "Does he scratch around in the straw?" or when the singing cows in a flavoured milk advertisement on television have male voices.

The habit of using the generic male is only one of a range of ways that females can be made 'invisible' in the curriculum and in everyday conversation in the school. In their well-known study of children's primary classrooms in Christchurch, Alton-Lee and Densem (1992) showed just how absent females can be in the curriculum. They analysed the number of times females were referred to in some primary school social studies lessons, and found that women were mentioned between 2 and 4 per cent of the time. In one curriculum topic, females made up only 3.9 per cent of the 13,027 mentions of people. The researchers record that of the few times women were mentioned in these units, it was virtually always in terms of their relation to a male (e.g. as his mother or wife). (See also discussion of the effects of gender stereotypes on what counts as geography by Nairn, 1993; Longhurst and Peace, 1993.)

Researchers argue that one of the effects of female invisibility in the curriculum is not only, as I have already said, that girls and boys learn that women's experiences and realities are less important than men's, but that children gain very little knowledge about women as active in history, science and public life. Women, it seems, do 'nothing much'. Such ignorance may be acted out in contemporary everyday life when girls or women find it relatively difficult to get their views, knowledge, needs and activities taken seriously – by themselves and others.

'Role Models'

A common lament from the 1990s is that there are 'not enough male role models' for boys in schools. Seventy-nine per cent of primary teachers and 53 per cent of secondary school teachers were women in 1999 (Ministry of Education, 1999: 23). Some boys' advocates argue that this 'feminisation' of teaching is at the root of boys' disadvantage. It is said that because boys tend to see relatively few male teachers in front of classrooms, they are encouraged to think that schoolwork is 'for the girls'. This argument, if we look at the statistics, can only legitimately apply to primary schooling where women have nearly always predominated in New Zealand.

It is the case that young New Zealand men tend not to see teaching, particularly primary and early childhood teaching, as a desirable career (Farquhar, 1997). One of the probable reasons is to be found in the strong relationship between teacher salary levels and the proportion of men in the teaching system. Those countries where teachers have higher salaries are able to attract more male teachers; where teaching is poorly paid, men tend to be scarce (Alton-Lee and Praat, 2000: 35). Another reason for men's avoidance of teaching young children is men's real fear, generated by the contemporary anxiety about accusations of child abuse (Jones, forthcoming), and the persistent view that looking after children is 'women's work'.

One of the problems with the feminisation-of-teaching argument is that it assumes that 'there was a golden age when there were many male teachers and no problems with boys' (Alton-Lee and Praat, 2000: 269). The fact that women have dominated primary school teaching in New Zealand for over a century, and men made up the majority of secondary teachers before women and men drew level recently, does not sit well with the sudden upsurge of concern about boys having too many female teachers. Indeed, there is no research consensus on the effects of a 'feminised' teaching profession on boys' views of school work. One international study in 1991 did show that a higher proportion of female teachers was associated with higher overall achievement rates (Alton-Lee and Praat, 2000: 172) suggesting that women teachers might benefit boys and girls!

According to some, the 'role model' problem is not that women are teachers, but that men predominate in decision-making. Although the situation has altered as more women gain positions of power and responsibility in education, in New Zealand schools it is still largely the case, as Neville (1988) said over ten years ago, that 'men lead, women follow; men manage, women teach'. In this situation, the message is reinforced for both girls and boys that men are – and should be – leaders and authorities. In 1999, although women made up 79 per cent of primary school classroom teachers, over two-thirds (64 per cent) of primary school principals were male. Indeed, of the total male teaching staff in primary schools 35 per cent were principals compared to 4 per cent of the total female staff (Ministry of Education, 1999b). In secondary schools in 1999, the situation was similar. While over half (53 per cent) of the classroom teachers were women, only 25 per cent of secondary principals were women, and many of these were in girls' schools. Positions of responsibility in secondary schools are still held mainly by men (ibid.).

Even when women do 'get to the top' many find that the styles of leadership they are expected to adopt and those which they would prefer, are two different things – which leads to conflict and stress (Irwin, 1992; Court, 1992, 1998). Court (1992) found that many women preferred a collegial, teamwork leadership style rather than a hierarchical one – although this was often in tension with more traditional notions of authority and efficiency. In relation to women's leadership in education, Irwin (1992) provides a particularly poignant view of 'becoming an academic' as a Maori woman. There is no doubt that many male leaders also prefer a less hierarchical authority structure in schools – though as yet there is little research on New Zealand male teachers' desired leadership styles.

One point that should not be overlooked is that, due to its traditional association with women, the classroom is one of the relatively few sites outside the home where girls can enact (non-sexualised) authority. If we go into any New Zealand primary school classroom we are likely to observe girls being 'little teachers', and telling boys what is, and is not, allowed. Bird's (1992) study in a Wellington primary school showed how girls gain authority through taking up the position of the (female) teacher – while boys' attempts at authority more often come from aggressive or bullying behaviour. One paradox of girls gaining power as mentors and 'little teachers' is that they can enact a sort of feminine disadvantage by putting the needs of others before their own, yet again.

In the face of the call for 'more role models' for both boys and girls in different sections of the school, there are points to be made about the slipperiness of the idea of 'role models'. The recruitment of 'reading guys' and 'non-smoking sporting heroes' and 'women explorers and scientists' into schools may be an excellent idea. But it is worth remembering that many untested assumptions are made about the good effects of introducing 'positive role models' to kids. We cannot control who or what might act as a model for young people (or anyone). Admired and influential heroes may be drawn from a variety of sources, including television, film, magazines and video. Any adults or peers – and not just 'real' ones, either

– may act as gender 'role models' for children (Middleton, 1992). A woman explorer may be seen simply as weird, compared with the 'normal' women on *Friends*. And Jonah Lomu in person may be too good/big to be true.

Possible role models do not just inhabit the principal's office and the classroom. There is clearly not a *lack* of adult male or female role models in the school. Adult males do exist in the school as principals, as cleaners and groundkeepers, as well as teachers (not to mention in curricula, book and screen images, and games). Women are not so often in the principal's chair, and work in the school in jobs such as teachers, secretaries, school nurses and tuckshop keepers. Many teachers and principals take seriously the idea that children do learn what is possible for themselves through regular positive encounters with adults. They attempt to invite into their classrooms and schools interesting people and resources which challenge the usual gender and ethnic stereotypes. They also take positive steps to ensure that positions of authority in the school and its curriculum can provide surprises regarding gender.

Truancy, Suspension and School Retention Rates

Girls and boys report that they skip classes at about the same rate, but boys are far more likely than girls to be suspended or expelled from school. Suspension figures indicate that of the 2 per cent of the school population who are suspended, 73 per cent of these are male. As with achievement figures any gender differences in suspension rates are completely overshadowed by differences between ethnic groups. The suspension rate of Maori (35.8/1000) is more than three times the Pakeha rate (10.9/1000), and the Pacific Islands rate is almost twice that of Pakeha (19.3/1000) (Sturrock, 1998).

Information on school retention rates also suggests that differences on the basis of ethnicity might require more attention than gender differences. According to Praat's (1999) report, males aged 16 and 17 years tend to leave school slightly earlier than females. When we examine these figures more closely and compare the rates of school retention for 'all' students with Maori students, we find major differences between ethnic groups, and within gender categories. In 1998, 40 per cent of Maori males and 43 per cent of Maori females aged 17 years remained at school, compared with 59 per cent of all males and 65 per cent of all females in the same age group. In terms of retention rates, Maori boys are the group that fare worst.

Single-sex and Co-ed Schools

There continues to be a certain amount of uncertainty in New Zealand about the benefits or otherwise of single-sex and co-ed schools. Faced with the range of schools in New Zealand in both the private and state sectors of the education system, some parents and students may have a choice. While examination results indicate that single-sex schools for both boys and girls collect the most examination passes (with girls' schools doing better overall), it is notoriously difficult to argue that these differences are the result of a one-gender school environment. There are several factors which complicate the possibility of answering clearly the popular question about whether it is better to send children to co-ed or single-sex schools at secondary level. Single-sex schools tend to attract students from higher socio-economic backgrounds (and wealth is positively correlated with educational attainment); parents may be more supportive of students at single-sex schools, having chosen to place them there; religious affiliations of many single-sex schools may impact on student behaviour and parental support.

Nash and Harker (1997b) conclude from their study of over 5,000 pupils in 37 New Zealand secondary schools that students do no better or worse as a result of the gender make-up of the school. That is, students' ability when they enter the school will tend to determine their scores, rather than whether the school is mixed or not.

There may be other reasons, aside from examination results, for students and their parents choosing single-sex or co-ed schools. Some argue that single-sex schools are better for girls because the distractions and harassment of boys are absent, and because there are a greater number of sporting and leadership opportunities, and more chance of high-achieving female peers. Boys, others say, are better off in co-ed schools due to the 'moderating influence' of girls, and mixed schools offer a more 'normal' social environment. On the other hand, a single-sex school may offer boys a more relaxed environment which caters more specifically to their interests and needs in sporting terms and in classrooms. Overall, it appears that research and opinion is equivocal, and single-sex or mixed-school choice may be a matter for individual preference.

Jones' (1988, 1991a) study of a girls' school in Auckland found that difference does not disappear in single-sex schools. She argues that the patterns of privilege and difference between boys and girls are simply replaced by those between ethnic and social class groups. At the school she studied, 'Girls' High' (an unusually mixed school in terms of social class and ethnicity), where boys could not dominate classroom talk and interaction, Pakeha middle class girls dominated, while the hard-working working class Pacific Islands girls were relatively invisible and silent peers.

Gender Matters 4:
Can we sensibly talk about 'boys' and 'girls' in school?

Discussion about gender difference and disadvantage rely on the use of the terms 'girls' and 'boys'. But although these terms are *necessary* to our talk about gender and education, they also fundamentally *limit* that talk, or *shape* it in particular ways.

When we talk about, say, *boys'* grade achievement and *girls'* school experience, we assume that boys and girls are coherent, unitary categories about which educational statements can be made. This assumption is obviously problematic. As we have already seen, the differences *within* the group 'girls' and *within* the group 'boys' are far more significant than the differences *between* them. When we look at achievement statistics as well as other measures of school experience, social class and ethnicity seem to be where the major differences and inequalities lie, rather than gender. In other words, the categories 'boys' and 'girls' are both severely fragmented, something we need to keep in mind when making generalisations about these groups.

This point, which has already been made by Maori educationists, is most starkly evident in school achievement statistics. Girls and boys as groups now have very similar achievement patterns, in fact, when you compare other patterns. In nearly all subject areas, the most marked differences in achievement seem to be associated *not* with gender but with social class and ethnicity. Nash and Harker's (1997a) analysis of the School Certificate results of 5,383 students in 37 schools showed that mean attainment in science, for instance, was over 20 per cent higher for students from upper professional families than for those whose parents were unemployed, on a benefit or semi-skilled. In their review of New Zealand's gender and education research literature, Alton-Lee and Praat (2000: 299) point out that in terms of school achievement, the girls and boys getting the least from schooling are those in low decile schools from poor communities – which have disproportionately high numbers of Pacific Islands and Maori students. They report that students from low decile schools did significantly worse on three-quarters of the assessed tasks or more in mathematics, social studies, literacy and information skills on the National Education Monitoring Project tasks.

While they are usually the measure for illustrating educational differences, grade achievement patterns are useful in only limited ways. For one thing, they divide the population into pre-determined groups about which we are then forced to speak. For instance, in New Zealand, the official national educational statistics collected by the Ministry of Education on examination grades normally use gender and particular ethnic divisions (European, Maori, Pacific Island, Asian and all candidates), though not social class groups. Truths about educational achievement develop around these 'official' categorisations, so we become concerned about particular 'ethnic' and gender groups, for instance, while remaining largely uninformed about social-class effects, and differences within ethnic categories.

However, for all their limitations, the official figures do give a dramatic and shocking sense of where the benefits of schooling are being received, and where they are not. If we look 'within' the gender categories it is clear that, for instance, Maori and Pakeha girls benefit very differently from secondary schooling. Maori girls achieve fewer educational qualifications, leave school earlier, score lower grades and are more likely to leave with no qualification, than Pakeha girls. For example, according to Ministry of Education school-leaving data, in 1998, while 26 per cent of Pakeha female school leavers left with Bursary, only 4 per cent of Maori girls and 5 per cent of Pacific Islands girls did. In the same year, 21 per cent of Pakeha boys left with Bursary compared with 3 per cent and 5 per cent of Maori and Pacific Island male school leavers. While 11 per cent of Pakeha female students left secondary school in 1998 with no formal academic qualification (compared with nearly 15 per cent of Pakeha males), over one-third (34.6 per cent) of Maori females (and 42 per cent Maori males) left with no formal educational credentials (Ministry of Education, 1999c).

Concluding their state-of-the-art review of gender and New Zealand school achievement, Alton-Lee and Praat (2000: 301) say: 'from our exploration of the research and assessment data available, considerations of gender need to be carried out with specific reference to the particular ethnicities, social class and cultural positionings, and school decile levels of particular groups of students'. They are clear that all research on school achievement continues to indicate the ongoing crisis in Maori education and in the education of Pacific Islands students, and as such they are at the very least calling for serious caution when we talk about 'boys' and 'girls' as groups in terms of grade achievement.

The main weakness with a reliance on achievement statistics to 'tell us the truth' about gender is that they make entirely invisible some of the most significant aspects of schooling and gender: how it is *experienced*. Making a difference to the statistics is only possible if we understand the ways that boys and girls, and their teachers, encounter and produce the gendered, cultural experience that is schooling. We have only begun to discuss some of those issues in this chapter. Educational researchers interested in gender in New Zealand have written about a wide range of topics which impinge on how education is gendered, including the erotics of teaching (Jones, 1996); how teachers have experienced changes in teaching over time (Middleton and May, 1997); education on sexuality, including stories about 'bodies, uniforms and discipline' (Middleton, 1998; Jones and Middleton, 1996); how Maori girls experience Maori boarding schools (Jenkins and Morris Mathews, 1995); students' experiences of being 'students' (Grant, 1993); Pakeha desires for Maori peers in feminist classrooms (Jones, 1999); the educational implications of the panic about touching kids (Jones, forthcoming), and so on. Samoan and other Pacific women researchers in education have also written about their experiences of schooling, indicating the predominant role which education has played in their lives and in their parents' hopes and expectations, as well as telling of their struggles to gain access to their fair share of educational resources (e.g. Tanielu,2000; Mara, 1995; Pasikale, 1996; Rogers, 1999; Tiatia, 1998; Tupuola, 1998, 2000; Jones *et al.*, in press).

Bibliography

Alton-Lee, A.G. and Densem, P.A. (1992), 'Towards a Gender-Inclusive School Curriculum: Changing Educational Practice', in S. Middleton and A. Jones (eds), *Women and Education in Aotearoa,* Vol. 2, Wellington: Bridget Williams.

Alton-Lee, A.G. and Nuthall, G.A. (1991), *Final Report: Phase 2 of the Understanding Learning and Teaching Project,* Wellington: Ministry of Education.

Alton-Lee, A.G. and Nuthall, G.A. (April, 1992), 'Student Learning in Classrooms: Instructional and Sociocultural Processes Influencing Student Interaction with Curriculum Content', in J. Fantuzzo (Chair), *The Analytic Study of Learning and Interaction in Classrooms,* Invited Symposium conducted at the meeting of the American Educational Research Association, San Francisco.

Alton-Lee, A. and Praat, A. (2000), *Explaining and Addressing Gender Differences in the New Zealand Compulsory School Sector (1989–1999): A Literature Review,* Commissioned by the Ministry of Education.

Bardsley, D. (1991), 'Factors Relating to the Differential Reading Attitudes, Habits and Interests of Adolescents', *Research Affiliateship Scheme Report* No. 1, Department of Education: Massey University.

Bell, B. (1988), 'Girls and Science', in S. Middleton (ed.), *Women and Education in Aotearoa,* Wellington: Allen and Unwin.

Bird, L. (1992), 'Girls Taking Positions of Authority at Primary School', in S. Middleton and A. Jones (eds), *Women and Education in Aotearoa,* Vol. 2, Wellington: Bridget Williams Books.

Burnett, P. (1998), *Balancing the Equation: Gender and Reading in the English Curriculum,* Paper presented to the NZARE Conference, Dunedin.

Carkeek, L., Davies, L. and Irwin, K. (1994), *What Happens to Maori Girls at School? Final Report,* Wellington: Ministry of Education.

Court, M. (1992), 'Leading from Behind: Women in Educational Administration', in S. Middleton and A. Jones (eds), *Women and Education in Aotearoa,* Vol. 2, Wellington: Bridget Williams Books.

Court, M. (1998), 'Women Challenging Managerialism: Devolution Dilemmas in Establishing Co-Principalships in Aotearoa/New Zealand', *School Leadership and Management*, Vol. 18/1, pp. 35–57.

Department of Education (1987), *The Curriculum Review*, Report of the Committee to Review the Curriculum for Schools, Wellington.

Department of Education (1989), *Countering Sexism in Education*, Wellington: Goverment Printer.

Dimen, M. (1992), 'Power, Sexuality, and Intimacy', in A. M. Jaggar and S. Bordo (eds), *Gender/ Body/ Knowledge: Feminist Reconstructions of Being and Knowing*, New Brunswick, N.J: Rutgers University Press.

Education Review Office (1999), *The Achievement of Boys*, Education Evaluation Report 3, Wellington: Education Review Office.

Elphick-Malone, J. (1986), 'What's Wrong with Emma? The Feminist Debate in Colonial Auckland', in B. Brookes, C. Macdonald and M. Tennant (eds), *Women in History: Essays on European Women in New Zealand*, Wellington: Allen and Unwin.

Farquhar, S. (1997), 'Are Male Teachers Really Necessary?', Paper presented at the New Zealand Association for Research in Education Conference, Auckland, December.

Fergusson, D. and Horwood, L. (1997), 'Gender Differences in Educational Achievement in a New Zealand Birth Cohort', *New Zealand Journal of Educational Studies*, Vol. 32/1, pp. 83–96.

Fergusson, D., Lloyd, M. and Horwood, L. (1991), 'Teacher Evaluations of the Performance of Boys and Girls', *New Zealand Journal of Educational Studies*, Vol. 26/2, pp. 155–163.

Flockton, L. and Crooks, T. (1996), *Reading and Speaking: Assessment Results 1996. National Education Monitoring Report 6*, Dunedin: Educational Assessment Research Unit, University of Otago.

Fry, R. (1985), *It's Different for Daughters: A History of the Curriculum for Girls in New Zealand Schools, 1900–1975*, Wellington: Council for Educational Research.

Fry, R. (1988), 'The Curriculum and Girls' Secondary Schooling 1880–1925', in S. Middleton (ed.), *Women and Education in Aotearoa*, Wellington: Allen and Unwin.

Garden, R. (1997), (ed.), *Mathematics and Science Performance: Results from New Zealand's Participation in the Third International Mathematics and Science Study,* Wellington: Research and International Section, Ministry of Education.

Gilbert, J. (1993), 'The Construction, Reconstruction and Deconstruction of Statements of Gender Equity in Two Science Curriculum Documents,' in J. Gilbert (ed.), *Feminism/Science Education,* Centre for Science and Mathematics Education Research, Hamilton: University of Waikato.

Gilbert, J. (1996), 'The Sex Education Component of School Science Programmes as a Micro-Technology of Power', *Women's Studies Journal,* Vol. 12, No. 2, pp. 37-57.

Gilbert, J. (November, 1998), '"It's Life, Jim, but Not as We Know It": The Trouble with Girls' Achievement in Traditionally 'Masculine' Subjects at School', Paper presented at the 'Girl Trouble: Feminist Theory and Young Women/Girls' Conference, University of Waikato.

Gilbert, J. and McCormish, J. (1990), 'Science Learning, Language and Feminist Pedagogy', *SAME Papers 1990,* Hamilton: University of Waikato Centre for Science and Mathematics Education Research: Longman Paul.

Grant, B. (1993), 'Making University Students: The Construction of Student Subjectivities', MA thesis, Auckland: University of Auckland.

Hamlin, R. (1989), 'Gender Characteristics of Secondary Science Texts', Unpublished assignment for EDUC 105, University of Canterbury.

Irwin, K. (1992), 'Becoming an Academic: Contradictions and Dilemmas of a Maori Feminist', in S. Middleton and A. Jones (eds), *Women in Education in Aotearoa,* Vol. 2, Wellington: Bridget Williams Books.

James, B. and Saville-Smith, K. (1989), *Gender, Culture and Power: Challenging New Zealand's Gendered Culture,* Auckland: Oxford University Press.

Jenkins, K. and Morris Matthews, K. (1994), *Hukarere and the Politics of Moari Girls Schooling 1875-1995,* Napier: Te Whanau o Hukarere.

Jones, A. (1988), 'Which Girls are Learning to Lose?', in S. Middleton (ed.), *Women and Education in Aotearoa,* Wellington: Allen and Unwin.

Jones, A. (1991a), *At School I've got a Chance: Culture/Privilege: Pacific Islands and Pakeha Girls at School,* Palmerston North: Dunmore Press.

Jones, A. (1991b), 'Is Madonna a Feminist Folk-Hero? Is Ruth Richardson a Woman? Postmodern Feminism and Dilemmas of Difference', *Sites*, 23, pp. 8-100.

Jones, A. (1992), 'Writing Feminist Educational Research: Am 'I' in the Text?', in S. Middleton and A. Jones (eds), *Women and Education in Aotearoa*, Vol. 2, Wellington: Bridget Williams Books.

Jones, A. (1993), 'Becoming a Girl: Post-structuralist Suggestions for Educational Research', *Gender and Education*, Vol. 5/2, pp. 155-166.

Jones, A. (1996), 'Desire, Sexual Harassment, and Pedagogy in the University Classroom', in *Theory and Practice*, Vol. 35/ 2, Spring, The Ohio State University, pp. 103-109.

Jones, A. (1999), 'The Limits of Cross-Cultural Dialogue: Pedagogy, Desire, and Absolution in the Classroom', in *Education Theory*, Vol. 49, No. 3, Summer, University of Illinois, pp. 299-316.

Jones, A. (ed.), (forthcoming 2001), *Teachers Touching Children*, Dunedin: Otago University Press.

Jones, A., Herda, P. and Suaalii, T. (eds)(2000), *Bitter Sweet: Indigenous Women in the Pacific*, Dunedin: Otago University Press.

Jones, A. and Jacka, S. (1995), 'Discourse of Disadvantage: Girls' School Achievement', in *New Zealand Journal of Educational Studies*, Vol.30/ 2, pp. 165-175.

Jones, A., Marshall, J., Morris-Mathews,K., Smith, G.H. and Smith, L.T. (1995), *Myths and Realities: Schooling in New Zealand*, Palmerston North: Dunmore Press (2nd edition).

Jones, A. and Middleton, S. (eds), (1996), *Women's Studies Journal* 1996, Vol. 12, No. 2, Spring. Special Issue: Educating Sexuality: The Women's Studies Association of New Zealand, University of Otago Press.

Kenway, J. (1992), *Revisions: Feminist Theories and Education*, Pilot Monograph, Geelong: Deakin University.

Kramarae, C. and Treichler, P. (1985), *A Feminist Dictionary*, London: Pandora Press, Unwin Hyman.

Lauder, H., Hughes, D., Watson, S., Simiyu, I., Stathdee, R. and Waslander, S. (1995), *The Smithfield Project, Phase One. Trading in Futures: the Nature of Choice in Educational Markets in New Zealand*, Third Report to the Ministry of Education, December 1995, Christchurch: University of Canterbury.

Longhurst, R. and Peace, R. (1993), 'Lecture Theatre to Classroom –
Feminist Geography', *New Zealand Journal of Geography*, October,
96. pp. 16–19

Mara, D. L. (1995), 'Te Puai no te Vahine: Pacific Islands Education Policy
and Education Initiatives in Aotearoa/New Zealand', Unpublished
M.Lit. Thesis, University of Auckland.

Martin, V. (1996), 'The Students', in R. Garden (ed.), *Mathematics
Performance of New Zealand Form 2 and Form 3 Students,* Wellington:
Ministry of Education.

May, H. (1992), *Minding Children, Managing Men: Conflict and
Compromise in the Lives of Postwar Pakeha Women,* Wellington:
Bridget Williams Books.

McDonald, G. (1994), 'Commentary: A Comment on 'Teacher Evaluations
of the Performance of Boys and Girls'', *New Zealand Journal of
Educational Studies,* Vol. 29/1, pp. 89–90.

MCEETYA (1995), Proceedings of the Promoting Gender Equity
Conference, Canberra: Gender Equity Taskforce of the Ministerial
Council for Employment, Training and Youth Affairs, February.

McGeorge, C. (1987), 'How Katy Did at School', *New Zealand Journal of
Educational Studies,* Vol. 22/1.

McWilliam, E. and Jones, A. (1996), 'Eros and Pedagogical Bodies: the
State of (Non) Affairs', in E. McWilliam and G. Taylor (eds), *Pedagogy,
Technology and the Body,* New York: Peter Lang.

Middleton, S. (1988a), 'A Short Adventure between School and Marriage?
Contradictions in the Education of the New Zealand Post-war Women',
in S. Middleton (ed.), *Women and Education in Aotearoa,* Wellington:
Allen and Unwin.

Middleton, S. (ed.), (1988b), *Women in Education in Aotearoa,* Wellington:
Allen and Unwin.

Middleton, S. (1992), 'Gender Equity and the School Charters:Theoretical
and Political Questions for the 1990s', in S. Middleton and A. Jones
(eds), *Women and Education in Aotearoa,* Vol. 2, Wellington: Bridget
Williams Books.

Middleton, S. (1993), *Educating Feminists: Life Histories and Pedagogy,*
New York: Teachers' College Press.

Middleton, S. (1998), *Disciplining Sexuality: Foucault, Life Histories and Education,* New York: Teachers College, Columbia University.

Middleton, S. and Jones, A. (eds), (1992), *Women and Education in Aotearoa,* Vol. 2, Wellington: Bridget Williams Books.

Middleton, S. and May, H. (1997), *Teachers Talk Teaching, 1915–1995. Early Childhood, Schools and Teachers Colleges,* Palmerston North: Dunmore Press.

Ministry of Education (1993), *The New Zealand Curriculum Framework,* Wellington: Learning Media.

Ministry of Education (1998), *New Zealand Schools. Nga Kura O Aotearoa 98,* Minister of Education. Report on the Compulsory Schools Sector in New Zealand, Wellington: Learning Media.

Ministry of Education (1999a), *March School Statistics Report,* Wellington: Learning Media.

Ministry of Education (1999b), *Table SL, FFTE of State School Teachers by Branch, Type of School, Designation, and Gender, as at March 1999,* Data Management Unit, Wellington: Learning Media.

Ministry of Education (1999c), *Table SL1, Level of Highest Attainment by Ethnicity and Gender,* Data Management and Analysis Section, Wellington: Learning Media.

Ministry of Women's Affairs (1985), *The 1984 Women's Forums: Policy Priorities,* Wellington: Government Printer.

Ministry of Women's Affairs (1996), *The Full Picture. Te Tirohanga Whanui: Guidelines for Gender Analysis,* Wellington: Ministry of Women's Affairs.

Nairn, K. (1993), *Who Participates in Class Discussion in Geography?* Proceedings of the Seventeenth New Zealand Geography Conference, Wellington: New Zealand Geographical Society, pp. 370–375.

Nash, R. and Harker, R. (1997a), *Progress at School,* Final Report to the Ministry of Education, Palmerston North: Massey University Educational Research and Development Centre.

Nash, R. and Harker, R. (1997b), *School Type and the Education of Girls: Co-Ed or Girls Only?* Paper presented to annual conference of AERA, Chicago, March.

Neville, M. (1988), *Promoting Women,* Auckland: Longman Paul.

Newton, K. (1992), 'John Says a Few Words, Margaret Listens: Sharing Time in the Primary School Classroom', in S. Middleton and A. Jones (eds) (1992) *Women and Education in Aotearoa*, Vol.2, Wellington: Bridget Williams Books.

Openshaw (1985), 'Contesting the Curriculum: A Case Study of a Conservative Pressure Group', in J. Codd, R. Harker and R. Nash (eds), (1990), *Political Issues in New Zealand Education* (2nd edition), Palmerston North: Dunmore Press.

Pasikale, A. (1996), *Seen But Not Heard: Voices of Pacific Islands Learners*, Wellington: Education and Training Support Agency.

Praat, A. (1999), *Gender Differences in Achievement and Participation in the Compulsory Education Sector. A Review of Information Held by the Ministry of Education 1986–1997*, Wellington: Research Division, Ministry of Education.

Quinlivan, K. and Town, S. (1999), 'Queer as Fuck? Exploring the Potential of Queer Pedagogies in Researching School Experiences of Lesbian and Gay Youth', in D. Epstein and J. Sears (eds), *A Dangerous Knowing: Sexuality, Pedagogy and Popular Culture*, London: Cassell.

Rogers, L. J. (1999), 'Samoan Women in Education: Four Samoan Women Reflect on their Educational Experiences in Aotearoa/New Zealand', Unpublished Research Report, Victoria University of Wellington.

Ryan, A. (1988), 'Remoralising Politics', in B. Jesson, A. Ryan and P. Spoonley (eds), *Revival of the Right: New Zealand Politics in the 1980s*, Auckland: Heinemann Reid.

Scott, A. (1992), 'A Girls-Only Science Class in a Co-Educational Secondary School', *SAME papers 1992*, Hamilton: Centre for Science and Mathematics Education Research, University of Waikato: Longman Paul, pp. 30–47.

Stephens, M. (1996), 'Fifth Form Boys' Sense of Self in the Secondary School Curriculum', M.A Thesis, Massey University.

Sturrock, F. (1993), *The Status of Girls and Women in New Zealand Education and Training*, Wellington: Ministry of Education.

Sturrock, F. (1998), 'Baseline Data on Suspensions in Schools', *Research Bulletin* No.8, Wellington: Ministry of Education.

Tanielu, L. (2000), 'Education in Samoa: Reflections on my Experiences', in Jones, Herda and Suaalii (eds), *Bitter Sweet: Indigenous Women in the Pacific*, Dunedin: University of Otago Press.

Tennant, M. (1986), 'Natural Directions: The New Zealand Movement for Sexual Differentiation in Education During the Twentieth Century', in B. Brookes, C. MacDonald and M. Tennant (eds), *Women in History: Essays on European Women in New Zealand*, Wellington: Allen and Unwin.

The Treasury (1987), *Government Management: Brief to Incoming Government*, Vol. 1, Wellington: Government Printer.

Tiatia, J. (1998), *Caught Between Cultures: A New Zealand-Born Pacific Island Perspective*, Auckland: Christian Research Centre.

Tupuola, A-M. (1998), 'Fa'asamoa in the 1990s: Young Samoan Women Speak', in R. Du Plessis and L. Alice (eds), *Feminist Thought in Aotearoa/New Zealand: Differences and Connections*, Auckland: Oxford University Press.

Tupuola, A-M. (2000), 'Learning Sexuality: Young Samoan Women', in A. Jones, P. Herda and T. Suaalii (eds), *Bitter Sweet: Indigenous Women in the Pacific*, Dunedin: Otago University Press.

Wagemaker, H. (1993), *Achievement in Reading Literacy: New Zealand's Performance in a National and International Context*, Wellington: Research Section, Ministry of Education.

Walkerdine, V. (1989), *Counting Girls Out*, London: Virago.

Walkerdine, V. (1990), *Schoolgirl Fictions*, London: Verso.

Watson, H. (1989), 'Getting Women to the Top', in *PPTA Journal*, Term 2, pp. 10–12.

Wylie, C., Thompson, J. and Kerslake Hendricks, A. (1996), *Competent Children at 5: Families and Early Education*, Report for the Ministry of Education, Wellington: New Zealand Council for Educational Research.

Young-Loveridge, J. (1992a), 'Girls and Mathematics: The Early Primary Years', in S. Middleton and A. Jones (eds) (1992), *Women and Education in Aotearoa*, Vol.2, Wellington: Bridget Williams Books.

Young-Loveridge, J. (1992b), 'Attitudes Towards Mathematics: Insights into the Thoughts and Feelings of Nine-Year Olds', *SAME papers*, University of Waikato.

Chapter 3

Social Class and Education in Aotearoa/New Zealand

Roger Dale

Introduction

Both key terms in the title of this chapter are separately matters of great interest and debate, and when they are put together they become especially significant for all of us[1]. Education systems are expressly set up to help achieve equality of opportunity and outcome; that may not be their only purpose but it is an absolutely central part of schools to the extent that people are willing to continue paying taxes to fund them. More broadly, education has been a central means of delivering the promise of modernisation, the idea that we are not slaves of 'fate' or accidents of birth, but are collectively, at a societal level, able to organise human society in ways that make it possible for us to achieve collective and individual ends. In the attempt to move from the *ascription* of social positions – the idea that our 'place' in society is determined by our parents' (or, usually, our father's) 'place' in that society, or by our gender, our ethnicity or any other factors over which we have no control – to *achieving* our place, on the basis of our own abilities and efforts, education has been seen as playing the dominant role. Its promise is to make possible an allocation of socially valued positions based on demonstrated merit rather than inherited attributes. By far the best known and clearest expression of that promise in this country is Peter's Fraser's statement that:

> Every person, whatever his (sic) level of academic ability, whether he be rich or poor, whether he live in town or country, has a right, as a citizen, to a free education of the kind to which he is best fitted and to the full extent of his powers.

In fact, there are three distinct and overlapping claims involved here. One is a 'universal social justice' argument: education can be made available and efficacious for all, so that all can partake in society on an equal basis and all positions are open to achievement. A second is a political argument, that all should participate in a common education in order to establish the basis of, as well as partake in, a unified (national) community. And the third, which may have become the most prominent if not the most important in recent times, is the economic argument: education's role is to guarantee the human capital on which the nation's economic survival depends, by identifying and nurturing the talent within the society.

From the perspective of the other key term in the title, it is not so much a commonplace as almost a defining feature of New Zealand national identity to deny the existence of 'class' or 'class structure', certainly in the forms that it has been supposed those take in Britain. It is often suggested that one of the main reasons that the original European settlers came to this country was to escape the kinds of hierarchy, snobbery and lack of opportunity that the British class system generated. It is certainly the case that such external markers of class as accent, dress and demeanour, that make its effects so palpable in Britain, are much less prominent in New Zealand. It is also the case that claims to 'Kiwi egalitarianism' and the desire and expectation that everyone will be given a 'fair go' contain some substance.

On the face of it, it might appear that the education system has done pretty well in advancing the claims made for it, and not to have been seriously affected by social class differences in doing so. For instance, it is clear that more and more jobs depend on possessing educational qualifications, and that more people now obtain educational qualifications than ever before. We all know someone from a very 'deprived' background who has nevertheless succeeded in education and in the labour market. However, those impressions and that anecdotal evidence are not confirmed by the information systematically collected by sociologists of education. In truth, the evidence on the relationship between people's social origins and destinations as it is mediated through the education system, a major part of whose reason for existence is its claimed ability to promote and foster equal opportunity, suggests very clearly that the system in New Zealand is no more successful than that of any other advanced Western country, be it class-bound Britain, the 'open' United States, Japan or Taiwan, or the former socialist countries of Eastern Europe, in attenuating the relationship between social origins and destinations. In an important study that included all these counties and more, Blossfeld and Shavit (1997) showed that in none of them were attempts to 'equalise opportunity' through education successful; in only two of the countries they studied, Sweden and the Netherlands, was any progress made towards equalising opportunity. In both of these cases the explanation lay in wider social policies (such as income maintenance, housing and so on) rather than in education.

The evidence seems to suggest, then, that the link between social class, educational achievement and occupational success is strong, tenacious and widespread. That does not mean, however, that it takes the same form everywhere. All the key components of the relationships – family patterns, education systems, labour markets and occupational structures – vary across countries, and the New Zealand experience is unique. In this chapter my aim will be to indicate the nature and consequences of those relationships, and to discuss why they might occur as they do. My task in doing this is made considerably easier, and the possibility of understanding what is happening and why is greatly enhanced, by the existence of two outstanding bodies of work in this area, produced by New Zealand sociologists of education. These are Lauder and Hughes' work on the Christchurch school leavers survey (1990a and 1990b) and the Smithfield project (see Lauder *et al.,* 1999), and Nash and Harker's several studies in this area, most notably their 'Access and Opportunity' and 'Progress at School' projects (on the former, see Nash 1993; on the latter see Nash and Harker 1997).

It may be most useful to begin by providing examples of what is being talked about when we refer to 'the relationship between social class and education'. One effective way of doing this is to set out quite starkly some key findings of the Christchurch school leavers survey. This survey involved collecting and analysing data on the measured academic ability, success in secondary school examinations, and occupational destinations of 2,500 Christchurch school leavers in 1982. Crucially, the reseachers also collected data on the students' socio-economic background, using the Elley-Irving scale of Socio-Economic Status (SES). This ranks the status of occupations on the basis of a combination of educational and income levels related to those occupations. The occupations are placed in six categories:

1. Professional
2. Managerial
3. Office, sales, technical
4. Skilled trades
5. Semi-skilled jobs
6. Unskilled jobs.

SES 1 – 3 are largely made up of people in non-manual occupations, and SES 4 – 6 of those in manual occupations.

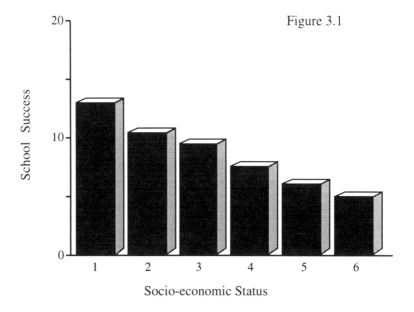

Figure 3.1

Socio-economic Status

Figure 3.1 illustrates the overall relationship between social class and educational achievement. It shows a rather direct relationship between the two; the higher the SES, the greater the level of school success and Lauder and Hughes (1990: 51) comment that the difference between the highest and lowest groups in terms of school success is the difference between a mean of University Entrance by accreditation and a mean of three School Certificate passes.

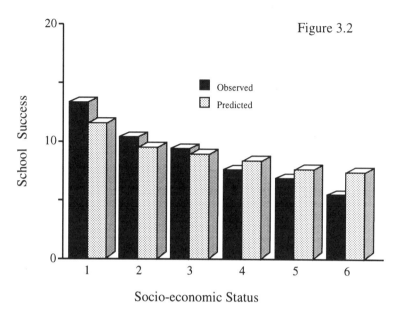

Figure 3.2

Figure 3.2 examines the relationship between social class and educational achievement a little more deeply, by seeing what happens when we hold measured ability constant; that is, it looks at whether the differences in school success can be put down to differences in ability. The graph shows the difference between students' observed success – what they actually achieved – and what would have been predicted on the basis of their measured ability alone. As Figure 3.2 shows, for the three highest SES groups the actual performance *exceeds* what would be expected on the basis of their measured ability. For the three lowest groups this is reversed: they *do worse* than would have been predicted. So, the relationship between SES and school success cannot be reduced to a matter of 'ability'; it appears to involve something more. This is a key finding (and one that is found in all the other countries, too), since 'difference in ability' is by far the most widespread 'commonsense' explanation of differences in educational success. Figure 3.2 shows that the issue is not so simple – or so fatalistic in its consequences.

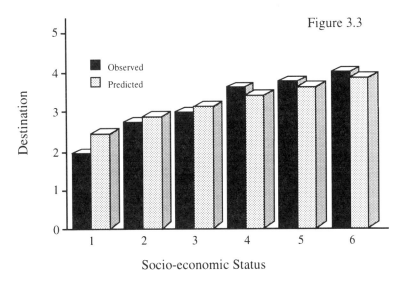

Figure 3.3

Finally, Figure 3.3 shows what Lauder and Hughes found when they compared school success and measured ability with SES in explaining the students' post-school destinations. The pattern of the findings is quite similar to that in Figure 3.2; students from SES groups 1, 2 and 3 were likely to find themselves in occupations at higher SES levels than would have been predicted on the basis of both their ability and their school success. And once again the reverse was the case for the students from SES 4-6.

Lauder and Hughes' evidence – which it should be repeated is quite similar to that found elsewhere – shows (1) that there is a strong association between SES and school success; (2) that the association is independent of possible differences in ability, that is, it is not explained by differences in ability; and (3) that there is a similar association between SES and post-school destination that is independent of ability and school success. At each stage in the process there is a strong association between social class and educational achievements and outcomes. This association is not explained by differences in ability, or, in the case of outcomes, by ability or achievement.

This evidence, then, highlights the issues. It confirms what has been found elsewhere. But on its own it does not enable us to understand the nature of the relationship between social class and educational achievement, and I shall be trying to shed some light on this in this chapter. However, there are some very important points to be made about what is at issue here. First, what the evidence so far has established is a *correlation* between a number of factors. That is to say, it has shown that, literally, these factors' values occur or vary together in a consistent manner. We cannot infer from this that one *caused* the other; in many cases we cannot even determine which of them *might* have caused the other. If we want to establish causes, we have to do this on the basis of theoretical analyses of the relationship: the facts do not (ever) speak for themselves; rather, their meaning(s) have to be established.

Second, there is no suggestion here that either SES background or education, or the two in combination, account for all the inequalities of opportunity and outcome in a society. It would obviously be absurd to suggest that they do, although it does seem that their relative importance is growing. The third important caveat is that the evidence we have presented, and will present below, is based on surveys of groups of the population. It does not tell us anything about *individual* students, or enable us to predict the likelihood or level of their educational and occupational success. And, of course, the opposite is also the case; just because we know some working class children who succeed does not mean that they will all succeed. The figures presented refer to categories of people defined in particular ways, and we cannot assume that any individual member of any category will display the same behaviour or achieve the same outcome as any other member of the category or of the category as a whole. We can, though, assess the chances of the category or group as a whole of achieving different levels of success.

The nature, causes, consequences and possible responses to the relationship between social class and educational achievement have been the subject of much, often passionate, debate. One simple way of characterising two of the main positions in this debate is by distinguishing 'equality of opportunity (or access)' and 'equality of outcome'. For the proponents of the first position we have done all we can when we have created a level playing field by removing all obstacles to access to education. So long as no one is prevented from entering any part of the education system by anything but their ability to benefit from it, we have achieved all the equality that it is possible (or desirable) to achieve. For the other side, this is an empty promise. To offer equal access to what amounts to a competition or race to people who we know from the start are not able, for reasons beyond their control, to compete on equal terms, is offering only the opportunity to fail. Moreover, declaring that access is open legitimates the basis of the competition and makes its (unequal) outcomes appear fair. Against this is put forward the idea of equality of *outcome*. In only a few extreme cases is this taken to mean that everyone must receive *the same* outcome. More commonly, the purpose is to ensure that more substance is given to the idea of equality of opportunity than is entailed in limiting it to equality of access. A representative statement of this kind of equality of outcome is the following, from a pioneer of the study of the relationship between social class and educational achievement by A. H. Halsey (1972: 27):

> ...a society affords equality of educational opportunity if the proportion of people from different social, economic or ethnic categories at all levels and in all types of education are more or less the same as the proportion of these people in the population at large. In other words the goal should not be the liberal one of equality of access but equality of outcome for the median member of each identifiable noneducationally defined group, i.e. the average woman or negro or proletarian or rural dweller should have the same level of educational attainment as the average male, white, white-collar, suburbanite. If not, there has been injustice.

The merest glimpse at Figures 3.1 and 3.2 shows us how far we are from such equality.

One other point that has so far been rather implicit in this argument concerns the relationship between educational achievement and occupational and social destinations. It often seems to have been assumed that equality of educational outcome would lead to equality of occupational entry. Figure 3.3 shows how false an assumption that is – and this is to disregard the extent of the gendered allocation of occupations, where girls' superior educational achievements are nowhere near being matched by their achievements in the labour market. So, we have to examine the effect of social class at two levels – how it relates to educational outcomes and how it mediates educational and occupational outcomes. In this chapter, for reasons of space, I will have to confine my comments largely to the first of these.

What is Meant by Social Class?

So far we have been assuming that SES, as measured in the Elley-Irving scale, is a wholly adequate way of representing what is meant by social class. This is not the case. Class is one of the most complex and contested concepts in the whole of sociology, not least in discussions of the relationship between social class and educational achievement. Unfortunately there is no space here to go into this in any detail. It is probably sufficient to point to what has been the major line of fracture in the debates about class, that between those who essentially follow the work of Karl Marx and those who are inspired by the work of Max Weber. For Marx, class was based on the relationship to the means of production. On the one side was the bourgeoisie, who owned the means of production, and on the other was the proletariat, who owned only their labour power. In order to survive the proletariat were forced to sell their labour power to the bourgeoisie, thus setting up a relationship of exploitation between the two classes as *groups*.

Weber, by contrast, emphasised the non-economic bases of the differences between groups; these may have been framed by but were not determined by, economic position. Here, class becomes broken down into, and related to, occupational groups whose 'status' differences are more significant than their structural similarities.

For our purposes what it is essential to note is that the position in the occupational structure is taken by both Marxists and Weberians to be the key determinant of other social relationships that individuals and groups enter into. In fact, more recent work on social class has tended to elide the differences between the two traditions, and to point to the relationship between the 'assets' or 'dispositions' associated with particular positions in the division of labour, and to how the differential potential of these assets and dispostions in different social circumstances influences social outcomes in patterned and highly significant ways (see Wright, 1997; Savage, 1992; Robertson, 2000; Bourdieu, 1997).

Perhaps the best known of this broad set of approaches is Pierre Bourdieu's notion of forms of capital. He distinguishes particularly two kinds of capital – and by referring to them as capital he intends these assets to be seen as equivalent to economic capital. The first is 'cultural' capital, which, Bourdieu (1997: 47) tells us,

> ...initially presented itself to me ... as a theoretical hypothesis which made it possible to explain the unequal scholastic achievement of children originating from the different social classes by relating academic success ... to the distribution of cultural capital between the classes and class fractions. This starting point implies a break with the presuppositions inherent both in the commonsense view, which sees academic success and failure as an effect of natural aptitudes, and in the human capital theories.

Cultural capital has three components – dispositions of body and mind, cultural goods and educational credentials. The last of these is particularly important not only because it operates in itself but also because it can act to 'confer entirely original properties on the cultural capital [they] are presumed to guarantee' (ibid).

The second form of capital is what Bourdieu calls 'social' capital, which he defines as:

> ...the aggregate of the actual or potential resources which are linked to possession of a more or less durable network of more or less institutionalized relationships of mutual acquaintance and recognition ... which provides each of its members with the backing of the collectively-owned capital, a 'credential' that entitles them to credit, in various senses of the word.

> (1997: 51)

To put it simply, but more colloquially, social capital is about 'who you know'. Like educational credentials, it acts both as a resource in itself and as a means of getting more out of other resources. (It is important to note that the use of SES as a proxy for 'social class' both elides the differences in the bases of the theoretical arguments over the issue, and, given the different forms and combinations of class-related assets that are bundled up in SES, makes it more difficult to tease out with any precision the nature of any causal relation between social class and educational achievement.)

One crucial conclusion that can be drawn from these approaches to social class reinforces the view that many existing studies of its relationship to educational achievement are distinctly partial, in both senses of the word: that is, they are both incomplete and (at least implicitly) biased. This is because they are based on an assumption that the 'causes' of working class children's relative educational underachievement are to be found in the 'failure' of those children and their families. They seek to establish schools to address this, and to find how those families can be enabled to 'catch up'. This assumption leads to both kinds of partiality, in that it neglects the possibility that the issue may be not so much the 'failure' of the working class as the 'failure' of the school, or the 'success' of the middle class. We will examine both these possibilities below, but in terms of the latter, what we see may be not so much the working class 'falling [further] behind', despite the best intentioned efforts of families, schools, teachers and policy makers, but the middle class 'staying [further] in front'. The middle class may be able to do this as a result of their efforts and ability to define the ends of education, mobilise their resources in order to ensure that they obtain an increasing proportion of the desirable ends of education, and to continue to reap disproportionate benefit from a system that is in any case moulded in their own image (this perspective is outlined in the introduction to Halsey *et al.*, 1997).

This perspective on the issue not only presents a much more complex set of questions to be examined and exposes a great number of facets of the relationship between social class and educational achievement, but also requires a somewhat more refined understanding of how class *works* in that relationship. One way of making this complexity easier to grasp is to impose a rather artificial, but for our purposes very practical, threefold breakdown of the way that class 'works': the effects of class-based *dispositions*; the different *resources* available to different social classes and how they are exploited; and the *power* they are able to realise through their control of various kinds of assets. All of these are crucial to an understanding of how social class, education and social mobility are related.

The Relationship between Dispositions and Success in School

It is highly significant that what is perhaps the single most encapsulating statement on the nature of class-related dispositions and their relationship to success in schools was made nearly 40 years ago, and that it could also have been made 40 minutes ago – and that, if we are pessimistic, it will still be possible to make 40 years from now:

> Members of different social classes, by virtue of enjoying (or suffering) different conditions of life, come to see the world differently – to develop different conceptions of social reality, different aspirations and hopes and fears, different conceptions of the desirable.
>
> (Kohn 1963: 471).

We can best examine the import of this argument in the New Zealand context by approaching it from two directions: what we might call 'the capacity to benefit from education', and 'school processes'. The relationships between 'dispositions' and educational success have received far more attention than the relationships between either 'resources' or 'power' and educational success. One reason for this is that the work described below is often regarded as belonging to two quite different sets of explanation. The account of this work in this chapter is divided into two sections corresponding to those two explanations. However, it is important to note the reason for both these decisions. It is that there is far more to the relationship between social class and educational achievement than can be perceived at the level of educational practice; and further, this may be the reason that research has so far been rather unsuccessful in establishing the nature of that relationship. This is not to say that we cannot believe the evidence that we will be looking at, or that it is not important, but that it does not speak for itself, and that we do not find the reasons for, or understand, the relationship between social class and educational achievement by focusing on the level of dispositions (albeit recognised as class related) and their classroom manifestations alone. It is for this reason, too, that I have combined the two sets of work, since, despite their quite different and often conflicting arguments, in essence the assumptions, nature and form of their explanations are very similar.

When we look at the body of work that I have referred to as 'capacity to benefit from education' (CBE), it is impossible to avoid discussing the so-called 'deficit hypothesis'. (This argument is most clearly set out in Flude (1974: 20-29), on which this account draws.) This holds that the social background of low status pupils contains elements, especially 'linguistic deprivation' and 'cognitive inadequacy', that constitute major obstacles to learning and educational success on the part of those pupils.

Flude argues that the early studies in education that discovered the correlations between social class and educational achievement led to the search for what precisely it was in pupils' home backgrounds and experiences that appeared, from those studies, to be the major determinants of CBE. In doing this, the studies imply a deficit in relation to the taken-for-granted mainstream culture and the assumed values of the school. As Flude (1974: 23) puts it, The 'deficit' model of working class and ethnic subcultures may be seen as a product of two interrelated assumptions:

> Firstly 'educability' is defined in terms of the background characteristics of those pupils who succeed in school. By implication, therefore, those pupils whose background is different are likely to experience difficulties in doing well at school. The manner then in which the problem is conceptualised makes it difficult for other accounts of educational failure to be fully considered. Secondly, the use of the term 'cultural deprivation' presupposes that judgements of comparison can be made between different groups in terms of ... values that are embodied in the 'mainstream or middle-class culture'.

In other words, Flude is suggesting that the form taken by the deficit hypothesis makes it impossible to test any notion of CBE that is not related to the mainstream values; it is impossible to establish whether working class children have a seriously diminished CBE when all we have to judge it against is a CBE based on a different set of values.

The use of deficit arguments in the New Zealand context has been taken up by Nash (1997). He argues that while they were once widespread, they are now quite discredited. However, this does not mean that 'the facts' from which the arguments wrongly, in his view, inferred the existence of a 'deficit' did not exist. Nash suggests that 'there can be little doubt that some children do enter school less well prepared to meet its demands than others' (1997: 70). He advances this in two ways, through discussions of how far schools can enable those less well-prepared (in terms of familiarity with school routines, the ability to sit and listen, verbal fluency and reading readiness) to 'catch up', and of what that would entail for schools and students. In terms of the former he is quite pessimistic. He points on the one hand to the 'dramatic' level of the difference in assessed intellectual level on entering school between working class children brought up in working class homes and those adopted by middle class parents. This suggests that there is no 'genetic' base to the class differences in educational achievement that we see. On the other hand, he is rather doubtful about how much 'catching up' can be achieved through the school, since

> ...there is cogent evidence ... that middle class parents, particularly those from the professional élite, are providing their pre-school children with literacy focused forms of socialisation, with the power – it must be quite literally – to structure the developing brain in configurations greatly suited to certain forms of abstract and literacy related cognitive processing.
>
> (1997: 62)

The forms of cognitive processing are those especially promoted and expected by schools. Nash quotes highly plausible New Zealand evidence that 'the differences to be observed in scholastic attainment and related test performance are established at such an early age that their origin probably lies outside the educational system' (1997: 63). (This argument is developed in greater detail in Nash, 1993, especially Chapter 7.)

Given this, what is the school to do? The first point to be noted here is that Nash's pessimism is, as he clearly recognises, based on the dominant assumptions made about what schools are for, their priorities, and the ways that they are organised to meet them. That is to say, we do not know whether schools would be able to help working class children 'catch up', because that has never been their highest priority.

Before leaving this section we should note that not all work on the relationship between class-based dispositions and educational achievement is directly related to a deficit hypothesis. One example is the work of Melvin Kohn, who has for many years been seeking to establish *how* class makes a difference. Interestingly, he has tested his central hypotheses cross-culturally – with comparative social psychological studies of the US, Poland and Japan, for instance. His argument can be distilled from Kohn *et al.* (1990). He defines social class primarily in terms of the ownership of the means of production and control over the labour power of others, and argues that class structure affects psychological functioning primarily because class position affects opportunities for occupational self-direction. He finds that men more advantageously placed in the class structure are more likely to value self-direction for their children, to be intellectually flexible and to be self-directed in their orientation (that is, to possess the qualities most valued in school settings). This work presents alternative hypotheses for the relationship between social class and educational achievement that have not been systematically investigated, though much of the qualitative work carried out for the Nash/Harker studies provides interesting opportunities to probe them further.

The possibility of improving the school's contribution to working class children's education without major changes in its mandate – what it is intended to achieve – lies at the heart of explanations of the relationship between social class and educational achievement that focus on the everyday processes and assumptions of schools. A central feature and purpose of these arguments is to go beyond what they perceive as the 'victim blaming' orientation that is seen to underlie some of the work on CBE. In essence, they focus on the 'match' between dispositions and school processes and expectations. Some of their ideas are contained in the CBE approach, but in the work to be described these are given a much more central explanatory role.

Once again, Flude sets out the basis of this work, and he succinctly refers to it as the 'cultural difference' model. It draws on the critique of the deficit model for its implicit 'normalising' or 'essentialising' of the dominant culture, in terms of which other cultures are seen as deficient. In its place it argues for the validity and strength of other cultural models, emphasising cultural *difference* in place of cultural deficit. In what might be seen as a defining statement of the approach, Baratz and Baratz state that:

> The educational problems of the lower-class culturally different Negro child, as of other groups of culturally different children, are not so much related to inappropriate educational goals as to inadequate means of meeting these goals.
>
> (quoted in Flude, 1974: 31)

These inadequate means take a number of different forms. However, they centre around what is seen as the imposition of the set of cultural assumptions and practices viewed as 'normal' and 'neutral' by the mainstream of groups upon those who do not share those assumptions and practices.

There is a wide range of examples that could be advanced to substantiate this argument, such as streaming, modes of discipline, forms of address and demeanour. The examples I will concentrate on here are those of pedagogy and curriculum, because they are both closest to the heart of what goes on in schools and least likely to be seen as constructed in ways that favour children from one social class over another.

It is possible to classify pedagogies in a range of different ways – progressive, instructional, child-centred, etc. The key point here is that none of these pedagogies is 'neutral' in terms of its implications for the relationship between social class and educational achievement. They all make assumptions about the 'ideal' pupil and the 'ideal' teacher-pupil relationship, and these are necessarily related in various ways to the differing dispositions that pupils bring to school. Again, these assumptions are more likely to be compatible with, and continuous with, middle class rather than working class dispositions. For example, students who go to school having experienced extensive and complex dialogue with their parents will be more likely to respond to pedagogies that expect students to act in similar ways with teachers, than students who have known a more hierarchical and dependent relationship with their parents.

Work by the British sociologist of education Basil Bernstein is very helpful here. Bernstein (1974) talks of different language codes that are systematically based in different class-based systems of socialisation. For example, to put it in extremely simple terms, he suggests that working class children tend to operate with a language code that assumes that the listener and the speaker share an understanding of the context. Therefore, for instance, such speech is characterised by a greater use of pronouns, assuming that the listener knows to what 'it' or 'they' refers. This context-dependence, or particularism, is compared with the context-independence, or universalism, that is more likely to be found in the language used by middle class children. The suggestion is that on the one hand, the language of the school is universal rather than particular, and, on the other, that universalism provides a better preparation for the kind of abstract thinking that is expected in education. Bernstein has also discusssed the class nature of pedagogies in some detail. He distinguishes what he calls 'visible and 'invisible' pedagogies, and argues that they have different consequences for different fractions within the middle class. As he puts it:

> The class assumptions of visible pedagogies are different from those of invisible pedagogies. These class assumptions carry consequence for those children who are able to exploit the possibilities of the pedagogic practices. The assumptions of a visible pedagogy are more likely to be met by that fraction of the middle class whose employment has a direct relation to the economic field (production, distribution and the circulation of capital). Whereas the assumptions of an invisible pedagogy are more likely to be met by that fraction of the middle class who have a direct relation not to the economic field but who work in specialized agencies of symbolic control usually located in the public sector.
>
> (quoted in Flude, 1974: 57)

In terms of curriculum, there has been considerable academic discussion about its 'class' nature. In what is still possibly the best known article on this topic, Michael F. D. Young (1972: 36) argued that knowledge is highly socially stratified, and suggested that high-status knowledge, the organising principle underlying academic curricula, is characterised by:

> ...literacy ... an emphasis on written as opposed to oral presentation: individualism (or avoidance of group work or cooperativeness) ... abstractness of the knowledge and its structuring and compartmentalizing independently of the knowledge of the learner; and ... the unrelatedness of academic curricula, which refers to the extent to which they are 'at odds' with daily life and common experience.

It does not seem implausible to suggest that these characteristics are such as to favour middle class rather than working class assumptions about the world and about the nature and value of education.

As a bridge to the next section, where we will look at the effects of differential class resources, it will be useful to consider the notion of the 'wisdom of class' put forward by Lauder and his colleagues. It is useful as a link because it is made up of a combination of cultural capital in the sense of 'the informal education received at home through the language employed within the family, books and other cultural artefacts', and 'the far higher educational aspirations and expectations of being able to act upon the world of children raised in middle class families' (Lauder *et al.,* 1999: 25). To this we might also add the suggestion that a significant reason for the achievement gap between working class and middle class children is that the former have no 'role models'; they typically come from families that have no examples of members having achieved educational success, and through it occupational success. They have necessarily limited understanding of the links between educational and occupational success and how they might be forged. As Lauder *et al.* put it:

> When these elements of class are taken together they combine to form quite different frames of reference within which education is understood by the different classes. The wisdom of class refers to the rules, norms, tacit assumptions and horizons which govern the understanding of education of different social classes.
>
> (ibid.: 43)

They put the idea to particular application in their analysis of education markets in New Zealand, which we will consider in the next section.

Class 'Resources' and School Achievement

Alert readers will have noted from the last section a further element of 'partiality' in the treatment of the broad issue: what that section implicitly suggests is not only that the causes of working class educational failure are to be found in the working class itself – the 'victim blaming' approach – but that those causes are confined to the direct experience of schooling. However, in the next two sections we will be arguing (1) that it is not sufficient to focus only on the level of practice and process if we want to understand the relationship between social class and educational achievement more adequately; and (2) that we need to bear in mind the 'middle class success' hypothesis as well as the 'working class failure' hypothesis. To do those things we need to understand both the contexts of those practices and processes, and the opportunity structures that they offer and to whom.

We will be looking at the contexts in a moment, but the point of this section is to show how middle class parents are able to convert their resources to ensure the benefit of their children. That is to say, the 'bias' in the education system towards the middle class is by no means confined to or exhausted by the greater continuities between middle class dispositions and the practices of the school, that were discussed in the last section. The point here is that this relationship is mediated through the differential – nay, preferential – *access* to enhanced opportunities for educational achievement that middle class parents are able to gain, retain and extend on behalf of their children. In part this argument parallels the one that suggests that 'the middle class get more of everything'. Certainly there is ample evidence that the middle class are able to employ their economic, cultural and social capital to get access to more resources (for an extensive discussion of 'middle class capture' of welfare benefits see Bertram, 1988).

At one level this is simply a matter of greater financial resources, which become more significant as the parental contribution to the costs of schooling continues to rise. The funding schools receive from the Ministry of Education does not meet the total of school costs, and while the evidence is clear that the additional funding that lower decile schools (all state schools in the country are placed in deciles based on the socio-economic basis of their population; decile 1 comprises the poorest schools in the country, decile 10, the wealthiest) receive from the ministry means that they have a higher overall income than higher decile schools, even taking into account the latter's far greater fund-raising abilities (through 'voluntary fees', events and so on), this neglects a number of key aspects of the differential ability to contribute to school costs.

This is partly a result of a rather restricted conception of what is included in school costs. The evidence from the School Sector Report (Ministry of Education 1999 and annually) does not include such increasingly important parental contributions as access to a computer at home, ability to purchase textbooks and other materials, educational visits, private tuition and so on. Nor does it take into account the less visible features of parental contributions that increase the school's finances, such as the possibility of free professional advice and services from qualified parents, to say nothing of such parents being able to use their networks for the benefit of their children's school. (On these issues, see Gordon (1994) and Dale (1996), who elaborates four 'mechanisms of differentiation' between schools:

(1) the Matthew effect – to he that hath shall be given (and from he

that hath not shall be taken);
(2) the marginality effect, which results from the extra impact of
income received outside core funding;
(3) the multiplier effect, that suggests that middle class schools are
able to derive extended benefits from each unit of input;
(4) the momentum effect, which refers to the tendency of the other
effects to combine in creating upward or downward spirals.)

However, the best evidence of middle class parents' ability to marshal their resources to enhance their children's chances of benefiting from the education system comes from studies of school choice in education markets. Once again we are fortunate to have a leading study in this area carried out in New Zealand. The Smithfield project (Lauder *et al.*, 1999) was set up and carried out in order to examine the nature, operation and effects of school markets in two large cities in New Zealand.

The book contains many detailed and important findings, but we will highlight some of those that are most relevant and significant for our current purposes. One central question that the researchers asked was whether, and how far, the introduction of an education market (brought about by the abolition of home zones, per capita funding of students and, to some extent, by the introduction of enrolment schemes by overcrowded schools) achieved greater fairness in the access to 'successful' schools ('freeing' working class children from being tied to their frequently less successful local school was a major claim made by the proponents of the scheme).

What the Smithfield researchers found was that the educational market had the opposite effect: it increased the likelihood of middle class children attending successful schools. Through a combination of greater access to resources such as cars, telephones and flexible work arrangements, all of which physically facilitate and expand choice of school, and the 'underlying confidence ... derived from their own cultural capital, success and familiarity with the conventions of middle class schooling ... they are able to exploit the market to their own advantage' (Lauder *et al.*, 1999). It should be noted, however, that middle class parents do not simply sit back and wait for the benefits of these resources to fall into their laps. They actively exploit them. Lauder *et al.* show how, at each step in the process of obtaining a place for their child in the school of their choice, middle class parents are both better informed and more able to ensure success in the process. This is not to say that working class parents lack the ambition or aspiration for their children to succeed, or that they do not understand that some schools provide greater opportunities to succeed than others, but that the resources to bring these things about are largely concentrated in the hands of middle class parents, who do not hesitate to exploit them. Nor, once again, is this just a matter of differences in measured ability. The Smithfield team (Lauder *et al.* 1999: 52, 53, 134) state their findings simply and starkly:

> Our results show that after controlling for achievement there is a highly significant relationship between SES and the probability of acceptance by a high circuit school ... [and] Whereas 93 per cent of high SES parents who 'prefer' a high circuit school have their son or daughter attending one, the respective figures for the middle and low SES parents are 82 per cent and 69 per cent [while] high SES parents are three times more likely to get their children into a high circuit school than their low SES counterparts.

In line with the 'middle class success rather than working class failure' argument that their work extends and substantiates, Lauder *et al.* conclude that the issue is not one of working class parents being somehow unable to compete on equal terms for desired educational credentials, or of whether all would eventually come to the market as equals, but why middle class parents would allow and indeed contribute to such an equality. 'The tactics used by middle class parents that we have documented clearly show that education markets serve to exacerbate the exclusion of working class and Maori students' (1999: 135).

One final, and in some ways even more telling example of this utilisation of resources for advantage, comes from Gary McCulloch's work on how school zones were drawn in Auckland (McCulloch, 1986). This demonstrates that even before education markets were set up, and in addition to the advantage that their relative wealth bestowed on middle class parents through their greater ability to buy a house in a desired school zone, middle class parents were able to have inordinate influence over how the zones themselves were drawn.

The evidence in this section is persuasive, in terms of the middle class success argument. There is, though, a danger that this may induce a form of 'middle class bashing' almost parallel to the victim blaming syndrome, and we should be careful to note that these arguments need no more rest on imputing venality to middle class parents than victim blaming arguments need rest on the 'unawareness' of the working class. In both cases, what we see is a system at work that carries with it particular structures of opportunity that enhance the chances of some groups at the expense of others. This is poignantly reflected in Ruth Jonathan's almost despairing analysis. She argues that since the rights of parents qua parents are grounded in their duties of truteeship or agency in serving children's actual or future interests (Jonathan, 1990: 122), whether they like it or not.

> Having (in an educational market) the opportunity only to try and secure an advantage for those whose interests they hold in trust, they are under pressure to adopt a conservative and prudential social stance. In a game structured like a prisoner's dilemma, trustees, far from having free choices, have no reasonable option but to make individualistic, competitive moves, even though this must entail a worse outcome for some of the young – and may arguably entail a worse outcome for all of them than would have resulted from a less competititve framework for decision.
>
> (ibid. 123-40)

Although parents may be loathe to exercise the rights they have been given to seek advantages for their own children, any such reluctance is likely to be acutely tested by the recognition that eschewing those rights will, as Jonathan puts it, 'simultanously expose our children to the consequences which follow from the similar exercise of those powers by others'(ibid.: 122).

Class Power and the Definition of Educational Achievement

The basic assumption that lies behind this section is that none of this happens randomly. The structure of the education system, which is what ultimately underpins both the structure of success and failure within that system and the ways that they are distributed, is neither 'natural' nor 'neutral'. We can recognise this readily when we look at other ways of arranging these things. Education systems differ from each other significantly along a number of dimensions: amount, nature and timing of curricular specialisation; extent of standardisation across the system; length of compulsory education; and so on. And we certainly need to recognise the continuities within education systems. There is little evidence that they are getting more alike, and strong theoretical reasons to believe that they are 'path dependent'; that is to say, that any changes they undergo are likely to be strongly shaped by their existing structures.

There are two crucial points of fundamental similarity to note here, however. First, if we take the path-dependency argument seriously, we can detect the continuing influence of the historical origins of schooling. In almost all the countries Blossfeld and Shavit (1992) and Shavit and Muller (1998) studied, for instance, education had developed as a means of providing a male, white élite with an education that marked its distinctiveness and prepared it for its position in society. That such education took many different forms at different times and places should not distract us from recognising the consistency of its purposes, and the nature of its clientele across all those societies, again irrespective of its precise forms and content. It therefore seems plausible to suggest, as feminist writers and anti-racist writers on education have done in their areas of concern, that a particular set of *class* assumptions is deeply embedded and embodied in the structures of schooling, and that these assumptions will tend, through the processes of path dependency, not only to survive but to continue to shape, albeit at the deepest and least conscious levels, changes in the organisation of schooling.

The second point requires us to recall the findings of Blossfeld and Shavit's (1992) study – that none of the countries they studied had policies that succeeded in attenuating the strength of link between class of origin and educational achievement. This suggests that there is something that the systems have fundamentally in common, that might account for the continuing and clearly very deeply rooted similarities. The most likely candidate for this is their broadly common system of production. While the study did include some East European (then) 'socialist' countries, their systems of production were not significantly different from those of the West (and we might also refer to the cross-cultural consistency of Kohn's (1990) findings). Elsewhere (Dale, 1989) I have suggested that the education systems of capitalist countries are permanently faced by three, contradictory problems – supporting accumulation, contributing to a context in which that accumulation can continue to proceed, and providing legitimation for the system. Crucially, the relative priority of these problems is not given, but varies. Susan Robertson and I have put forward an account of how they vary and how and why the support of accumulation has become very dominant over the other problems in the past two decades, and outlined some of its consequences (Robertson and Dale, 2000). One of our arguments is that recent changes in the global economy and New Zealand's attachment to it have led to education being primarily seen as a major contributor to economic development, and that this explains the current emphases in the system. However, it should again be stressed that this is a particular form of a deeply embedded relationship, and that to understand the basic links between social class and educational achievement we need to look into that relationship.

This has recently been done clearly and impressively by David Livingstone (1998). He argues that:

> As both Marxist class theorists and some Weber-inspired social closure theorists recognize, the principal powers of definition and exclusion have accrued to those with the ownership of substantial private property. These powers generally have been accorded greater protection than other social rights by the legal and coercive sanctions of the state. This 'deep structure of closure' as Murphy calls it, and the related control of material resources by large capitalist owners and top private and state sector managers, profoundly limits the clear public expression of contending claims of competence, skill or value by those not allied with the interests of property owners. As Murphy (1998, 82) argues, more derivative and contingent forms of social closure such as those attempted by members of occupational specialisations, have owed much of their success to the extent of their complementarity with this deep structure: 'The success of any credential group in carving out a monopoly depends on its success in propagating the claim that its credentials certify the presence of some skill (and that their absence indicates lack of that skill) and that the skill itself is necessary and of value.' Such success is not a matter of intellectual rigor, but rather of ideological struggle, itself founded on the structure of power in society. It is not just a question of the power of that particular credentialed group, but the structure of power in society within which the group can carve out its own position of power.
>
> (Livingstone, 1998: 201-2)

This extended quotation points us very neatly to the key issues that underlie the structures of power that frame the relationship between social class and educational achievement. As an illustration of how that works we might look briefly at the question of the definition of 'skill'. As the quotation from Murphy indicates, defining skill is not so much a technical as a political matter. As he argues, it is a question of who has the greater power to impose their definition, which is always contested because so much depends on it. Two brief examples show this. First, we have really only to ask why there have traditionally been so many more 'skilled' jobs for men than for women. It does not take excessive attachment to conspiracy theories to recognise that it has more to do with the gendered distribution of power in society than with men's greater skill, or even with the 'skill' component of men's and women's jobs. Second, it is clearly the decline in power and influence of trade unions over the last decade and a half that has led to a decline in the number of 'skilled' jobs, which both require an extended apprenticeship and command a remuneration premium, rather than the development of any superior ways of carrying out those jobs.

It is significant that we have moved here to referring to 'credentials', which indicate a general level of educational attainment, rather than qualifications, which indicate an increased capacity to perform a particular job. We should indeed go further and acknowledge that, increasingly, credentials are taking on the character of 'positional goods', that is goods that are valuable only to the extent that no one else has them. The usual analogy to describe such goods is that of standing up while watching a public performance in order to get a better view. This only works for as long as no one else does it. In educational terms, we might say that it means that if everyone had a Ph.D. it would not be worth having, at least not for its 'exchange value'. What all this means is that the competition for educational credentials becomes intensified and extended, with ever-higher stakes – which may go some way to explaining parents' efforts to ensure that their children have the best opportunity to collect such credentials.

There may be debate over whether competition – and hence inequality, because there can be no winners if there are no losers – is necessary, but it appears to be inevitable. And that has a further consequence for the core problem of legitimation. There is a powerful strand in the sociology of education that has seen the legitimation of wider social inequality as a major purpose – and achievement – of education systems. As Pierre Bourdieu (1974: 39) puts it:

> By giving individuals educational aspirations strictly tailored to their position in the social hierarchy, and by operating a selection procedure which, although apparently formally equitable, endorses real inequalities, schools help both to perpetuate and legitimize inequalities. By awarding allegedly impartial qualifications (which are largely accepted as such) for socially conditioned attributes which it treats as unequal 'gifts', it transforms *de facto* inequalities into *de jure* ones and *economic and social* differences into *distinctions of quality*, and legitimates the transmission of cultural heritage. In doing so, it is performing a confidence trick. Apart from enabling the 'élite to justify being what it is, the *ideology of giftedness*, the cornerstone of the whole educational and social system, helps to enclose the underprivileged classes in the roles which society has given them by making them see as natural inability things which are only a result of their inferior social status, and by persuading them that they owe their social fate (which is increasingly tied to their educational fate as society becomes, more rationalized) to their individual nature and their lack of gifts. The exceptional success of those few individuals who escape the collective fate of their class apparently justify educational selection and give credence to the myth of the school as a liberating force among those who have been eliminated, by giving the impression that success is exclusively a matter of gifts.

However, the evidence of the most recent and thorough work on the problem in New Zealand, that we have reviewed here, seems to suggest that the gap between the classes is not narrowing. It suggests a plausible reason for this is in the operation of educational markets. What does this mean for the traditional response to the legitimation problem, when it appears that opportunities are becoming more unequal? One response has been that, in education as in other sectors, the benefits of the competitive system will 'trickle down' to the population at large. However, the evidence is no more compelling in education than elsewhere. Indeed, given its inherently competitive nature, it could not be; it is not possible for the winners' winnings, in a positional goods competition to trickle down to the losers.

A further major problem with schools being able to choose students rather than vice versa, and an associated significant polarisation of schools on social class lines, is that educational opportunities tend to be distributed *by school* rather than by either individual ability and disposition, which is the basis of the market model of allocation of opportunities, or by bureaucratic allocation, which is essentially what zoning schemes are. That this is seen as a serious problem can be inferred from the Ministry of Education's reaction, which has been to set up the School Support Scheme as a 'safety net' for failing schools (see Ministry of Education, 1999). Whether, or how far, such schemes can restore the opportunities for educational success that are promised in the National Education Guidelines is, at the time of writing, unclear.

Conclusion

In this chapter I have sought to demonstrate the nature of the link between social class and educational achievement in New Zealand and to consider, briefly, some possible explanations of that relationship. I began by establishing that the commonsense explanation of the relationship, that it was due to different ability, did not stand up to scrutiny. Having considered some theories of social class we adopted a threefold version of the way it makes a difference – through dispositions, resources and power. Each of these was seen to contribute to working class relative lack of success in education. Different dispositions mean that children arrive in school with an enormous shortfall already – so great that it may not be possible for it to be made up – in their capacity to benefit from education. In school this range of dispositions comes into contact with processes and practices, such as pedagogy and curriculum, that are implicitly and unconsciously based on patterns more amenable to middle class children.

I also considered the possibility that the relationship could be explained by 'middle class success'; I looked at the operation of education markets in this light. One thing that was implicit throughout is that any relative improvement in the achievements, both educational and occupational, of working class children would necessarily be at the expense of middle class children. With educational credentials taking on the character of positional goods, one person's success has to be at the expense of another's failure. If Halsey's prescriptions for equality of outcome were to be met, that would imply an increase in the numbers of working class children in high-achieving groups but, again necessarily, a matching decrease in the number of middle class children in those groups. All of these things suggest that middle class defence of and closure around the factors and strategies that underpin their existing relative educational success are unlikely to be significantly weakened or willingly surrendered.

Two main themes emerge from this very brief survey of the relationship between social class and educational achievement. One is the sheer mass of the assumptions, practices, processes and expectations that embed that relationship. These are so great, for instance in the gap that already exists in children's capacity to benefit from education by the time they start school, as to make the problem of catching up almost seem impossible. The other is the significance of middle class defence of their continuing superior ability to benefit from a system that is formed in their image, rather than that of the working class.

From these two themes two conclusions might be highlighted. One is that it would be wrong to think of what is happening as a conspiracy, or as intended. It is a matter of how the education system as a whole works. Yet while there is no reason to doubt the sincerity, dedication and ability of those teachers, administrators, policy makers, Board of Trustees members, parents and others who are committed to improving working class children's educational opportunities and success, there has to be reason to doubt how far they will be able to significantly raise the level of working class children's success without reforms of the system that would be far more radical, and more exclusively targetted to that purpose than has ever been attempted anywhere.

The final point to be made is much more positive. It is to highlight the huge success of the efforts that have been made to attenuate the relationship between working-class children and education failure. The sheer array of evidence we have considered here presents massive odds against any kind of success for working-class children. Yet we know that many, many teachers and schools and parents and families do succeed in helping their children overcome these odds. Things are not getting as dramatically worse as would be expected from the unmitigated and unmediated play of the forces we have been considering in this chapter. And so we might call, finally, for praise rather than condemnation for those efforts. The plight of working-class children would be much worse without them.

Note

[1]Note that this chapter does not distinguish between Maori and non-Maori members of different social class. The relationship between Maori ethnicity and class membership is a very complex one (see, for example, Nash and Harker (1997, Appendix D)). While it is clear that most Maori occupy lower social class positions, it is also the case both that the majority of members of lower social-classes are not Maori and that Maori experience of schooling is different from that of non-Maori at all points in the social-class spectrum. Further discussion of these issues is found in Chapter 4 .

Bibliography

Bernstein, B. (1971), 'Education Cannot Compensate for Society', in B. Cosin *et al.* (eds), *School and Society (Second Edition),* London: Routledge and Kegan Paul.

Bernstein, B. (1974), *Class Codes and Control: Structuring of Pedagogic Discourse,* London & Boston: Routledge and Kegan Paul.

Bernstein, B. (1990), *The Structuring of Pedagogic Discourse,* London: Routledge and Kegan Paul.

Bertram, G. (1988), 'Middle Class Capture: A Brief Survey', in *Report of the Royal Commission on Social Policy, Volume III, Part Two, Future Directions,* Wellington: Royal Commission on Social Policy.

Blossfeld, H. P. and Shavit, Y. (1992), *Persistent Inequalities: Changes in Educational Opportunities in Thirteen Countries,* Boulder: Westview.

Bourdieu, P. (1974), 'The School as a Conservative Force', in J. Eggleston (ed.), *Contemporary Research in the Sociology of Education,* London: Methuen.

Bourdieu, P. (1997), 'Forms of Capital' in Halsey *et al.* (eds), *Education: Culture, Economy, Society,* Oxford: Oxford University Press.

Dale, R. (1989), *The State and Education Policy,* Milton Keynes: Open University Press.

Dale, R. (1996), 'The '4Ms': Processes of Differentiation between Schools', in A. Pollard and S. Tan (eds), *Readings in Primary Education,* London: Cassell.

Elley, W. and Irving, J. (1976), 'Revised Socio-economic Index for New Zealand', *New Zealand Journal of Educational Studies*, 11, 25-36

Flude, M. (1974), 'Sociological Accounts of Differential Educational Achievement', in M. Flude and J. Ahier (eds), *Educability, Schools and Ideology*, London: Croom Helm.

Gordon, L. (1994), 'Rich and Poor Schools in Aotearoa/New Zealand', *New Zealand Journal of Educational Studies*, 29, 2, 113-25.

Halsey, A.H.(ed),(1972), *Trends in British Society Since 1990: a guide to the changing structure of Britain*, London: MacMillan and New York: St Martin's Press.

Halsey A. H. *et al.* (eds) (1997), *Education: Culture, Economy, Society*, Oxford: Oxford University Press

Hughes, D. and Lauder, H. (1990), 'Public Examinations and the Structuring of Inequality', in H. Lauder and C. Wylie (eds), *Towards Successful Schooling*, Brighton: Falmer.

Jonathan, R. (1990), 'State Education Service or Prisoner's Dilemma? The 'Hidden Hand' as a Source of Education Policy', *British Journal of Educational Studies* XXXVIII, 2, 116-32.

Kohn, M. (1963), 'Social Class and the Parent-Child Relationship', *American Journal of Sociology* 69, 471-93.

Kohn, M. *et al.* (1990), 'Class Structure and Psychological Functioning in the United States, Japan and Poland', *American Journal of Sociology* 95, 4, 964-1008.

Lauder, H. and Hughes, D. (1990a), 'Social Inequalities and Differences in School Outcomes', *New Zealand Journal of Educational Studies*, 25, 1, 37-60.

Lauder, H. and Hughes, D. (1990b), 'Social Origins, Destinations and Educational Inequalities', in J.Codd, R.Harker and R.Nash (eds), *Political Issues in New Zealand Education (2nd Edition)*, Palmerston North: Dunmore Press.

Lauder, H. *et al.* (1999), *Trading in Futures: Why Markets in Education Don't Work*, Buckingham: Open University Press.

Livingstone D. W. (1998), *The Education-Jobs Gap: Underemployment or Economic Democracy*, Boulder: Westview.

McCulloch, G. (1986), 'Secondary Education Without Selection? School Zoning Policy in Auckland', *New Zealand Journal of Educational Studies* 21, 2, 98-112.

McCulloch, G. (1991), 'School Zoning, Equity and Freedom: The Case of New Zealand', *Journal of Education Policy* 6, 2, 155-68.

Ministry of Education (1999), *Report on the School Sector*, Wellington: Ministry of Education.

Nash, R. (1993), *Succeeding Generations: Family Resources and Access to Education in New Zealand*, Auckland: Oxford University Press.

Nash, R. and Harker, R. (1997), *Progress at School; Final report to the Ministry of Education*, Massey University: ERDC.

Nash, R. and Harker, R. (1998), *Making Progress: Adding Value in Secondary Education*, Palmerston North: ERDC Press.

Nash, R. with Major, S. (1997), *Inequality/Difference: A Sociology of Education*, Palmerston North: ERDC Press.

Robertson, S. (2000), *A Class Act: Teachers' Work in Comparative Perspective*, Brighton: Falmer.

Robertson, S. and Dale, R. (2000), 'Competitive Contractualism:A new Social Settlement in New Zealand Education', in D. Coulby, R. Cowen, and C. Jones (eds), *Education in Times of Transition: World Yearbook of Education 2000*, London: Kogan Page.

Savage, M. (1992), *Property, Bureaucracy and Culture: Middle-Class Formation in Contemporary Britain*, London: Routledge.

Shavit, Y. and Muller, W. (1998), *From School to Work*, Oxford: Clarendon Press.

Wright, E. O. (1997), *Class Counts: Comparative Studies in Class Analysis*, New York: Cambridge University Press.

Young, M. F. D. (1972), 'An Approach to the Study of Curricula as Socially Organised Knowledge', in Young (ed.) *Knowledge and Control*, London: Macmillan.

Chapter 4

Maori Education Policy:
A State Promise

Kuni Jenkins and Alison Jones

The Promise of the State

The Ministry of Education, in March 1999, made a bold statement of
purpose. This purpose announced on their web page 'About-Us' is:

> Te Ihi, Te Mana, Te Mātauranga: Empowering Education

These terms have huge meaning, but the web document does not spell out
how they are to be interpreted. Collectively, the Maori words in the slogan
are not equivalent to the Pakeha words. 'Empowering Education' suggests
that Maori are still to become 'powerful', and that via education they will
become 'empowered'. In other words, the English part of the slogan
suggests that the people lack mana. By contrast, the Maori part of the
slogan is positive, and full of excitement and pleasure because of the
recognition of Te Mana. The intrinsic, self-determining power of Maori is
contained in this term. Within the slogan, then, is a serious contradiction.
On the one hand is the wish for power for a 'powerless' people; on the
other is the assertion of existing power. This contradiction signals more
than an unintentional use of catchy terms in a policy slogan. The tension
in the slogan lies at the heart of contemporary education policy for Maori
in Aotearoa/New Zealand.

Prefacing their March 1999 statement of purpose, the Ministry
declares that the government is not a provider of education:

The Ministry's influence on education outcomes is indirect. We are not a provider of education and our purpose reflects this.

Rather than providing them to the people directly, the ministry contracts others to provide the services of education; the government sees itself as enabling and facilitative rather than as being directive. It sees its role as an influencing and encouraging one, which fosters a policy environment which is able quickly and effectively to respond to social and economic impacts. In this sort of policy environment, Maori and others are theoretically 'empowered' to take some control of education, through being the devolved providers of education 'for' the state.

According to the ministry, a devolved education system for Maori should be structured around language revitalisation and te reo me ona tikanga. As *Nga Haeata Mātauranga* (1994: 4), the Strategic Direction Policy Document for the Ministry of Education, put it:

> Kua hangaia e te Tāhuhu o te Mātauranga ōna kaupapa mātauranga Māori i runga i te tuapapa o tō tāua nei reo rangatira. Kia aha ai? Tuatahi, kia mau ki tō tāua nei reo me ōna tikanga mō ake tonu atu. Tuarua, kia piki ake ai tātou ki ngā taumata mātauranga hei oranga mō tātou.
>
> The Ministry of Education has structured its policies on Maori language revitalisation: Why? Firstly for the sake of the retention of Maori language and customs in perpetuity, and secondly for increasing successful outcomes for Maori from education (translation by Kuni Jenkins).

This text shows how extensive the state 'promise' is for Maori language revitalisation. The Ministry's promise for the language and its customs suggests government commitment to deeply rooted change. For example, 'kia mau ... mo ake tonu atu' (to be maintained in perpetuity) is a long-term promise for supporting the language and customs. The text goes on to a second part which also emphasises the commitment of the Ministry: 'kia piki ake ai tātou (so that we can all ascend [and thereby achieve]) ki ngā taumata mātauranga (to the ultimate levels of knowledge [to which we aspire]) hei oranga mō tātou (so that we can survive [as positive outcomes])'. If the Ministry is serious about these kinds of aspirations, then it really is talking about the intrinsic power of the people (Te Mana) to bring these objectives to fruition. It would be a realisation of what Matiu Rata was talking about in 1979 when he said:

> We will no longer tolerate policies which take no account of our language, customs and lifestyle, nor will we continue to accept being governed or administered by anyone who does not understand the way we think or appreciate our values.
>
> (cited in Walker, 1990: 228)

Rata's comments not only establish the notion of mana, of power and status of the people to define and control their world, but they also reflect the notion of ihi, another of the words in the 1999 policy slogan. Within the framework of ihi are ideas of power, authority and rank. These are the ideas behind the first Maori term in the Ministry's slogan. The third idea presented in the slogan, Te Mātauranga (knowledge), presumably refers to Maori knowledge.

The policy statements from the 1990s above indicate, at least in the Maori text, a commitment of the state to real power for Maori, for a partnership in education which expresses and ensures Maori mana. But will the Pakeha words, the state's notion of 'Empowering Education', be more prominent than Te Mana and Te Ihi? Will the Maori concepts operate in tandem with 'empowerment', or will they determine the way Maori language revitalisation and schooling proceeds? Or will Pakeha ideals for Maori decide how the promises of the policies are played out?

Graham Smith's (1997) work suggests that Pakeha influences will dominate and control Maori education and especially Maori knowledge (Te Mātauranga), even while the ministry appears to be devolving Maori education to Maori. He points out how the recent market forces in education have served to commodify and appropriate Maori knowledge. He gives some examples of how the state, through its agency the New Zealand Qualifications Authority (NZQA), has developed mechanisms for appropriating particular divisions of Mātauranga which are pivotal to the way Maori cultural frameworks operate:

> The New Zealand Qualifications Authority has moved to give 'official' recognition to Maori knowledge through the qualifications

> structure. In this way Pakeha have assumed the power to determine
> and to exercise control over Maori definitions of knowledge. For
> example, kaumātua (elders), tohunga whakairo (carvers) ... have
> various qualification criteria that have been established by the
> Qualifications Authority ... The Kohanga Reo Trust award
> kaumätua certificates which bears the Trust's name and the
> Qualification Authority's insignia of endorsement. In these instances
> the right to control and to determine what counts in regard to
> traditional Maori knowledge has become appropriated by the state.
>
> (Smith 1997: 384, 399, 414)

Smith also points out that the National Government of 1990 removed the compulsion clauses of equity and the Treaty obligations which were included in the charters for Tomorrow's Schools – a removal which probably pleased many high-decile schools around the country. The government saw that equity and the Treaty were barriers to the 'freeing up' of the market.

It is not only Smith who has expressed concern about the promises of the state to Maori education. The Waitangi Tribunal (cited in Te Puni Kokiri, 1999:6), in its monitoring role of the state's performance, has spoken of the 'slippage in the Crown's commitment' to education. For Maori, the Treaty continues to be the benchmark by which the state is held to its obligations of guaranteeing education as a 'right and privilege'. The Tribunal was concerned at how there had been inadequate care since 1991 of attending to Maori language and culture as a taonga. The Tribunal pointed out how the state needed to be more vigilant at ensuring it had strategies and resources to ensure the protection of the taonga:

> We believe that the evidence submitted demonstrates that the Crown
> has not been adequately fulfilling its obligations in relation to Māori
> language and culture, especially since 1991, when there has been
> some slippage in the Crown's commitment to, and support for them
> in education and broadcasting. It is not sufficient for the Crown to
> rely on existing institutions. In view of the crisis in Māori language,
> every means must be employed to ensure the survival of the
> language.
>
> (Waitangi Tribunal, cited in Te Puni Kokiri, 1999:6)

By monitoring the state's performance and how it keeps to the Articles of the Treaty, especially the Third Article which promises to 'impart to them [Maori] all the Rights and Privileges of British subjects', the Tribunal assists Maori with the task of implementing te reo me ona tikanga (the language and customs). While the Ministry has tried to declare that the government/ state is not a provider of education, clearly the Waitangi Tribunal holds them directly accountable as providers of education under the Treaty. Part of the Tribunal's mandate is a monitoring of how the state is making provision for Maori education under the Treaty. The Ministry's plea that it is not a provider of education contributes to 'the slippage' about which the Tribunal is concerned.

The contradictions and double-speak of the March 1999 statement of purpose appear to continue a recent tradition in Maori education policy. In the late 1980s, the education policy document *Te Urupare Rangapu* (Ministry of Maori Affairs, 1988) explained how devolution for Maori should work. Graham Smith (1997: 384) discusses how initially Maori saw the potential in this policy for taking increased control over their own tribal affairs. At that point, the 'hands off' approach supposedly characteristic of the free market and the mechanism of devolution, should have facilitated Maori entry into the educational market-place and assured them of resources and other provisions. But, as Smith explains, the government interfered and pulled back on a lot of promises, and so did not devolve to Maori the range of services it said was possible.

It might be perceived that the Ministry of Education's phrase '*Te Ihi, Te Mana, Te Mātauranga: Empowering Education*' does appear to signal a move towards a full devolution package or at least a real space for ihi Maori to flourish. However, it is clear from past experience that Maori need to be mindful that the Ministry has built-in parameters which define its own interpretations of Maori concepts. Maori understandings of the reo used so freely in the Ministry documents differ from Pakeha interpretations. The Maori words become merely worthless tokens when they are used without understanding or serious intent. It will be interesting to see how state agencies like NZQA and state policies of the NEGs (National Educational Guidelines) and NAGs (National Administration Guidelines) will deal with the new slogan and its concepts of Te Ihi, Te Mana, Te Mātauranga. Can Te Ihi and Te Mana, as very abstract and traditional Maori terms, be commodified and domesticated in the way Smith discussed? How will the slogan assist in contributing to the policy aim which since the 1980s has been 'closing the gaps', and 'raising achievement and reducing disparity'?

What is the 'Disparity' in Maori education?

Among the state's strategies for reducing disparity and 'reducing the gaps' and overcoming Maori low achievement levels is, of course, continuation of increasing the 'dosage' of English and Western culture. There is still a ploy of trying to get Maori families to model their homes on Pakeha cultural styles. Maori pupils are still encouraged, through Home Economics programmes, to organise their households 'properly', to learn about 'better' dietary foods and to learn about cleanliness and always, at any given opportunity, to speak and write better English. In the past, such models were described as 'enrichment' models, but they are now described by the state as 'empowering education'. Such ideals may contribute to meeting the peripheral needs of Maori, but how educational programmes in mainstream schooling will be able to translate the ideas of Te Ihi, Te Mana, Te Mātauranga from the depth of Maori cultural frameworks into educational practice is far from evident.

Many Pakeha educational policies identify the 'disparity' between Maori and Pakeha in terms of different schooling outcomes, so that the aim in reducing disparity is to make Maori outcomes look more like those of Pakeha. But the great disparity Maori seek to address is the chasm between the Pakeha world in which they are isolated and the Maori world of which they are the keepers and in which, paradoxically, they often cannot speak with confidence. In the process of accessing existing education resources, many Maori become disoriented and dislocated from the mana of their communities. When Maori can speak with confidence because they 'know' their own world, then the 'disparity' will have been reduced and they will understand more fully what it means to possess Te Ihi, Te Mana, Te Mātauranga.

Maori are not, of course, indifferent to statistical disparities in achievement. Statistical data continues to be produced through class rolls, progress and achievement registers, and national examinations. These statistics present the measurements by which we can see how great the disparities are between the achievement and retention rates of Maori pupils and non-Maori pupils. While the data from the early 1990s revealed that the gap remained alarmingly wide, at close of the millenium, the Ministry takes hope from a very faint improvement in the statistics. It remains the case that Maori get far less from schooling than their Pakeha peers, as the state continues to fail in its promises of Te Ihi, Te Mana, Te Mātauranga. The 1997 school-leaving statistics show that 17.8 per cent of Maori left with a seventh form award, compared with 47.6 per cent of Pakeha. Those leaving with no qualifications are also starkly contrasted, with a shocking 37.7 per cent of Maori as compared with 12.2 per cent of Pakeha leaving school with no formal outcome. While, according to the statistics, the number of Maori students leaving school with no formal qualifications has reversed the spiral of increase since 1993, Maori may not be impressed by the 1.3 per cent decrease shown in the 1997 figures (Ministry of Education, 1998).

Other statistics illustrate the correlation between academic attainment and economic status. In decile 1-3 schools in 1997, the percentage of those leaving with a seventh-form qualification was 26 per cent, while in decile 8-10, that percentage was 59 per cent. At the other end of the scale, 28 per cent of students in decile 1-3 schools had no leaving qualifications, compared with 7 per cent in decile 8-10 schools.

Faced with statistics like these, disparity is obvious, but reducing the gap between rich and poor is not likely to be a feat which Maori strategies, aimed at revitalising Maori language and customs, will be able to begin to achieve. After all, the culture of the rich never connects with the culture of the poor; the gap will never be bridged. The poor have always been exploited by and divided from the rich. Racial barriers merely accentuate those divisions.

While the state is riveted to reducing disparities in order to enable Maori to enter the market-place in greater numbers, Maori are very likely to disappoint those whose measure is dollar-based. The Maori measure of achievement is not only economic, but based on possession of fluency in te reo me ona tikanga. And, while making comparisons between rich and poor schools may work for explaining non-Maori achievement, there are many Maori who do not accept explanations which are simply related to economic wealth. We are not promoting an idea that Maori are not interested in money, they are, and the programmes they want are going to cost a lot of money. Perhaps one day Maori enterprise will again make money as it did in the 1840s, in the initial history of the relationship between Maori and Pakeha.

In the past, statistical data has 'quietly' monitored the disparity between Maori and Pakeha. However, with the appointment of the state's 'policing' agency ERO (Educational Review Office) to monitor all facets of state-funded schooling, the statistics have been more publicly available. Not just the statistics, but the details of the management in schools became public information which newspapers could publish. The 1990s was a decade of school 'scandals' as several of the badly performing schools were 'marked' by the ERO inquisitions and further ridiculed by the publicity they received. Strangely enough, the rich schools mostly missed out on the limelight, and through their 'invisibility' continued to expand and get richer. Among the first schools to feel the heat of ERO in the early 1990s were Nga Tapuwae College, then rural schools in the central North Island (with large Maori populations), and finally the Maori boys' boarding schools, especially Te Aute, St Stephens and Hato Petera.

All of the negative publicity for Maori education served to sow the seeds of a new message about the lack of desirability of Maori schools. These messages become mechanisms for reinforcing the deficit theories of the 1960s when Maori were blamed for their own underachievement. The messages also serve to 'prove Maori incompetence', propped up by the statistical claims about low achievement in low-decile schools. Public sympathy is therefore lost as scenes of truancy, bullying and violence reported in the ERO documents become associated with 'the Maori problem'. The desire Maori have to revitalise their language and their customs becomes linked to these negative images in many Pakeha minds. Visions of a Maori-speaking community moulds people's fears into thinking of the Maori language initiatives as a return to savagery.

Recent research studies done by the University of Auckland into the incidence of truancy (Research Unit for Maori Education, 1996), and bullying and violence (Adair *et al.* 2000; *NZEI Rourou*, April 1999: 3) show that Maori do not have a monopoly on these problems. In fact, the studies show how widespread these problems are among all schools, both primary and secondary, and how the rich schools suffer as much as the poor schools from such elements. The rich schools can simply hide it better.

Wider Contexts for Te Ihi, Te Mana, Te Mātauranga

As a new century begins, old problems which plagued Maori in the last century still haunt them. Crime rates are still burgeoning at a level Maori would prefer not to have to address, health statistics continue to be very negative, employment levels are abysmal with no respite it sight, and credential inflation has moved the goal post off the playing field. Who would be a Maori in such a negative environment? For Maori in this context, pursuing the goals of Te Ihi, Te Mana, Te Mātauranga seems like a worthy option given that most all else has failed in the schooling system – according to the Ministry's statistics. The 'old problems' exist in a new economic and social environment. The debates on multi-culturalism seemed to subside in the decade of the 1990s as the country struggled to cope with its free-market policies and the selling-off of state assets which dominated the political arena. Communication networks went as did the railways, the Post Office, the telephone network, the television networks, the postal services, Air New Zealand and others. The citizenry of New Zealand hardly raised a murmur as the billions of dollars of New Zealand-owned assets went under the hammer and thousands of New Zealanders became unemployed in the name of privatisation. But the noise of Maori protest, and the litigation grievances they presented over the sales, created some real headaches for the government. In order to deal with the weight of those grievances, the role of the Waitangi Tribunal considerably expanded. The grievances can be viewed as challenges to the loss of Te Ihi, Te Mana, Te Mātauranga and how the sales were not in the least 'empowering' for Maori (and for many other New Zealanders).

Enacting Te Ihi, Te Mana, and Te Mātauranga in the 1990s was not only at the heart of protest about the implications of the economic changes, but also played a major role in engaging critically with the implications of the huge scientific advances in gene technology and exploitation. Donna Gardiner's (1997: 51) study of the Genome project carried out among her iwi in Tauranga provides an example for considering the way Te Ihi, Te Mana, Te Mātauranga operates at a community level. Her study emphasised the interference to cultural and intellectual property rights and the bodies of her own people caused by scientific projects in her home area. Her major concern was how life had taken on new meaning, without having to coincide with the moral and traditional codes which human beings have come to understand as the basis of reproduction and life. As such her study demonstrates the way Te Ihi, Te Mana, Te Mātauranga were so easily disturbed and downtrodden in her region. So how does education expect to uphold these principles in schools?

Some Positive Outcomes of Maori Schooling

There have been some positive outcomes from Maori initiatives over the past decade, especially in the area of Maori language revitalisation. Margie Hohepa (1999) uncovered statistics which show how, in 1996, a considerable increase in support for Maori-medium education happened, not just in Kura Kaupapa Maori options but also in Maori-medium options being offered within the state. She said:

> There were 3,222 children who were enrolled in 43 kura. In comparison, the number of conventional or 'mainstream' schools offering instruction through the medium of Maori increased from 50 to 251 between the years 1987-1993. By 1996, the total number of Maori primary school students in some form of 'Maori medium education' including Kura Kaupapa Maori was 27,669, 20% of all Maori school-aged students (Te Puni Kokiri, 1997: 17). ... By 1998, forty-two new Kura Kaupapa Maori had been built and seventeen existing state schools had been re-designated as Kura Kaupapa Maori.
>
> (1999: 36)

It is interesting to note from Hohepa's extract that seventeen state schools had changed their designation to become Kura Kaupapa Maori. The latest statistics from the *Directory of Schools* (Ministry of Education, 2000) show the numbers of Kura Kaupapa Maori to now be at 53, the result of several more state-controlled schools re-registering as kura. Early in the 1990s it had been the promise and policy of the state to build five new kura per year until the demands for such establishments were met. However, the last kura to have been built as a brand new establishment was Te Kura Kaupapa Maori o Maungarongo in Mt Albert in 1998.

A slogan such as 'Te Ihi, Te Mana, Te Mātauranga: Empowering Education' does seemingly commit state support for Kura Kaupapa Maori options, but is Smith (1998) right? Is the slogan simply an example of the commodification of Maori-medium education, and ultimately getting Kura Kaupapa Maori, with its meagre resources, to take the blame if its programmes fail to meet Maori demand, as Smith (1998) suggests? Is this simply the market-place setting itself up to sort out the 'weak traders' (helped along by ERO, perhaps) and get rid of them in the process of producing a better, more efficient service? Under the Treaty, the state is supposed to guarantee the provision of schooling to Maori, not make Maori do the providing of schooling. The message from the government that we are not a provider of education' is contradictory to the role Maori expect of it. The basis of the Treaty of Waitangi was the promise made by British representatives of the Crown that they would provide a system of governance. Among the provisions was education. Proper provisioning from those promises should result in the outcomes signalled in the Ministry of Education's report Nga Haeata Mātauranga (1994: 4):

> Tērā ka puta mai ngā hua, ka tutuki ngā wawata, ngā moemoeā o ā tāua tīpuna mātua
> ...and from that (successful outcomes) we can expect to come to fruition the hopes and dreams of our ancestral heritage (translation Kuni Jenkins).

But, so far, the hopes and the dreams of the ancestors remain just that.

Mechanisms for Teaching Te Reo me ona Tikanga

The mechanisms used by the state in the 1980s to cater for all pupils wanting to learn aspects of Maori language were Taha Maori curricula, bilingual education and total immersion programmes. Shifts in perceptions of these programmes was another characteristic which marked the changes of the 1990s. Taha Maori was recognised for its tokenism and became sidelined in favour of a more meaningful implementation of te reo me ona tikanga. The Resource Teachers of Maori (RTMs) who used to travel around schools and who had signalled an interest in Taha Maori programmes, were redeployed to work only in schools who were pursuing bilingual (reo-rua) or total immersion (rumaki) classes.

It was believed that teaching through the mechanisms of bilingualism would contribute to the regeneration and revitalisation of languages which are endangered, and that there was a need to encourage and foster in New Zealanders at least one additional language. Such aspirations in New Zealand schools that adopted bilingual programmes ran alongside the ideal of removing the impediments to learning. It was thought that an emphasis on Maori language might offer new ways of motivating Maori learners. But the catch was that these learners were first and foremost to be committed to an English-driven mainstream curriculum. Pupils who entered bilingual classes soon learned to carry a double load, that of carrying through the languages of English me ona tikanga and Maori me ona tikanga. And the tikanga which generally takes precedence is tikanga Pakeha/ English. Ideas of Te Ihi, Te Mana, Te Mātauranga have a specified and controlled – and therefore almost impossible – existence within such a context.

Many of the Maori teachers involved in bilingual education soon found how difficult it was to maintain the bilingual approach because the fluency levels of teachers were frequently lower than those of the pupils. There were also many cases where bilingual classes were fronted by non-Maori teachers whose fluency levels in Maori were still developing, or where their protocols were hard to connect with tikanga Maori. The *NZEI Rourou* magazine, April 1999, presented views of Maori teachers who were agitating for 'more Maori faces in front of Maori classes'. Schools soon found Maori families voting with their feet and leaving to join other schools which were offering immersion Maori classes.

Other people involved in the management of schools, such as administration assistants, made comments in *NZEI Rourou* (28 July 1998) like:

> Working as an administrator in a kura, you can only speak to the children in Maori. For much of the time you are in a no-English zone. You need to work hard to develop a fair understanding of the language (pp. 4-5).

Teachers at the 1998 Hui-a-tau (annual meeting of NZEI, Maori section) were concerned about being able to grow the language and being able to control what was happening in Maori education. These teachers took quite a radical position by insisting on a Maori Education Authority (Te Areare). In their eyes, such a move, if it were adequately funded, would be a mechanism for reducing the disparity between Maori and Pakeha educational achievement and at the same time increasing the fluency of Maori language of both teachers and students.

The new Associate Minister of Education, Parekura Horomia, meeting a delegation of NZEI Te Riu Roa (Maori members of NZEI) in Wellington in May 2000, said he wanted to monitor kaupapa Maori education in the mainstream and how Maori education policy and practice was fitting in with other developments in schools. One of the executive members told him of the present reality in schools – that most of the 80 per cent of Maori students in mainstream schools have little or no access to their culture. The member wanted to see a scenario where all Maori children have access to te reo at school. Her comments served to highlight how depressed – indeed, non-existent – are the aspects of Te Ihi, Te Mana, Te Mātauranga in mainstream schools, because of the insecurity of Maori language.

Te Puni Kokiri's National Maori Language Survey (1997) was important in reviewing the gap between fluent Maori speakers and non-fluent Maori. Based on the results, which showed continuing falling rates of fluent Maori speakers, Te Puni Kokiri, as a state agency, was then positioned to decide how it would advise educational agencies about where the real needs lay in Maori education. Te Puni Kokiri would also indicate how educational agencies should deploy their resources to assist in achieving the state's expressed policy of 'raising achievement and reducing disparity'. 'Raising achievement' for Te Puni Kokiri meant increasing fluency in te reo me ona tikanga. 'Disparity' was defined in terms of the levels of non-fluency which existed in communities. The report of their survey contained the following results:

> Although more than half the Maori adult population speaks some Maori, only 8% are highly fluent. Of the highly fluent, 33% are aged over 60 and 38% are aged between 45 and 59 years.
>
> (Te Puni Kokiri 1997: 6)

While the statistics show a dismal picture of Maori fluency in te reo for all age levels, the lowest fluency rate they reported (via Benton, 1991: 25) was for the youngest age brackets from ages 0-35. The use of Benton's figures is problematic because they are outdated, though they are presented as 1991 figures. In addition they give no sense of the fluency levels of the 1990s emerging from Te Kohanga Reo and Kura Kaupapa Maori. At present, the very young from Te Kohanga Reo and school age pupils are making significant gains with te reo, and it is the age group from upper secondary levels where the noticeable non-fluency and non-familiarity with Maori language occurs. This phenomenon continues to be present among the 20-60 year olds. It is our opinion that the 'problem' groups, who might be called the 'lost generations', are largely in those age brackets.

Having said that, it is the 'problem' group who are agitating to eliminate, and not just reduce, the disparity which exists for te reo me ona tikanga. Many of this age group do not want to reproduce a situation where 'being Maori' means to be an observer of the demise of their own culture. Loss of cultural frameworks, they argue, have greater impact for Maori than do the educational measures of 'school failure' documented in the school retention and national examination statistics.

Despite this belief about the centrality of language and culture, negative myths about Maori language learning are still to be heard through whispers of how 'Maori language won't get you a job', and how 'attending Maori schools is a return to the past'. In the Maori Education Commission Report (1999:10) were included papers from the International Symposium for Bilingual and Biliteracy Conference. Among them was a paper by Fishman (1999) which outlined myths of the negative impacts of bilingualism on educational achievements. Fishman (1999:10) said:

> Myths perpetuated by majority, authoritarian, societies include bilingualism having negative impacts on intelligence and educational outcomes. Bilingual education in all its forms has been accused of 'playing tag with the intelligence of students' by lowering their achievement potential.
> (Fishman, cited in Maori Education Commission Report, 1999:10)

He went on to say how the myths linked bilingualism and poverty, and, even worse, how 'bilingual education leads to poverty, alienation and social disorganisation'. Fishman showed how faulty associations are easily made which lead to negative thinking about bilingual education.

Summary

This chapter has outlined some of the issues which concern Maori educationists at the beginning of the twenty-first century. The policy promises of the government have sought to 'reduce' education gaps and disparities for Maori – and in doing so have defined what counts as disparity and achievement. Their definitions have been in fundamental tension with other elements also present in education policy – namely Te Ihi, Te Mana, Te Mātauranga, and the protection for te reo me ona tikanga. These latter ideas begin to name Maori aspirations for education policy. But not only are their meanings ignored, at the same time existing Maori educational initiatives struggle in a mainstream policy and monitoring environment which defines success in its own terms. The paradoxes remain particularly stark for Maori who set up Kura Kaupapa Maori. Among their reasons for taking this initiative was dissatisfaction with the results of Maori support for state education for more than a century. Their long-term support had merely led to low achievement levels for Maori in mainstream schools and the virtual loss of te reo me ona tikanga. Those who joined the kura movement had decided they could not do any worse by trying to run their own educational establishments, with their own curriculum of study. Now the state has turned to co-opt their efforts, and the efforts of those who continue to labour for Maori in mainstream schooling, through using Maori concepts which promise much, while failing to have any regard for these meanings and promises.

Bibliography

Adair V.A. *et al.* (in press), 'Ask Your Mother Not to Make Yummy Sandwiches: Bullying in New Zealand Secondary Schools', *New Zealand Journal of Educational Research*.

Benton, R. A. (1991, 1997), *The Maori Language: Dying or Reviving?*, East-West Centre, Alumni-in-Residence Working Paper Series, Wellington: NZCER.

Fishman, J. (1999), 'The Sociology of Bilingualism and Bilingual Education', Paper presented to the Bilingualism and Biliteracy through Schooling Conference, International Symposium, Long Island University, New York, cited in Maori Education Commission,

Report Four to the Minister of Maori Affairs, Wellington, September.

Gardiner, D. (1997), 'Hands Off Our Genes: A Case Study on the Theft of Whakapapa', *Cultural and Intellectual Property Rights: Economics, Politics & Colonisation*, Volume Two, Auckland: IRI/ Moko Productions.

Hohepa, M. K. (1999), Hei Tautoko i te Reo: Maori Language Regeneration and Whanau Bookreading Practices, Unpublished Ph.D. thesis, University of Auckland.

Maori Education Commission (1999), *Report Four to the Minister of Maori Affairs*, September 1999.

Ministry of Education Web-page, 5 June 1998, *Education Statistics*, News Sheet, Volume 8, No. 5.

Ministry of Education Web-page, March 1999, 'About Us'.

Ministry of Education (2000), *Directory of Schools*, Wellington.

Ministry of Maori Affairs (1988), *Te Urupare Rangapu*, Wellington.

Nga Haeata Mātauranga (1994), Annual Report 1993/94 and Strategic Direction for 1994/95, Wellington: Ministry of Education.

NZEI Rourou (1998) Vol. Nine, Number Seven, 28 July.

NZEI Rourou (1999) Vol. Ten, Number Three, 13 April.

NZEI Rourou (2000) Vol. Eleven, Number Four, 3 May.

Rata, M. (1979), cited in R. Walker (1990), *Ka Whawhai Tonu Matou: Struggle Without End*, Harmondsworth: Penguin Books.

Research Unit for Maori Education (R U M E) (1996), *Te Kupenga: Children Adrift in the Truancy Crisis*, Report presented to Ministry of Education.

Smith, G. H. (1997), The Development of Kaupapa Maori: Theory and Praxis, Unpublished Ph.D. thesis, University of Auckland.

Smith, G. H. (1998), 'Iwi Wars: Neo-Colonisation in Aotearoa', *Fisheries & Commodifying Iwi*, Auckland: IRI/Moko Productions.

Te Puni Kokiri (1997), 'National Maori Survey', Wellington.

Te Puni Kokiri (1999), 'National Maori Language Survey', cited in Maori Education Commission, *Report Four to the Minister of Maori Affairs*, September.

Chapter 5

Education Policy for Pacific Nations Peoples

Eve Coxon and Diane Mara

Pacific Nations education is concerned with the study of educational issues pertaining to both education in Pacific countries and to Pacific peoples in Aotearoa New Zealand. In order to provide a critical analysis of education policy in both arenas, this chapter is presented in two parts, both of which employ the inclusive term 'Pacific Nations' to refer to six or seven distinct ethnic and linguistic groups, with their own social structures, histories, values, beliefs and practices. It should be noted, however, that this term does not account for the diversity between its constituent groups, such as the differences between the resident peoples of each island country; and, within migrant communities, between individuals born in their island of origin and those born in Aotearoa/New Zealand. We should also be mindful of differences within groups, such as gender role differences, intergenerational differences, social class differences, differences in educational attainment and so on.

New Zealand's Influence on Education Policy in the Pacific

Over the past century New Zealand has played a significant role in the development of education policy and practice in the Pacific. In order to demonstrate the shifts in New Zealand's education policy for Pacific countries – especially those having close historical and cultural links to New Zealand – we need to outline New Zealand's historical location in the region during the periods of colonialism and decolonisation, and refer briefly to the educational relationships developed during these periods. (For an account of Pacific education prior to colonial times refer to Mara, Foliaki and Coxon, 1994: 182-190.)

We then move to a discussion of the post-colonial period, during which New Zealand's influence has been maintained largely through the educational aid provided under the New Zealand Official Development Assistance (NZODA) programme, with a focus on developments during the 1990s. Our concern here is to analyse critically the effects of New Zealand's economic restructuring and education policy redirection over the past 10-15 years, for education in the small, underdeveloped island countries of the Pacific. Our discussion explores the implications of shifts in the policies underpinning the NZODA programme for Pacific education, and its administration through the Ministry of Foreign Affairs and Trade. Of particular concern is New Zealand's promotion of neo-liberal economics, the dominant ideology within the global economy, as the only effective development strategy for Pacific states. Notable also is the extent to which the NZODA programme has been used to promote New Zealand as the ideal of the market-friendly state, upon which Pacific States should model themselves.

Although New Zealand's educational and wider policies during the time period under consideration are explicitly located as part and parcel of wider globalisation processes, due recognition is also paid to the historical and cultural particularities which shape how New Zealand's educational relationships with Pacific countries were, and are, played out.

Colonialism

New Zealand's official involvement in Pacific education began at the turn of the century when the New Zealand government took control of the Cook Islands and Niue under the Pacific Islands Annexation Act, 1901. This event arose from a longstanding imperial ambition, dating from the early years of New Zealand's own colonial history. New Zealand's desire for a Pacific 'empire' had not been satisfied, however, so when, on the outbreak of World War I, Britain requested that New Zealand seize Western Samoa 'as a great and urgent imperial service' (Field, 1991: 2), New Zealand was keen to oblige. In 1925 the islands of Tokelau came under New Zealand's administration. Also, from the early years of the century, New Zealand played a significant role in education, on behalf of the British colonial administration, for Fiji, Tonga, Kiribati and Tuvalu (then known as the Gilbert and Ellis Islands).

The New Zealand-based bureaucrats and politicians responsible for education policymaking for Pacific countries promoted the notion of state responsibility for a secular system of schooling (which had underpinned New Zealand's education system since the 1870s). However, the administrators in the Pacific countries concerned were keen to avoid the financial expenditure involved in a fully state-controlled system, so tended to work with the various Christian missions which had established schools in each of the island countries. Under these arrangements existing primary schools were maintained according to missionary beliefs and practices, and school systems expanded only according to what was perceived as being in the political and economic interests of the New Zealand authorities.

Officially, what constituted education policy depended on which of two schools of thought on 'native' education in New Zealand's Pacific dependencies was prevalent at the time. One view saw the educational needs of Pacific Islands people as ordained by their 'natural' role as cultivators of the land, and believed that schooling beyond a very basic level could be both economically and politically counterproductive because it would make them discontent with village life. The other saw education as an efficient agency of assimilation (New Zealand's official policy for Maori education). Those upholding the latter view proposed a schooling system which would produce a limited number of graduates with the attitudes and skills which would enable them to fill minor roles in the public service, to work in clerical and sales positions in the commercial sector, and to train as primary school teachers, nurses and tradespeople.

There was no coherent development of either of these broad policy directions. With a growing number of New Zealand teachers working around the region, however, as stated in Mara, Foliaki and Coxon (1994: 193):

> Much of what was offered was based on that practised in New Zealand Maori schools – described in official policies as 'in accordance with the latest developments in the education of native races'.... What this meant in practice was a very limited curriculum and schooling being used as a form of social, economic and political control.

Pacific peoples during these years consistently sought more, and higher levels of schooling. Their leaders objected consistently to these education policies which they recognised as having the intention of stifling their aspirations. They made repeated requests to the colonial authorities for better primary schools, the establishment of secondary schools and teacher education institutions that would produce local teachers of a good standard. Their requests were just as consistently declined by those who wished to avoid the creation of an educated population which might threaten New Zealand's political authority.

Decolonisation

As for the rest of the colonised world, the end of the Second World War in 1945 triggered significant political, economic and social changes throughout the Pacific. This included a process of decolonisation resulting from the demands of nationalist movements among colonised peoples struggling for self-government (the most notable Pacific example being the Mau Movement of Samoa – see Field, 1991). Combined with this was a changing international order that reduced the power of the centres of colonialism such as Britain and France and supported the ascendancy of USA and USSR – both avowedly anti-colonial. The New Zealand Labour Government of the time was supportive of the wish for political sovereignty among colonised peoples, and also recognised the need to redefine its role in this rapidly changing global order.

New Zealand's Pacific policy became specifically geared to preparing its colonial territories for some form of self-government, and education was perceived to be essential to the preparation of colonised peoples for this self-government. In 1945, at the instigation of the Prime Minister, Peter Fraser, who on his official visit to Samoa the previous year had noted the 'appalling condition of the education system' (Barrington, 1968: 80), New Zealand's Director-General of Education, Clarence Beeby, led a delegation of New Zealand educators on a fact-finding tour of the region (Beeby, 1992).

As a result of this and a further tour led by Beeby in 1954, primary schooling was upgraded and secondary schooling established or expanded. A scholarship scheme, under which the most academically able students were sent to New Zealand for senior secondary and/or tertiary education, was established. Many more New Zealand teachers worked on contract in

Pacific schools. Curricula, pedagogy and evaluation systems were increasingly prescribed by the New Zealand Department of Education. Growing numbers (though still a very selective group) of Pacific students sat New Zealand School Certificate (NZSC), and in later years, New Zealand University Entrance (NZUE). Some were then selected for scholarships for higher secondary and tertiary education in New Zealand.

Further significant initiatives arising from Beeby's recommendations were the establishment of an Islands Division within the New Zealand Department of Education, and the appointment of an Officer for Islands Education to coordinate the education systems of New Zealand's Pacific dependencies (Ma'ia'i, 1957: 229).

During the 1960s and 70s, the NZODA programme (initiated in 1960) was geared to assisting both the decolonising New Zealand administrations and the newly independent Pacific states in the achievement of education policy goals perceived as necessary for enabling underdeveloped countries to 'catch-up' to so-called developed countries. The immediate requirement was for qualified people to run the state, while the more long-term requirement was for a workforce with the 'modern' skills and attitudes deemed necessary for economic development. Central to both was the need for more senior secondary schooling and tertiary education with a vocational focus. Larger numbers of Pacific students were entered in the New Zealand senior secondary examinations. Together Britain, Australia and New Zealand were the driving forces behind the 1968 establishment of the University of the South Pacific (USP) to serve the 'manpower' needs of the eleven countries formerly under their administration (Baba, 1992).

Education was promoted by both the Pacific governments and the aid donor countries as the key to development, and investment in human capital through education as the best way to ensure economic growth. These understandings were incorporated into national development plans and informed education policies for the emerging Pacific states. A further aspect of the relationship between New Zealand and her ex-dependencies, which upheld the dominance of New Zealand schooling structures throughout their school systems, was that New Zealand's expanding industrialisation of the time created a need for unskilled labour which could not be met from within the existing population (even after the urban migration of rural Maori). Employers looked to the Pacific for recruitment of a cheap and convenient labour force. For Pacific countries, the rapid population growth of the early post-war years (largely due to improved health services), and the subsequent increases in the school-age population, meant that despite their improved and expanded school systems, educational demands could not be met. Neither could Pacific peoples' aspirations for wage-paying jobs in the modern sectors of their economies. The perception of better educational opportunities and the availability of wage employment, combined with other factors such as improved transport services, resulted in a flood of Pacific migrants to New Zealand. Preparation for life in New Zealand was increasingly seen as a legitimate policy goal for Pacific education.

Post-colonialism

By the mid-1970s there was much dissatisfaction with the outcomes of this policy approach. Educators were concerned about the appropriateness of what was offered which they saw as addressing the needs of only the small number of academically successful students. They proposed a shift to education more 'relevant' to the needs of the majority of students who would return to village life at the end of their schooling. Politicians and bureaucrats were concerned about the social tensions arising from urban unemployment, as increasing numbers of rural dwellers moved to urban areas in pursuit of educational and employment opportunities. Another area of concern was education's failure to deliver the promised economic growth despite the (relatively) large amounts of resources expended. Added to these concerns were those from New Zealand about the effects of the world-wide economic recession on the New Zealand economy. The reduced need for migrant labour contributed to a shift of emphasis in NZODA policy in Pacific education; preparation for life in New Zealand was no longer perceived as a desirable objective for island schools. The combined effect of these concerns was the development of policies for the localisation of curricula and assessment. A number of countries developed dual secondary systems which offered agricultural – technical programmes in schools located in rural areas and an academic programme to selected students in urban-based schools.

Throughout the 1980s, localisation – at the national level for primary and junior secondary, and the regional level for senior secondary and tertiary – was the major policy thrust in Pacific education, and the promotion of self-reliance became the overriding policy goal informing NZODA. National teachers colleges and curriculum development units, with the assistance of aid donors, developed programmes seen as relevant to the Pacific context. In 1980 the establishment of the South Pacific Educational Assessment Board in Fiji led to significant changes in what was included in curricula and who controlled assessment processes. National fifth form awards replaced NZSC, and a regional sixth form certificate replaced NZUE. New Zealand continued to provide assistance with the construction of exam papers and processing of results as and when requested. The University of the South Pacific Foundation Programme was used as a seventh form equivalent programme by all member countries.

NZODA's policy emphasis on self-reliance encouraged a responsiveness to needs defined by Pacific countries themselves – an approach reflecting a 'bottom-up' view of development. It recognised the need to provide the educational assistance which would enhance Pacific educators' objective of developing teaching and learning processes relevant to their contexts. A notable measure of NZODA's positive contribution was that Pacific academics/educators were frequently invited to participate in aid-funded activities throughout the region, so strengthening USP and national educational institutions and building up a regional pool of educational expertise and knowledge.

The 1990s

The restructuring of New Zealand's public sector, in accord with the general neo-liberal policy environment of the late 1980s and the 1990s, included the refocusing of aid-funded development policies towards Pacific education. This was first signalled in 1988 by the relocation of Pacific Education from the International Division of the Department of Education to the Ministry of Foreign Affairs and Trade. The public servants employed by the Department of Education because of their knowledge of and familiarity with Pacific education policies and practices, and their close professional relationships with regional educators, lost their institutional base. Those who wished to continue working in the field became private sector consultants competing for contracts. As such, they were no longer in a position to contribute to the institutional memory built up over the previous 40 years about Pacific education.

In 1991, in a speech entitled 'New Zealand in the South Pacific', New Zealand's Minister of Foreign Affairs 'charted a new emphasis on New Zealand's policy in the region'. The speech focused on the need for New Zealand to pursue its own economic interests in the region. The means for fulfilling this overriding policy goal included strategies for encouraging Pacific governments to follow the neo-liberal path New Zealand was undertaking. This was reinforced by the NZODA policy document *Investing in a Common Future*. The use of NZODA as a means of 'encouraging' recipient countries to model themselves on New Zealand is seen in the statement, 'New Zealand's aid policy reflects our own development path' (Ministry of Foreign Affairs and Trade, 1996: 6).

New Zealand's upholding of itself as a model of development, given the social and economic costs of the development path taken, must be subjected to critical analysis. By the end of the 1990s we had a huge balance of payments deficit and high foreign debt, serious unemployment, and our education and health systems were unable to cope with the consequences of poverty and increasing inequalities. Despite fifteen years of sacrifices by the majority of New Zealand's population, there was nothing to indicate that by continuing to pursue such a path the situation would improve. That New Zealand's aid programme should have been utilised as a means of exporting this model to the fragile and vulnerable economies of the Pacific is alarming to say the least.

The 'new emphasis' in New Zealand's Pacific policy was incorporated into the policies and procedures of NZODA, the primary means by which New Zealand's influence on Pacific education, as the major recipient of NZODA, is maintained. A review of the principles underpinning the aid programme led to the development of a new policy framework in 1993, which reflected the new emphasis in both the management of educational projects and the kind of project which attracts aid-funding. Although notions such as 'equity' and 'sustainability' are upheld as desired outcomes of NZODA policy, the focus is on education as a delivery system, the efficiency of which is determined by centralised rational decision-making according to cost-effectiveness in the use of resources.

This 'top-down' managerial approach, which presents education as a matter of technical inputs and measurable outputs, downplays the processes and structures of teaching and learning – curriculum, pedagogy and assessment. Teaching and learning are presented as technical, rather than social and cultural processes. Furthermore, as the consequences of the educational reforms undergone in New Zealand over the past 10-12 years demonstrate, the managerial-technical formula, from which NZODA education policy appears to be derived, fails to acknowledge the tensions between notions such as equity on the one hand and the tenets of market discourse such as efficiency on the other (see Codd, 1993).

Concluding Comments

New Zealand's adoption of a managerial-technical approach to educational development in the Pacific means that during the 1990s there has been, at policy level, limited recognition of contextual factors. This is in contrast to the growing recognition in the 1980s policy approach that the solutions to Pacific education problems should be devised by Pacific educators according to the needs of Pacific students. As indicated earlier, during the decolonisation and early post-colonial periods, New Zealand's Pacific policy, while undoubtedly working in New Zealand's strategic and other interests, had also been responsive to the needs and interests of Pacific countries as voiced by Pacific peoples themselves. It could be argued that New Zealand's promotion of a top-down development model represents a recolonisation process – in which the aid donors become policy-makers, while those receiving aid are expected to fill the role of policy-takers.

By the end of the 1990s it was clear that there was an urgent need to resist and counter the neo-liberal ideology being promoted by New Zealand to the small states of the region, as the only effective approach to development. As argued by Pacific writers (for example, Emberson-Bain, 1994; Fairbairn-Dunlop, 1996; Hau'ofa *et al.*, 1993), a model of development based on such an ideology would serve to break down the ethics of redistribution, reciprocity and inclusiveness which still characterise the economic structures embedded in Pacific societies and cultures, and thus threaten their very survival.

If the outcomes of projects and activities supported through NZODA are to achieve the very worthwhile goals of sustainable and equitable educational development, then they must anchored in local values and structures. This requires a focus on local, social, cultural and educational factors rather than the application of a managerial-technical formula devised elsewhere.

Education Policy for Pacific Nations Peoples in Aotearoa/New Zealand

As previously stated, the rapid increase in migration of Pacific peoples to Aotearoa/New Zealand during the 1960s was the consequence of a combination of factors. In New Zealand the 60s were years of economic diversification and the need for unskilled labour could not be met from within the country. Circumstances in Pacific Islands countries at the time – rapid population growth, lack of sufficient employment and educational opportunities soon meant they were ripe for recruitment as the cheap and convenient labour force required for New Zealand's economic development. What has been referred to as a 'flood' of Pacific migrants arrived in New Zealand throughout the 60s and early 70s mostly to the main cities but also to forestry towns like Tokoroa. Most of the Pacific Nations people living in New Zealand today are those who arrived during that time, or their New Zealand-born children and grandchildren.

In order to look critically at developments in education over the past thirty years or so for New Zealand-based Pacific Nations peoples in Aotearoa, as well as present education policy directions, we need an understanding of the political, social and economic context of Pacific communities since the time they became a significant minority population within Aotearoa/New Zealand. Useful here is the employment of the sociological concept of 'marginalisation' to describe how social, political and economic mechanisms, structures and policies operate to exclude the interests, views and perspectives of minorities from the 'mainstream' life of a society, and confine them to a subordinate position.

Research during past decades has illustrated the subordinate class location of Pacific workers (see for example, Spoonley and Shipley, 1982). The structural position of Pacific Islanders in the economy of New Zealand is reflected in the high proportions who are unemployed or who occupy unskilled and semi-skilled jobs. More recent statistics show very little improvement in the social and economic status of Pacific peoples in the 1990s (see 'Pacific Island Population and Dwellings' in the 1991 Census by the Department of Statistics), and indicate the extent to which Pacific communites are indeed marginalised. Such indicators demonstrate clearly the social and economic marginalisation of Pacific Nations populations in Aotearoa.

The point made in the chapter on social class about the complexities involved in the correlation between ethnicity and socio-economic status for Maori is also applicable to Pacific peoples. The interrelationship between social class and ethnicity underpins the socially constructed reality for these groups, and for Pacific women the factor of gender reinforces existing inequalities. Pacific women support their unemployed male partners; they shoulder extended family responsibilities; they support their church congregations; they hold down one or more low paid jobs; they run language nests; they run culture groups at the local school and so on.

It is maintained here that inequalities in our education system reflect social class, ethnic and gender differences in wider society, and that there is no physical or 'natural' basis for the different educational achievement levels between groups. The fact that these differences exist in a supposedly egalitarian system – one that claims to provide equal opportunities to achieve for all students – indicates that the system itself, and its relation to wider society, needs to be critically investigated. What needs to be explored is why some groups of students persistently fail in our educational institutions; and Pacific nations students' failure rates are higher than for any other group. We need to ask whether and what education policies and practices have been or can be put in place in order to ensure equity of access, treatment and outcome in educational provision for all social groups across all levels of the system from early childhood through to tertiary.

Initiatives of the 1970s

As educators we accept that a factor in educational success or failure is that of high parental expectation and the value placed on educational achievement by a student's family. As is characteristic for migrant populations, Pacific communities have always shown a keen interest in working hard and providing better opportunities for their children than would have been available in their country of origin. The following comment, written at the time that Pacific migration was at a peak, indicates the educational motivation which underlies migration for many (Challis, 1970: 26-7):

> To many parents in Western Samoa and in the Cook and Niue Islands the desire to give their children a good education is almost a passion. Facilities for education, particularly higher education, are still

limited .... The parent sees that his [sic] children have little opportunity, unless they are quite talented, of gaining a place in the government secondary schools. He [sic] knows that in New Zealand all children must go to school and stay there until they are fifteen .... Many families come to New Zealand with the purpose of giving this opportunity to their children.

This discussion outlining the educational initiatives established and implemented throughout the 70s aimed at assisting Pacific Nations people to fulfil their educational aspirations, draws attention to an increasingly widening contrast between the efforts and energies of Pacific communities themselves and the *ad hoc* responses of those in power.

A significant initiative for the time was the Pacific Island Polynesian Education Foundation (PIPEF), established in 1972 by Act of Parliament. Its purpose was 'to promote and encourage the better education of Polynesians and to provide financial assistance for that purpose' (Clause 5 of the Act). The Board of Trustees and the Chairman of PIPEF were to be appointed by the Governor-General (on government recommendation) and five trustees were to be appointed on the recommendation of their respective Pacific communities: Niuean, Cook Islands, Samoan, Tokelauan and Tongan. However, the fact that the PIPEF Act stipulates which Pacific communities are able to benefit from the available assistance has long been contested. Lobbying from the Pacific communities over a number of years for an amendment to cover all Pacific peoples, rather than only those from Polynesian cultural groups, has been ignored by successive governments. The communities themselves believe that Fijians, for example, as non-Polynesian Pacific Islanders resident in Aotearoa, should qualify for PIPEF awards (particularly given their involvement in fundraising for PIPEF).

The effectiveness of PIPEF has always been a matter of debate, but it would be true to say that throughout its history it has not maintained a large financial base. Unlike the Maori Education Foundation which receives monies and endowments from Trust Boards and lands, the Pacific communities (lacking similar economic bases) have not consistently resourced PIPEF. One explanation for the lack of community support could be that remittances to the home countries, church and family obligations had greater priority in the earlier days of Pacific Islands migration to

Aotearoa. Despite a substantial donation to PIPEF from PACIFICA Inc (Pacific Women's Council) in 1978, PIPEF has been unable to meet the increasing demands from Pacific students for educational grants. PIPEF was previously administered through the Department of Education and is now administered by the Ministry of Education.

The subsequent establishment of educational trusts and scholarships which are aimed at promoting educational achievement and training (such as the Pacific Youth Leadership Trust), and a range of scholarships offered by government departments, has supplemented the work started by PIPEF. The Pacific Island Business Development Trust (set up under the auspices of the Ministry of Pacific Island Affairs) publishes a yearly magazine called *Achievers*, a compilation of the seventeen or so awards and scholarships that are available to Pacific students.

In July 1974, the Minister of Education Phil Amos invited Pacific community leaders and educators to a week-long Lopdell House Conference to discuss the nature of educational provisions for Pacific peoples in New Zealand. The group produced 74 recommendations in a report to the Minister covering the teaching of English, continuing education and social services, curriculum and staffing, pre-school education, teacher education, pre-vocational and vocational education, and the role of the media in education.

One of the main recommendations of *Educating Pacific Islanders in New Zealand* (1975) was implemented in 1976 with the establishment of the Pacific Island Education Resource Centre (PIERC) in Herne Bay, Auckland. PIERC's foundation objectives were as follows:

> ... assist Pacific Islanders to overcome language, social and other difficulties faced when settling in New Zealand and to provide training facilities for Islanders to make a professional contribution in schools. At the same time it would provide training for teachers to permit them to acquire a better appreciation of the cultural background of Pacific Islanders and their special educational requirements. To these ends a variety of teaching materials and resources would be developed.
> (Report on the Review of the Pacific Islanders Educational Resource Centre, 1987a: 11)

In its first years the centre published educational resource materials, including in 1978 *A Handbook for Teachers of Pacific Island Children.* The Centre also provided resources for the teaching of English as a Second Language, aimed initially at Pacific Islanders but increasingly for migrants from Asia. In 1983 PIERC opened an outpost at Nga Tapuwae in Mangere to be closer to another large population concentration of Pacific communities.

A further initiative was the conference called in 1978 by PIPEF and the Department of Education of representatives from a wide range of Pacific organisations and interests. It was an attempt to fulfil the 1974 recommendations to establish an advisory committee to the Minister of Education.

In summary the 1970s were characterised by educational initiatives for Pacific peoples that occurred because there was a changing political and social context within which the growing needs of distinctive ethnic minorities were becoming acknowledged. Pacific Nations populations were rapidly increasing in the satellite suburbs such as Otara and Porirua and in towns like Tokoroa. The social agencies – social welfare, health, immigration, justice and education – had at that time the resources available to meet the consequences of the changes in ethnic composition of communities in Aotearoa/New Zealand.

The 1980s

The 1980s could be described as a decade in which hope was replaced with disenchantment. The social consequences for all groups in Aotearoa/New Zealand of the economic problems and policies of the 1980s were amplified for Pacific communities. Any significant or positive consequences for educational policy development, educational outcomes and educational provisions were, generally speaking, minimal.

In 1981 Peter Ramsey of Waikato University published his report on schools in Otara and Mangere called *Tomorrow May Be Too Late.* One result of his report was the setting up of two Resource Experimental Developmental Centres (RED Centres) in 1983. As was the case with other initiatives, the success of the centres relied on the goodwill and energy put into them by the community, including Pacific peoples, while the overall system underfunded them by just redeploying existing discretionary resources to set them up. There was also an expectation that existing agencies in the community, such as schools and unpaid or low paid community workers, would provide the ongoing support for such initiatives. Ramsey had anticipated this in his demand that any initiatives arising from his report should be adequately and appropriately resourced.

In areas such as South Auckland a myriad of social agencies (central and local bodies) were utilised to the extent they could be, to sustain community initiatives. This perpetuated an already *ad hoc* problem-solving approach. Groups were constantly lobbying (as a result of reports on social crises) to get 'emergency funding' in order to fund what were, in actuality, ongoing projects. This situation meant that many groups spent their time not only serving the needs of their people as best they could, but also lobbying, developing submissions, meeting bureaucrats, and being endlessly researched and consulted as to community needs.

The community consultation process continued in 1981 with the Department of Education's decision to hold a series of district conferences on Pacific Islands education in order to involve growing Pacific communities in areas such as the South Island. A total of eleven meetings were held over 1981 and 1982, with some follow-up meetings in 1983. Recommendations from these meetings were beginning to articulate more particular concerns about such issues as educational success, the retention of one's first language, the involvement of parents in schools, the request for more exact Pacific education statistics and the need for more Pacific teachers at all levels of the education system from pre-school to tertiary.

Strong community lobbying, following the establishment of PIERC in Auckland, led to the Department of Education, establishing the Wellington Multicultural Resource Centre (WMRC) in 1981 in an attempt to meet growing educational needs in Wellington. Its focus, however, was wider than Pacific nations; its targets were extended to include Asian, Greek and other ethnic communities. Both centres also ran English as a Second Language programme for these communities.

At a further Lopdell Centre course in 1984 the Pacific teachers who attended reviewed the recommendations from all previous conferences and submissions. This group developed and submitted to the Department of Education over 50 recommendations on such areas as parental involvement in education, guidance counselling, vocational guidance, teacher education (pre- and inservice); and a number that focused on language development through English language support, first language maintenance, bilingual education and the introduction of Pacific languages in schools.

By the mid-80s the Teacher Unions (PPTA, NZEI) had become involved in lobbying and promoting the needs of Pacific teachers and students. In 1985 PPTA sponsored a Pacific Islands Education Forum which involved parents, students and teachers to talk about educational issues which concerned them. The recommendations which came out of that forum were presented later that year to the PPTA Annual Conference, and formed the basis of its Pacific education policy.

The establishment in 1985 of the Ministry of Pacific Island Affairs in Wellington, albeit with a limited budget and a small number of staff, was a significant means of giving Pacific peoples a voice at government level. Its main task was to inform the Minister of Pacific Island Affairs on matters of policy, including education policy, affecting Pacific peoples in Aotearoa. The Ministry's function was also to monitor all government policy to ensure the needs and perspectives of Pacific communities were being incorporated in that policy development. As with previous developments, despite the efforts and energies expended by individuals and some important gains, it has been difficult for a small team to make any real impact on policy when the volume of policy developed across all government ministries is enormous.

In 1986 the Department of Education made three Education Officer appointments to its staff: two Education Officers in Pacific Islands Education (one in Auckland and one in Wellington), and one Women's Education Officer in Maori and Island Education. A fourth Pacific Islands Education Officer was appointed to Continuing Education. Again the observation can be made that despite the commitment of the individuals appointed, the lack of political will and the structural and the institutional barriers, which were largely insurmountable, meant that their net impact on mainstream educational policy was minimal (Mara, 1993).

It was during the early to mid-1980s that the growth of Pacific Islands Early Childhood language groups, the first of which was established by Cook Islands women in Tokoroa, accelerated. Aoga Amata (Samoan), Punanga Reo (Cook Island) and Niuean, Tongan and Tokelauan groups were being established by women in each of these communities. In recognition of the consequences for tangata whenua of the loss of language and culture, and thereby identity and self-esteem, Pacific Islands women decided that action must be taken to ensure the future educational success of their children. Stimulated by the early efforts of Cook Island and Samoan women in such places as Tokoroa, Otara and Newtown, and the lack of access to mainstream early childhood education which sets the basis for later educational success, Pacific communities began their early childhood groups in church halls, homes, garages, spare classrooms at schools, and community halls. The establishment of these groups relied almost completely on the community's own resources with minimal playgroup funding from the government. For the Niuean and Tokelauan communities, the greater majority of whom now live in Aotearoa/New Zealand, the issue of language maintenance has become an issue of cultural survival.

In order to respond to the need for parent and home-based support approaches to early childhood education, PACIFICA, in conjunction with the Department of Education, developed a submission to the Bernard Van Leer Foundation of the Netherlands for funding for an early childhood intervention programme. The proposal was accepted and the project began its work in 1988 in Auckland, Tokoroa and Wellington. This project is called the Anau Ako Pasifika Project. It works with parents in their own homes assisting them to participate in their children's learning by using everyday and culturally relevant resources. It also gathers together Pacific parents and supports their move into established early childhood services in their community – which could include a Pacific language group. It is significant and ironic that the most important development in Pacific Nations education in Aotearoa/New Zealand in the 1980s was funded by an overseas trust.

The hopes of all involved in education for Pacific communities were raised when the Department of Education Report in 1987 included a statement that the department had given 'considerable thought to the educational implications of multiculturalism' and recommended 'a comprehensive set of proposals for the teaching of the languages of the main ethnic communities in this country'. It went on to suggest that the full implementation of these proposals required 'a firm, long-term commitment by government' (1987b). Despite this and the ongoing consultations with the Pacific communities throughout this period, the Department of Education and the governments of the time still failed to see the need for an overarching policy in Pacific Nations education. Such a policy should have included all the issues raised during the protracted consultation processes, which served only to raise expectations that could not be fulfilled, and indeed were not.

The last significant development of the 1980s was the inclusion in the 1988 Royal Commission on Social Policy of the first comprehensive structural overview of Pacific Islands and migrant education policy. The commission, in outlining policy in this area, stated that 'Currently we have a situation where minority groups are recognised only for their disadvantage or deprivation in assimilationist terms' (1998 Vol III, Part 2, 5: 235). The report also questioned the effectiveness of an assimilationist policy in which members of ethnic or cultural minorities had not been given full opportunity to attain equitable positions in employment and other measures of social 'success'. In focusing on educational attainment and educational qualifications as a key determinant of 'success', it identified the lack of policy in the area as a matter of concern, pointing out that:

> The Education Department has appointed staff to positions with particular responsibility for areas of concern (e.g. Pacific Island advisers in Maori and Island Education section from 1986 onwards) before developing a coherent policy or having a clearly articulated understanding of what their underlying purpose and direction should be.
>
> (1988, Vol III:235)

The Commission's Report continued (ibid.):

> In effect, people from the groups concerned have been appointed to positions in which it is possible for them to develop programmes in consultation with their constituent groups- yet these programmes are having to be developed in isolation from any government policy on the nature and preferred direction of New Zealand society, including education.

Pacific Nations' Policy Developments in the 1990s

The report of the Royal Commission was sidelined by the political process, however, and the situation described above still applied in the early 90s. What 'progress' had been made in the area of Pacific Nations education had been either largely as a response to what the communities themselves have initiated, or to a more limited extent, what had been able to be accommodated within wider policy at little expense.

It was hardly surprising, given the policy environment of the late 80s and early 90s, that there was minimal development in Pacific Nations education during these years, and perhaps even less surprising that some of the Pacific Nations leaders in education (despite some isolated initiatives) had become cynical about political support and acknowledgement of the urgency and extent of their educational needs. As discussed in previous chapters, 1988 saw the beginnings of a far-reaching reform of the administration of the education system in Aotearoa/New Zealand. Initially there was considerable support for a reform which promised more parental and community involvement in the running of schools. For Pacific Nations communities it held the promise of flexibility in the system which would be responsive to the particular needs of their children. However, as the reforms advanced, Pacific parents were not elected in large numbers to Boards of Trustees. Those who were found themselves in the role of accountant or employer and deluged with mountains of circulars and printed information from the Ministry of Education which was, with some exceptions, framed in educational jargon. School principals in lower socio-economic and predominantly multi-ethnic areas found they were often the only member of the Board of Trustees whose first language was English and/or the only member with educational qualifications beyond a secondary level.

In response to the increasingly urgent crisis in Pacific Nations education, as evidenced by statistical data about access and outcome, however, the past few years have seen an increasing number of Ministry of Education initiatives through policy documents, targeted programmes, and contracts for delivery of educational services to Pacific Nations students.

In 1994, Lesieli Tongati'o, who held the position of Pule Maata Pasefika in the Ministry, produced a paper entitled *Challenging Success: Developing Pacific Islands Education in Aotearoa, New Zealand.* It summarised past developments in Pacific education and provided a 'current achievement background' of Pacific students. The paper identified key tasks that lay ahead if the ministry was to implement policies to meet the needs of Pacific students. They included :

> ... identifying the educational needs of the Pacific Island community within the New Zealand Curriculum Framework, providing advice

and information on the appropriate implementation of approved
policy, identifying and providing a Pacific Islands perspective on
relevant policy development projects, developing a Pacific Islands
data base.

(Tongati'o, 1994: 29)

This paper formed the basis for the subsequent development of the Ko e
Ako 'a e Kakai Pasifika policy plan, published in 1996. It was described
as a 'plan to promote Pacific Islands peoples' success in New Zealand
education' and contained goals for each of the education sectors: early
childhood, primary, secondary and tertiary. Descriptions of a number of
initiatives, some of which the ministry was supporting or planning to
support, were included.

This was a very significant policy development for Pacific Nations
education, as Ko e Ako 'a e Kakai Pasifika was linked into the Strategic
Plan of the Ministry of Education and related to at least four of its 'Key
Result Areas'. A second report, covering the period January 1997 to October
1998, reviewed the targets and achievements outlined in the 1996 document.

The Education Review Office had also included Pacific students in its
1995 Barriers to Learning Report, which signalled an examination of
structural barriers in schools which contribute to learning disadvantages
for certain groups, including Pacific students. As stated in the report:

> Few schools recognise that their own policies and procedures may
> impose barriers and disadvantage students. Teachers who are ill-
> prepared, who use outdated teaching resources, who fail to capture
> the interest of students or who have low expectations of their
> students create their own classroom-based set of barriers to learning
> and achievement.
>
> (Education Review Office, 1995:154)

Although this report was interpreted by some teachers as an attack on their
professionalism, researchers of the AIMHI initiative, Kay Hawke and Jan
Hill, found that in their interviews, some of the Pacific students' perceptions
of teachers and schools as being racist bore out this criticism.

In the area of early childhood education the challenges faced by Pacific
Nations communities in changing their community-based groups into fully
licensed and chartered centres have been enormous (Mara, 1998b). These

include financial challenges, property provision, management processes and procedures, the provision of trained and qualified staff, liaising with Pacific parents and communities, seeking resource consent and meeting local government regulations. Despite the struggles, Pacific Islands early childhood centres provide care and education alongside long-established providers such as kindergartens, child care centres, playcentres, kohanga reo and other private providers. The number of licensed and chartered centres nationwide is approximately 70 with further development likely as a result of increased government funding. The Pacific centres are also required to implement the Early Childhood Curriculum: *Te Whariki*. A pilot study completed in 1998 for the Ministry of Education (Mara, 1998a) identified some of the challenges faced by Pacific educators, families and communities in implementing *Te Whariki*.

The rapid growth in the Pacific early childhood education sector has been characterised by the concurrent growth of Pacific organisations and individuals gaining contracts from the Ministry of Education to provide support for groups becoming licensed and chartered; for professional development contracts in implementing the Ta'iala (Samoan Curriculum); and contracts for implementing statutory requirements called Desirable Objectives and Practices (DOPs). Early Childhood Development (ECD) is an agency which has a Pacific network to deliver its contracts. PIECCA, Kautaha Aoga Niue and other Pacific individuals and organisations have become providers to their own communities. There is a need to examine whether the competitive nature of the process of bidding and winning contracts will result in a duplication of services, or worse still, confusion at centre-level in regards to which organisation is delivering which contract and for how long?

In 1996 NZEI Te Riu Roa, the Ministry of Education, the New Zealand School Trustees Association and the State Services Commission held a forum in Wellington: Pathways to Success: Pacific Peoples in Education. Pacific educators raised issues concerning teacher education, recruitment of Pacific teachers, Board of Trustees training, school-community liaison and health matters as they relate to learning. The report is a valuable resource for educators. In 1999 the first Pacific Educators conference was held in Auckland. The proceedings, published by the Ministry of Education and titled *Educating Pasefika Positively,* contain a record of the range of involvements of Pacific educators and as such is another valuable resource for all teachers (Ministry of Education, 1999a).

This renewed interest in Pacific Nations education by the Ministry of Education is reflected in the collation of data and published reports, newsletters and statistics that are accessible to interested and informed educators. In July 1999, for example, the first of a series of newsletters, *Talanoa Ako: Pacific Education Talk,* was published. At the end of 1999 the Ministry was a signatory (alongside nine other ministries and government departments) to the *Pacific Vision Strategy* that emerged from the Pacific Vision Conference held by the Ministry of Pacific Affairs in June, 1999, and for which one of the key strategic priorities was to 'Significantly improve educational achievement of Pacific peoples' (Ministry of Pacific Island Affairs, 1999: 8).

From Policy to Practice

A critical examination of education policy requires educators to look beyond the surface and to question how such factors compound inequality for marginalised groups in society. Pacific parents and students consistently demonstrate their desire for the knowledge, skills and qualifications educational institutions have to offer. Although equity objectives have been given prominence in the policies informing the ongoing restructuring of our education system, the strategies needed to address the lack of equity for Pacific students are largely unknown. Fortunately, there is a growing body of research in Pacific Nations education issues in Aotearoa/New Zealand, much of which is carried out by Pacific researchers. The recent establishment of the Research Unit in Pacific Education at the University of Auckland provides an ongoing focus for the coordination, collation and promotion of Pacific educational research that should increasingly inform relevant and appropriate educational policy and practice.

The imperative for educators to develop a critical understanding in the area of Pacific Nations education is vital. Teachers must actively engage in a process to increase their awareness of their own cultural identity and their own role in the achievement of educational equity. What is required is a going beyond sensitivity and awareness of the needs of their pupils towards a thorough-going knowledge of the structural and ideological factors which perpetuate marginalisation of minority students. What does engender optimism is that Pacific students in a growing number of schools are learning in culturally appropriate ways, and learning through the medium of their own language. Pre-service teacher education programmes are actively recruiting trainees from Pacific communities, and in-service opportunities focusing on the learning and teaching needs of Pacific students are increasingly available.

Recent policy developments, and changes in assessment methodology and measures of achievement will impact on educators attempting to incorporate the needs of Pacific students into their teaching practice. Group assessment techniques, the inclusion of cultural knowledge and skills as valid areas of assessment, the need for parents to be informed about their own child's progress clearly and in a meaningful way, are some aspects requiring implementation. The keeping of profiles of achievement which show a more extensive picture of the academic, social and cultural skills and knowledge of pupils will assist in communicating the achievements and abilities of Pacific students to parents and the wider community. The expansion of opportunities for students to learn in their own Pacific languages has led to the development of appropriately designed assessment measures.

In order to build on these initiatives, educators must find out about the different migration histories of Pacific students in their classrooms. They need to be aware of the diversity within and between Pacific nations in terms of language, values and the cultural adaptations they have made as successive generations are New Zealand-born. Christian values are widespread amongst all Pacific communities, and attendance at church, youth groups and Sunday schools are still a feature of the students' daily lives. Educators must take into account the demands such involvements mean in terms of time and responsibility.

Educators of Pacific students must inform themselves about Pacific concepts associated with valued knowledge, teaching and learning. For example, Konai Helu-Thaman uses the metaphor of the Kakala to provide an insight into Tongan values of learning, knowledge and wisdom and their relevance to modern education (Helu-Thaman, 1995). The relationships between ako (Tongan education), poto (to have sense, intelligence, to be clever) and ilo (finding out, discovery, knowing) are fully explained and accessible to all educators.

In the Cook Islands context, Teremoana MaUa Hodges is developing the Tivaevae (traditional bedspread) model of knowledge and learning. Just as the tivaevae is planned and designed in response to the patterns of the environment, and just as many individuals contribute to ensure the whole bedspread is completed and given as a gift (never sold), then so is knowledge formed and transmitted within and amongst the people. Alternative, and equally valid, systems of knowledge occur in other cultures, and educators must become aware of the ways of learning and teaching that are indigenous to Pacific cultures.

Schools and teachers are increasingly asked to work alongside and support Pacific parents and communities as they work together to enhance the academic achievement of Pacific students in their schools. To encourage school – community liaison, in 1996, the Ministry of Education set up a project called the 'Pacific Islands School-Parent-Community Liaison Project'. Clusters of schools with a high proportion of Pacific students were offered the opportunity to apply for funds to support strategies to enhance their home-school relationships. Each of the successful clusters employed a Pacific Liaison Officer who established such things as mentoring programmes and homework centres, and programmes for the promotion of positive achievements, visits to Pacific parents, professional development for teachers, and many other initiatives to improve home-school communication. An evaluation of the project, undertaken by NZCER for the Ministry of Education, reported unanimous support for the liaison people and a request for extension of the project (Mara, 1998a).

Concluding Comments

This past decade has seen significant inclusion of Pacific education issues in policy development at a national level. There still remains the need to evaluate whether these initiatives, at the level of policy, have resulted in the educational achievement of Pacific peoples, and their subsequent employment profile, being significantly improved over time. Will the indicators of success relate only to gaining of academic qualifications in a wider context of qualification 'inflation', or will other factors such as equitable representation at all levels of the education system be the preferred outcomes of all this policy attention? Will this result in better life chances or life choices for Pacific Nations students? Only time will tell.

Pacific parents continue to have high expectations of their children.

The challenge for both the policy-makers at the national level and those who make decisions at the individual school level is to bring parents into the joint enterprise of education, so that home and school work together to give the students both the cultural and the academic skills they need to survive in the modern technological world. Any compromise on the standards or quality of educational provision will perpetuate unequal outcomes.

Bibliography

Baba, T. L. (1992), 'Higher Education and the Development of Small States', Keynote Address: Small States Higher Education Meeting, Brunei, 14-18 June 1992.

Barrington, J. M. (1968), 'Education and National Development in Western Samoa', Unpublished Ph.D.Thesis, Victoria University.

Barrington, J. et al. (1987), 'New Zealand in the Pacific: Exporting Education, Some Trends and Consequences', Directions, 9/1, pp. 12-25.

Beeby, C. E. (1992), The Biography of an Idea. Beeby on Education, Wellington: New Zealand Council of Educational Research.

Beaumont, C. (1992), 'Assisting the Maintenance of Pacific Languages in New Zealand', Paper presented at Third National Community Languages Conference, Auckland.

Challis, R. L. (1970), Pacific Islanders in New Zealand, Wellington: School Publications, Department of Education.

Codd, J. A. (1993), 'Equity and Choice: The Paradox of New Zealand Educational Reform', Curriculum Studies, 1/1: 75-89.

Coxon, E. (1992), Senior Secondary Education in the Pacific, Report to the Churchill Trust.

Coxon, E. (1996), 'The Politics of 'Modernisation' in Western Samoan Education', Unpublished Ph.D Thesis, University of Auckland.

Department of Education (1982), Recommendations from Pacific Islands Education Conferences, Internal Report.

Department of Education (1987a), Report of the Review Committee on the Pacific Islands' Educational Resource Centre, Wellington: Government Printer.

Department of Education (1987b), Report to Parliament for Year Ending March 31.

Department of Statistics (1992), Pacific Islands Population and Dwellings, *1991 Census of Population and Dwellings*, Wellington: Government Printer.

Dunn, A., Pole, N. and Rouse, J. (1992), *The Education Sector Workforce*, Wellington: Ministry of Education.

Education Review Office (1995), *Barriers to Learning;* Wellington: Education Review Office, 9, Winter.

Emberson-Bain, 'A. (ed.) (1994), *Sustainable Development or Malignant Growth? Perspectives of Pacific Island Women*, Suva: Marama Publications.

Fairbairn-Dunlop, P. (1996), Sustainable Development or Going Back to the Pacific Way, in R. Grynberg (ed.), *Economic Prospects for the Pacific Islands in the 21st Century*, Suva: School of Social and Economic Development, USP.

Field, Michael J. (1991), *Mau: Samoa's Struggle for Freedom*, Auckland: Polynesian Press.

Glenn, C. L. 1989, 'Just Schools for Minority Children', *Phi Delta Kappan*, June, 777-9.

Hau'ofa, E. *et al.* (1993), *A New Oceania. Rediscovering Our Sea of Islands*, Suva: School of Social and Economic Development, USP.

Hawk, K. and Hill, J. (1996), *Towards Making Achieving Cool: Achievement in Multi-Cultural High Schools (AIMHI)*, Auckland: ERDC, Massey University, Albany Campus.

Helu-Thaman, K. (1995), 'Concepts of Learning, Knowledge and Wisdom in Tonga, and their Relevance to Modern Education', *Prospects*, XXV,(4).

Lopdell Centre Course 1984, 'Pacific Islands Education Issues', Unpublished Report. Ma'ia'i, F. (1957), 'A Study of the Developing Pattern of Education and the Factors Influencing that Development in New Zealand's Pacific Dependencies'. Unpublished Masters Thesis, Victoria University.

Mara, D.L. (1993), Forward Together? A Pacific Islands Woman's Viewpoint: 1972-1993 and Beyond. Paper presented to Women's Study Conference.

Mara, D., Foliaki L. and Coxon E. (1994), 'Pacific Education', in E. Coxon *et al.* (eds), *The Politics of Learning and Teaching in Aotearoa – New Zealand,* Palmerston North: Dunmore Press.

Mara, D. L. (1995), 'Te Puai no te vahine: Pacific Islands Education Policy and Education Initiatives in Aotearoa/New Zealand', Unpublished Masters Thesis, University of Auckland.

Mara, D. *et al.* (1996),'Evaluation Report of the Anau Ako Pasifika Project: A Home-Based Early Childhood Intervention Programme for Pacific Islands Families in New Zealand', Unpublished Report,Tokoroa.

Mara, D. L. (1998a), 'Pacific Islands School-Parent-Community Liaison Project: An Independent Evaluation', Wellington : NZCER.

Mara, D. L. (1998b), 'Progress towards Licensing and Chartering Pacific Islands Early Childhood Centres in New Zealand', Wellington: NZCER.

Mara, D. L. (1999), 'Implementation of Te Whariki in Pacific Islands Early Childhood Centres: Final Report to the Ministry of Education', Wellington : NZCER.

Ministry of Education (1993), *The New Zealand Curriculum Framework,* Wellington: Learning Media.

Ministry of Education (1996), *Ko e Ako 'a e Kakai Pasifika: Pacific Islands Peoples' Education in Aotearoa, New Zealand towards the Twenty-First Century,* Wellington: Learning Media.

Ministry of Education (1998), *Ko e Ako 'a e Kakai Pasifika Report: January 1997 – October 1998. Pacific Islands Peoples' Education in Aotearoa, New Zealand towards the Twenty-First Century,* Wellington.

Ministry of Education (1999a), *Educating Pasefika Positively:* Conference Proceedings: Pacific Islands Educators Conference, Auckland, 13-15 April, Wellington: Learning Media.

Ministry of Education (1999b), *Talanoa Ako: Pacific Education Talk,* Newsletter 1, July, Wellington: Learning Media.

Ministry of External Relations and Trade (1993a), *Refocusing NZODA to Education and Training in the South Pacific.*Wellington, New Zealand.

Ministry of External Relations and Trade (1993b), *Guiding Principles and Policy Statements. New Zealand Official Development Assistance Programme,* Wellington: Government Printer.

Ministry of Foreign Affairs and Trade (1996), *Investing in a Common Future: A Policy Framework for the New Zealand Official Development Assistance Programme,* Wellington: New Zealand.

Ministry of Pacific Island Affairs 1999, *Pacific Directions Report: Pacific Vision Strategy*, Wellington: MPIA.

New Zealand Royal Commission on Social Policy (1988), *Future Directions*, Vol 111, Part 2: 234-251.

Pacific Islands Business Development Trust (1992), *Achievers Magazine: A Guide to Pacific Islands Scholarships*, Wellington.

Pacific Islands Education Resource Centre (1978), *A Handbook for Teachers of Pacific Island Children*, Auckland.

Pasikale, A. (1996), *Seen But Not Heard:Voices of Pacific Islands Learners*, Wellington: ETSA.

PIPEF Foundation Act 1972 and Amendments 1972, 1975, 1981, 1982, Wellington: Government Printer.

Ramsay, P. K. (1981), *Tomorrow May Be Too Late: Final Report of the Schools with Special Needs Project*, Hamilton: University of Waikato.

Report of the South Pacific Policy Review Group 1990, *Towards a Pacific Island Community*, Wellington.

Spoonley, P. and Shipley, S. (1982), Polynesian Unemployment Rates, *NZERSG Newsletter*, 3, (1), State Services Commission/NZEI.

Te Riu Roa (1997), *Pathways to Success: Pacific Peoples in Education*, Report of Forum Proceedings, December 1996, Wellington.

Tamasese, K., Masoe-Clifford, P. and Ne'emaia-Garwood, S. (1988), Pacific Islands Peoples Perspectives, *Royal Commision on Social Policy Report*, Vol. IV, Wellington: Government Printer.

Tongati'o, L. (1994), *Challenging Success: Developing Pacific Islands Education in Aotearoa, New Zealand, Report 1*, Wellington: Pule Maata Pasefika, Ministry of Education.

Waite, J. (1992), Aoteareo: Speaking for Ourselves, *Ethnic Community Languages*, Part B, Wellington: Ministry of Education.

Chapter 6

Bright Futures and the Knowledge Society

James Marshall

The Knowledge Society and the Knowledge Economy

In launching the *Bright Future* package in 1999, outlining a set of new policies to enable New Zealand to prosper in the oncoming knowledge society and knowledge economy, the New Zealand Government claimed that in order to approach the issues and opportunities that will face New Zealand in the twenty-first century we need to bring together 'the education, research, business and government sectors' (Shipley, 1999). In his contribution to the *Bright Future* package, Max Bradford (Minister of Enterprise and Commerce and Tertiary Education), said that the world is changing into a global market-place as we go through a revolution in information and communications technology: 'increasingly what is in our heads is becoming as valuable as what's in our pockets' (loc. cit.). In what follows, the term *Bright Futures* will be used to refer in general to the above document and to two further documents on this topic from the Ministry of Research, Science and Technology (MoRST, 1999) and the Information Technology Advisory Group to the Minister of Information and Technology (ITAG, 1999).

Bradford is talking about the knowledge economy, which is a term 'used to describe an economy where the value tends to be created by people's knowledge rather than investment in plant and natural resources or straight physical labour'op.cit. According to the Ministry of Research Science and Technology (MoRST, 1999), common features of the knowledge economy include:

- knowledge and information as major sources of creating value

- rapid changes in technology
- greater investment in research and development
- greater use of information and communications technology
- growth of knowledge-intensive businesses
- increased networking and working together
- rising skill requirements.

MoRST reiterates Bradford's point that knowledge is the key to creating wealth and improving the quality of life in this 'knowledge revolution'. The knowledge revolution is driven, MoRST says, by:

- globalisation of the world's economies, which has fuelled competition and spurred the gathering of knowledge to get ahead economically;
- the technologies for gaining, sharing and applying knowledge, which are changing rapidly – for example, the rise of computers and the Internet;
- the growing role of research, science and technology in creating knowledge to solve business, social and environmental problems;
- knowledge growing at exceptional rates. Whereas the resources of the industrial society, for example fossil fuels, tended only to be used once, existing knowledge can be used to create new knowledge, speeding up the rate at which knowledge is created.

Another closely aligned term is 'the knowledge economy'. In a submission to the Government from the Minister of Information and Technology's Information Technology Advisory Group (ITAG, 1999), neo-classical and 'modern' economics (new growth theory) are contrasted. The advisory group states that the former recognised only two factors of production – labour and capital – whereas the latter recognises *knowledge* as the key factor. In neo-classical economic theory, knowledge, productivity, education and intellectual capital were seen as factors which were external to economics. Now knowledge and technology, with their increased ability for rapid production, have become a third factor internal to 'leading economies'.

Some economists make a stronger claim, to the effect that knowledge is now *the* basic form of capital. Thus economic growth depends upon the accumulation of knowledge; technology can raise the return on investment which, if reinvested, makes technology more valuable; and technological breakthroughs can create technical platforms for further innovations, which in turn become the drivers of economic growth.

However, economic growth doesn't just happen. What is needed is immense investment in technology and human capital for the development of knowledge. As 'New Zealand companies need to better understand and use the concept of intellectual capital', so also must they 'unlock the value of their hidden assets, such as the talent of their employees, the loyalty of their customers, and the collective knowledge embedded in their systems, processes and culture. They must learn to turn their unmapped, untapped knowledge into a source of competitive knowledge' (ITAG, 1999).

Clearly education has a role to play here and, it would appear, this has become one of its allotted roles for the first years of the twenty-first century, as the *Bright Future* package heralded major advances and scholarships and the priming of teachers for the immanent knowledge economy.

Initial Comments

Most readers will have heard of some of these *Bright Futures* ideas. At school they will have been encouraged to get qualifications and technological skills. More mature readers will have heard talk of the new technologies and wondered, if they were unemployed, how they could re-enter the workforce, if at all. But what did it all mean, when there was such vast unemployment in New Zealand from the mid 1980s? Would this provide new jobs, or would technology merely reduce labour costs by bringing about further unemployment? Indeed accompanying talk of being prepared to adapt to several occupations during one's working life seemed to imply just that.

So just what are these *Bright Futures*-type policies about? Listening to the political rhetoric in just those three documents above (there are many others), it would seem that little has happened to prepare us for the knowledge society and economy in the last two decades, and that new and urgent polices are required. It will be argued that this is far from being the case for there had been a raft of earlier policies, because of a major restructuring of the New Zealand economy including both welfare and the education system (at all levels), beginning as long ago as 1988. The groundwork was laid even earlier in education, with a number of major criticisms of a traditional liberal education system which, by the contemporary international criteria, was performing well. But all systems in Western education in the developed nations were to undergo major critiques and major structural changes as precursors to globalisation, the knowledge society and economy, and rapidly moving capital.

In order to make sense of the opening remarks, and to understand just what these new *Bright Future* policy initiatives are about, we will need to consider a number of notions or concepts. These, in the order in which they will be discussed, are:

- neo-liberalism
- knowledge and information
- technology and the self
- vocationalism and liberal education
- globalisation.

Neo-liberalism

The structural changes which have taken place in New Zealand since the mid 1980s are usually described as neo-liberal, sometimes by the slightly wider concept of *new right*. New right ideology is made up of two major elements: a neo-liberal element, which is committed to the free market and to the substitution of market-like arrangements for the state; and, a neo-conservative element, which is committed to fundamentalist and conservative moral values. These elements are united by the belief that state intervention to promote egalitarian social goals has been responsible for the present economic decline, and has represented a violation of individual rights and initiative. From this combined view, the new right believes that equality and freedom are incompatible, and that freedom construed in individual and negative terms (i.e. freedom from intervention) is indispensable for economic vitality and well-being. The theoretical underpinnings for this view are to be found, in part, in a contemporary rejuvenation of classical liberal economic theory which privileges both the market, as an institution above all others, and market values over all other values (see further Peters, Marshall and Massey, 1994).

The main theoretical elements of the new right can be summarised as follows:

1. A commitment to the free market, which involves two sets of claims: (i) claims for the efficiency of the market as a superior allocative mechanism for the distribution of scarce public resources; (ii) claims for the market as a morally superior form of political economy.
2. A return to a form of individualism which is competitive, 'possessive' and construed in terms of consumer sovereignty.
3. An emphasis on freedom over equality, where 'freedom' is construed in negative and individualistic terms. Negative freedom is freedom from state interference, which implies an acceptance of inequalities generated by the market.
4. An anti-state, anti-bureacracy stance. The attack on 'big' government, made on the basis of both economic and moral arguments, tends to lead to corporatisation and privatisation strategies to limit the state.
5. A moral conservatism, based on fundamentalist and individualist values which are anti-socialist, anti-feminist and anti-Maori.

In educational terms commitment to the free market involves the belief that 'excellence' and 'quality' in education will be served, and scarce public resources better utilised, by adopting market-type arrangments such as de-zoning, institutional decentralisation and competition between schools. That the market is seen as morally superior is evidenced by the opportunity to *choose* between schools, and the accompanying claim that this promotes freedom.

The assumption here is that society is constituted by competitive and possessive individuals, capable of making choices which are in their best interests. For such individuals education becomes a commodity purchased by individuals for individuals, and utilised by those individuals for their own personal advancement. Obscured in this notion of individualism and education are the beliefs that knowledge is shared and the outcome of agreement and social interaction, and a more traditional belief that education is not only for the good of the individual but also for the good of society, where society is construed not merely as a collection of individuals but as a cohesive, intrinsically social community. Contrasted here are the notions of society as an atomistic, fragmented, hedonistic collection of self-interested individuals, and of society as a community based upon shared interests (Dewey, 1916), public goods, and the notions of altruism, empathy and respect for persons.

The concepts of freedom and equality pose tensions in liberal thought, even though the notions of liberty, equality and fraternity were the catch-cry of the French Revolution and of the Enlightenment. Nevertheless, these are contested concepts. In the new right framework, freedom is interpreted in the negative sense of freedom *from*; the positive sense of freedom *to* is generally excluded. Thus, when freedom is extolled in the call for less state intervention in the welfare state and education, little is said about how disadvantaged groups are to effect their choices, which they are said to be free to make in the competitive markets of education, and of course health. Equality is also a contested concept, as we have seen above. Whilst the new-right framework makes some concessions to equality of opportunity, in general, freedom *from* overrides fully fledged notions of equality that have inspired various versions of democracy. For some new right thinkers (for example, Strike, 1982) even notions of democracy are contrary to neo-liberal thought, because they might involve constraints upon that negative sense of freedom. In Strike's case this has considerable implications for what can be offered in education, particularly to ethnic minorities, who would wish to preserve their language and culture as a self-determining right. Such preservations for minorities require the understanding, if not assistance, of members of the majority group. This may require induction of the young into languages and cultures other than their own, and contrary to the wishes of their parents.

The attack on 'big' government (i.e. the welfare bureaucracy) is reflected in the devolution of responsibilities from former state agencies, such as the now defunct Department of Education, to schools and other educational institutions. An emphasis on knowing the per capita costs of education can provide structures and mechanisms which could lead ultimately to the full privatisation of education. The point here is that once the true cost of educating an individual is known, then it matters little who pays the bill – the state or the individual parents.

Finally, the morality underlying new right thought is inherently conservative. Either conservative and traditional values are imported hand-in-hand with the revision of this individualistic doctrine, or morality and social justice are deemed to be the outcome of exchanges generated by the market (Hayek, 1978). This conservative tradition is exemplified clearly in the Sexton Report on Education produced by the New Zealand Business Roundtable in 1991. There are blatant appeals to objective views on knowledge and values, and an overt attack upon cultural differences. This ethnocentrism is a result of holding and universalising British colonial attitudes. The effects upon education of adopting the Sexton Report would have been serious for disadvantaged groups, reinforcing a monocultural, middle-class and male-oriented set of values and institutions (Marshall, Peters and Smith, 1991).

An evaluation of the educational reforms of the late 1980s in New Zealand requires an understanding of the wider policy context in which the principles of neo-liberal thought are clearly exposed.

Knowledge and Information Skills

Knowledge

The type of knowledge which the knowledge society 'needs' can be identified as 'surfacing' as early as 1993, in *The New Zealand Curriculum Framework* (MoE, 1993). There we find a move away from traditional approaches to knowledge, and notions of disciplines or subjects defined by different kinds or forms of knowledge (see the work of Paul Hirst on forms of knowledge, for example Hirst, 1983). Thus forms of knowledge can be structured by key concepts, general principles, and different ways of establishing truth claims (cf. geometry with history).

In the proposals for curricula for schools in that document there is a silence regarding basic and fundamental philosophical questions about the nature of knowledge. Central to a consideration of curricula are *epistemological* questions about what counts as knowledge, how it is defined and controlled, and whose knowledge is selected for inclusion – who decides, and on what basis? What counts as important knowledge also defines what is seen as *not worth knowing*. Consequently, the interests of different gender, class and ethnic groups may be unequally represented in what is, and what is not, included in the curriculum. Philosophers, since at least the time of Plato, have traditionally seen such questions as important!

Philosophers, have also drawn a distinction between knowing *that,* in the sense of knowing that something is the case, and knowing *how*, that is knowing how to do things in practice. The distinction can be illustrated, for example, by considering the difference between knowing that it is raining outside and knowing how to ride a bicycle. In the New Zealand literature there is a very explicit emphasis on getting skilled, wherein learning as a *process,* and of knowing *how to do* things, has replaced knowing some *content* or thing. No longer is the curriculum presented in terms of disciplines, but in terms of learning areas, of getting skilled in those areas, and of knowing how to do things within those areas. In the ministry documents the justification for these learning areas is either blatantly pragmatic or rests on economic considerations. The term 'knowledge' is not employed to justify these areas, but at best becomes some pragmatic outcome of skills and information acquisition in these areas.

In the areas of attitudes and values in the curriculum documents, it is an attitude towards learning (as a process) that is valued, and not an attitude towards knowledge (as something known). It is the processes, the ever ongoing learning and reskilling, that are seen as of paramount importance. There are parallels here with the support for approaches to the curriculum which can be called, broadly, constructivist. In constructivist approaches to pedagogy what is important is the process of construction, and not the object constructed. This is especially so in radical versions of constructivism (see *Access,* 13(2), 1995) .

All students must study in the essential learning areas: languages; mathematics; science; technology; social sciences; the arts; and health and physical well-being. These essential learning areas are said to be broad categories of knowledge and understanding, which take into account the common curriculum experience of schooling today, both in New Zealand and overseas. But how these categories have been developed is not clear. If they are not subjects *per se*, are they merely descriptive of what goes on? If so, to talk of the curriculum being directed by the principles seems a little inflated. Curriculum principles should be *principled,* providing general grounds for evaluation of what should be in a curriculum. But the essential learning areas seem more like a list, and a tick-off list at best. There is no rationale, based upon a coherent notion of knowledge, provided for the essential learning areas in the alleged principles.

Knowledge has, in effect, been replaced by *skills* and *learning.* Everything which might have been seen as obtaining knowledge – an *object* of an activity – seems to have moved into an activity mode, where what is important is a *process.* Knowledge, in the sense of knowing that something is the case, has been replaced by knowing how, with the explicit emphasis on getting skilled. Learning as process has replaced knowing some thing, in the notion of learning areas, getting skilled and in the area of attitudes and values (MoE,1993:21). This is in part because the outcome of all this is not knowledge but *information*. And because it is (merely?) information, it has to be continuously 'relearned', readjusted and restructured to meet the demands of the consumer in the service of the new society in the Age of Information.

These points are clearer in MoRST (1999). MoRST talks about different kinds of knowledge, introducing this terminology: know-what and know-why; know-who; know-where and know-when. According to MoRST, know-what or knowledge about facts (i.e. information) is nowadays diminishing in relevance. This is contrasted with know-why: understanding or explanatory knowledge about the natural world, society, and the human mind. But this contrast is essentially the difference between *information* and *knowledge,* which was drawn above. If know-what (i.e. information) is no longer important, why the emphasis in *NZCF* on information? In other words, information *per se* is not really important. Why then the emphasis on information and skills required of young people so that they can acquire information (see below)?

In my view a possible explanation, apart from general confusion, is that information is important in one sense, in that it is part of what can be sold. However, deeper knowledge and understanding is required to continually develop new information to sell on, and this is explanatory knowledge or 'know-why'. This latter kind of knowledge is scarcely mentioned in *NZCF*. But a possible outcome is the producers of information – the beavers who continuously work information which is not in itself important, as it will be turned over almost immediately. What of those who develop know-why? Is that to be the province of a very highly educated élite? Politically and educationally something needs to be said about this potential for a two-tiered education system.

Know-who 'refers to the world of social relations and is knowledge of who knows what and who can do what' as 'knowing key people is sometimes more important to innovation than scientific principles' (MoRST,1999). Know-where and know-when are important in a flexible and dynamic economy. The subsumption of knowledge to economic principles could scarcely be more blatant. But at least MoRST has done what *NZCF* could not do, and that is talk of *knowledge* in the strong sense of understanding and its critical importance. They finally refer to know-how or skills.

Information Skills

When *The New Zealand Curriculum Framework* is searched under the skills section, what is found again is information. In that section it is said that students will (p.18):

- identify, locate, gather, retrieve and process information from a range of sources
- organise, analyse, synthesise, evaluate and use information
- present information clearly, logically, concisely and accurately
- identify, describe, and interpret different points of view, and distinguish fact from opinion
- use a range of information-retrieval and information-processing technologies confidently and competently.

Students are also meant to have problem-solving skills. These seem to be the normal liberal-educational set of critical skills, which are part of the educated person's abilities. But what they are given to operate on is the problem. Whilst it is said that fact should be distinguished from opinion, that 'endeavour' rests in the mode of information and, on the schema of skills outlined, would amount to testing bits of information against other bits of information because the fundamental concepts are in the information mode. There is no attempt to distinguish information from knowledge (or in MoRST language knowing facts from knowing why), or any 'flash of insight' that these notions might be different. Indeed, it is knowledge or knowing-why which may well be needed to test information.

R. S. Peters (1966) made the point on education that information without knowledge and understanding of a general theoretical kind was worthless. What is lacking in an education which concentrates on information (know-that) is that general theoretical understanding (know-why), to which Peters draws our attention, permits information to be critically assessed (and, for Peters, even understood). Another point is that the general knowledge and understanding which Peters points us towards, is to be located in modern technology in the software and hardware, and cannot, therefore, be subject to criticism, as it is presupposed in any 'critical' approach within the programme. In fact the general knowledge and understanding that Peters made much of becomes redundant for many operators and users of knowledge, but at tremendous critical cost.

At best there is a demand for *quality* of information in a cry for fact, but quality of information will be decided by the consumer, not the provider. It is use value which overrides issues of *truth,* and it is the consumer in the information economy who will decide. Within the New Zealand educational scene this point has been made very clearly by the neo-liberals and by the New Zealand Qualifications Authority.

Technology and the Self

As has been noted, the New Zealand education system was launched into a number of 'stunning' changes in 1988. These changes are caught well by Jean-François Lyotard's (1984) concept of performativity. He argues that liberal education systems have abandoned notions of the development of leaders and an educated élite, as they have been subsumed under wider demands for the efficient functioning of economic and social systems. If these proposals for change in New Zealand were launched initially as administrative changes, they were soon seen as educational *reforms*; if initially they were seen as providing a more efficient delivery of educational services, they were soon said to be capable of providing a *better* education. If Lyotard is correct, however, the changes should be seen as part of the worldwide subsumption of education systems under wider demands for the efficient functioning of economic and social systems. They are therefore far from administrative changes in the delivery of education.

Technology Documents

In this section, I wish to concentrate upon technology and its recent formal and explicit introduction into the New Zealand curriculum. As we have seen, there is a great emphasis in the policy statements and proposals – *Bright Futures* – upon this new age of information (see Poster, 1990 on the new *mode* of information), electronic communication and technology. However, I wish to raise a number of philosophical questions about the nature of technology. In general, technology has been seen in New Zealand curriculum documents as unproblematic, as being neutral means to ends seen as part of human activity, and to be decided and implemented so that humans retain mastery over technology. I derive my arguments about the nature of technology from Martin Heidegger (1977), but the sources from which I develop my concerns are within New Zealand. First we will look at what is said about technology in the primary sources in New Zealand. There are two major documents that we need to consider.

In her Foreword to *The New Zealand Curriculum Framework (NZCF)*, Secretary of Education Dr Maris O'Rourke says that the *NZCF* (MoE, 1993: 1): 'Promotes new emphases in learning areas which are important to the country's health and growth, such as technology, second language learning'.

O'Rourke is clearly aligning technology with growth (cf. *Bright Futures*). *NZCF* is said to describe 'a framework for learning and assessment' which defines the national curriculum (MoE, 1993: 3). It states the *principles* for the direction of all teaching and learning, specifies seven *essential learning areas* and sets out the *essential skills, attitudes and values* to be developed in this curriculum. Elsewhere I have commented that the principles are essentially instrumental if not outright economic, that the notion of learning areas (technology is one) is unclear (are they subjects, or disciplines, or forms of knowledge, for example?), that there is a downplaying of knowledge to skills and information. I have also argued that there is a lack of such holistic and traditional liberal values as the good citizen, the autonomous person, etc. (Marshall, 1997a,b), and any awareness of how the self might be constituted differently in the mode of information. Technology, then, is said to be one of the four essential learning areas.

Technology in the New Zealand Curriculum (TNZC) (MoE, 1995) is the first national curriculum statement to have been developed in New Zealand in the area of technology. It was developed through a phase 'which included scrutiny of technology education developments occurring in many other countries'. It is not therefore a document produced in some idiosyncratic colonial environment, and much that might be said about it can also be said about those documents from other countries which make similar assumptions about the nature of technology.

Technology was introduced into *NZCF* as a separate learning area, but is also seen as a neutral means to enable learning in the other learning areas. In *TNZC* however, it is the instrumental theme of neutral means which is pursued in O'Rourke's introduction. The introduction of technology into the curriculum is said to be 'part of a broad initiative aimed at improving student achievement', and that it 'aims to develop technological literacy through three integrated learning strands to enable students to participate fully in the technological society and economy in which they will live and work'. Furthermore, the technology curriculum 'seeks to enable and empower students with the know-how they will need to make informed choices about technology, and to be the technological innovators of the future' (MoE, 1995: 5). The notion of technology as neutral means to societal and economic ends, and the idea that one can choose between the means, is clearly an instrumental approach to technology.

In the first section, Introducing Technology, the following is said:

> Technology is a creative, purposeful activity aimed at meeting needs and opportunities through the development of products, systems, or environments. Knowledge, skills, and resources are combined to help solve practical problems. Technological practice takes place within, and is influenced by, social contexts ... (for we) ... live in a technological world. Technological practice affects our environment, our standard of living, and our quality of life. Technology plays an increasingly important part in our health care, choices of food, transport, and the very functioning of our society. The technologies used today have built on the ingenuity, traditions, observation, and knowledge of people who, throughout history, have sought to improve their lives, solve problems, and satisfy their needs and wants. ... This process of continual incremental development and testing is essential for people to meet challenges and fulfill their expectations.
>
> (MoE,1995: 6)

There is, however, a *suggestion* here that technology is deeply embedded in our social system and the functioning of our society and, thereby, is not merely a means to some other ends. But this suggestion is faint, for the instrumental tone quickly reasserts itself. Technology 'helps people make new connections', 'adds value to traditional products and services and creates new ones to improve people's quality of life, and help New Zealand's continuing development as a successful nation', for 'New

Zealand is rich in energy resources and primary products which can be processed into higher value products, through ideas and products yet to be developed'. Technology, then, presents us with a challenge, a challenge of mastery over resources, of how to extract, store, and invest in them. This challenge, it is said, 'provides exciting opportunities for all students', for 'technology is challenging and rewarding and open to everyone'(ibid.). Thus technology is essentially conceived as neutral and challenging, but capable of being mastered by us.

Technology Education

Technology education, on the other hand:

> ... is a planned process designed to develop students'competence and confidence in understanding and using existing technologies and in creating solutions to technological problems. It contributes to the intellectual and practical development of students, as individuals and as informed members of a technological society.
>
> (MoE,1995: 7)

The aims of this education are stated to be:

> ... to enable students to achieve technological *literacy* [my emphasis] through the development of:
> • technological knowledge and understanding
> • technological capability, and
> • understanding and awareness of the relationship between technology and society.
>
> (ibid.: 8)

Students are, however, to face environmental questions. But these are restricted to the investigation of options in relation to 'authentic' problems, so that students can appraise the appropriateness of technological solutions to environmental concerns. Thus the theme which is pursued is still that technology is neutral, and certainly nothing like a challenge to humanity in Heidegger's sense (to be developed below). At best, technology carries the sense of challenge as seen in video advertisements where Sir Edmund Hillary climbs mountains – i.e. as something which we can master if we work hard enough at it.

If students are to become technologically literate and aware of the interplay between technology and society (past, present and future), they are also to become empowered in choosing the appropriate technology and 'feeling empowered to contribute to a technological society'. But being aware of the interplay of technology and society and empowering students are but two of the nine listed attributes of technology literacy (MoE,1995: 9). The remaining seven, if we are to stay with the metaphor of literacy, are rather like the characteristics which are those of a *functional* literacy. Functional literacy permits one to operate within a society, but it tends not to provide a real literacy which permits one to read into the edicts and requirements of how to function in society the underlying assumptions and power structures that *constitute* that society. Functional literacy, then, tends to disempower people. In what sense can technological literacy be empowering as opposed to merely functional? In my view, our curriculum planners offer us little in this document on technology which is more than a functional form of technological literacy.

When we turn in *TNZC* to the section on Technology and Society (MoE, 1995: 41), we are told that 'understanding the nature of the relationship between technology and society is vital to technological practice', acknowledging that 'no technology is value-free'. But this is to acknowledge only that in its *applications* technology is not value-free. This is far from an acknowledgement that, in *essence*, technology is value-laden and therefore *not* neutral. Thus the whole section on technology and society does not question the orthodoxy that technology is, in its very nature or essence, *neutral*. Instead, it is merely a question of resolving the issues that arise from 'the culture, beliefs, and values that influence decision making in that society'. Thus the factors that make technological choices value-laden are those that inhabit the particular contexts or situations, and these must be made explicit because they are 'sometimes overlooked'. Nowhere is it suggested that technology *per se* should be questioned. In other words, the technology curriculum does not encourage students to raise themselves above the level of a functional technology literacy. Just as functional literacy does not provide the 'tools' to question the structures that underlie it, nor does technology literacy, as envisaged in these documents, provide the ability to pose questions concerning technology.

The Neutrality of Technology

Martin Heidegger, the German philosopher, provides major arguments to the effect that technology is not neutral in his essay, 'The Question Concerning Technology' (1977). Heidegger is concerned to question, through *questioning* as a way or path, the essence of technology. By 'essence' Heidegger does not mean simply what something is *now*, but also the way in which it pursues its course, the way in which it endures through time, or the way in which it 'reveals' itself to us, and hence the ways in which we can respond to it. It is not something static which can be ascertained by answering *the* question, 'What *is* technology?', for that demands a mere temporal and situated, here-and-now type of answer. Instead, there must be an ongoing questioning. Hence, in Heidegger, the present continuous sense of the verb 'question'.

Heidegger makes the point that the essence of a tree cannot itself be a tree which we could encounter, for what we are seeking is something which pervades all trees. By analogy, when seeking the essence of technology we should not seek something which is itself technological, but something which pervades or dwells in all forms of technology. Nor should we seek something which is neutral for, common and persuasive as this view might be, it 'makes us utterly blind to the essence of technology' (1977: 4). Heidegger's main argument starts from traditional accounts of what technology is – what he calls the *instrumental*.

Heidegger says that while the instrumental view is uncannily correct about technology (ibid.: 5), it is not the *truth* about technology, and it conditions every attempt 'to bring man into the right relation to technology', because we tend to see that relation as one of mastery over instrumental technology, of not letting it get out of hand. To say something which is correct about an object is not to give the truth about that object – to say that petrol is a fuel for motor cars is correct, but it is not to say the truth about petrol, for example that burning petrol pollutes the atmosphere. And truth, for Heidegger, must be revealed.

Heidegger's claim is that *enframing* (ge-stell) is the essence of modern technology; it is 'that challenging claim which gathers man thither to order the self-revealing as standing reserve' (1977: 19). The difference from ancient technology, where what is in nature is (merely?) revealed by a bringing forth, is that in modern technology enframing involves a *challenging* or *demanding* of nature, a demand placed upon nature by modern man, that it not only reveal nature, but nature as standing reserve. Enframing means the way of revealing which holds sway in the essence of modern technology and which is itself nothing technological. On the other hand, all those things that are so familiar to us and are standard parts of an assembly, such as rods, pistons and chassis, belong to the technological. The assembly itself, however, together with the aforementioned stock parts, falls within the sphere of technological activity; and this activity always merely responds to the challenge of enframing, but never comprises enframing itself or brings it about.

Because enframing reveals the real as standing reserve, and man is challenged to reveal nature as, above all, a standing reserve, Heidegger argues that modern technology is neither merely a human activity nor a mere means within such activity. As enframing is outside human agency, and 'sent' to us by the real (i.e. being), therefore value does not merely accrue to human agency. Thus the instrumental view of technology as means to an end, and the ethical enjoinder to master technology as providing the *truth* about technology, are untenable, he maintains.

Heidegger says that the questions asked about man's relationship to technology and of the essence of technology come too late if we think that we can enter into any such relationship *subsequently*. This would presuppose a revealing of the essence of technology as standing reserve independently of and prior to any human relationship with it. But these must be simultaneous; we must enter into such relationships for the essence to be revealed, for our very experiences and our experiences of ourselves have to be challenged by the essence of technology as standing reserve, for this enframing to 'come to presence' (1977: 24).

In brief, then, technology is not neutral and is not merely a means to an end, but a challenge to 'man' to reveal both nature and 'him'-self as standing reserve, as a permanent resource to be utilised or consumed.

Vocationalism and Liberal Education

The Traditional Distinction

Whilst it might be thought that we are entering a new age of vocationalism in education, it will be argued that we are not, at least if we understand the issue in a traditional manner in which vocational education is to be defined *against* a liberal-arts-humane education. This is no longer the case, for we are entering a total education and training culture in which the vocational, and business values, so permeate the culture that 'vocationalism' has little or no meaning (Marshall, 1997a). This is because there appears to be no *other* form of education, in the realm of educational discourse, to define it against. Nevertheless the issue remains, for even if liberal education appears hidden or occluded by vocationalism's demands, it may still be drawn forward, out of the darkness so to speak, by a suitable critical problematic.

Arthur Wirth (1988: 5) puts the traditional liberal-vocational issue on schooling quite bluntly: 'the choice ... is whether schools are to become servants of technocratic efficiency needs, or whether they can act to help men and women humanise life under technology'. But the historical dilemma for families, one which is still relevant in the twenty-first century, is clearly stated by Corson (1988: 12):

> The workplace has become separated from the home: occupational roles have become distinct from kin based roles and relationships; labour market values have penetrated into family decisions about the future of offspring; parents have come to see that children's job prospects are far removed from any form of socialisation that they can possibly receive within the family and parents are not usually placed to make the social connections necessary to put their children in touch with work that might suit and satisfy their wants and talents.

On vocational grounds, what were working class families to do? Choose a bookish, élitist education that *might* lead to a leisured and safe life, perhaps to the professions, or opt for an education that would guarantee a vocation and perhaps security, if not happiness?

Bertrand Russell believed this distinction to be mistaken. He argued (Russell, 1926: Chapter 1) that education had always had a vocational element, and that the distinction between the ornamental and the useful in education was spurious. But he also believed that education was best served by the development of creative powers through rigorous study in the disciplines. Dewey also believed the distinction to be spurious, but for different reasons (Dewey, 1916). Because Dewey argued for the importance of technology, and because in this new vocationalism we are entering what can be called the mode of information (Poster, 1990), we will look at how Dewey attempted to collapse this dualism and 'harness' technology for the development of intellect, whilst at the same time dismissing the view that we should become servants of technocratic efficiency needs.

Dewey on Vocationalism

According to Dewey: 'The demands of an industrialised and technological society cannot be ignored' (Dewey, 1935: 89). But how those demands were to be met was another matter, as he resisted narrow versions of vocationalism most strongly. However, the context in which his arguments were formulated has changed, raising questions as to their applicability today. The new arguments which are required must take a different form, and one which is 'on line' with the new technological and information society.

Like Dewey, I believe that there must be some relationship between education and the world of work. However, he sees the relationship as being necessary:

> There is the necessity that these immature members (of society) be not merely physically preserved in adequate numbers, but that they be initiated into the interests, purposes, information, skill and practices of the mature members [otherwise the group will cease its characteristic life] (author's enclosure).
>
> (Dewey, 1916: 2)

According to Dewey, because of the complexity of modern life, schools are necessary for this education to take place. He is proposing therefore a strong, or causally necessary, connection between education and schooling and the social world, including the world of work. Dewey saw the antithesis between liberal-humanistic education and vocational education as an outcome of a number of several other closely aligned dualisms (Dewey, 1916: 306). According to him these dualisms were 'deeply entangled ... with the whole subject of vocational education' (loc. cit.), and had to be collapsed.

Whilst Dewey accepted the need for the reform of schools and was part of a general reform movement, he parted company quite strongly with an element in that 'movement' which was advocating a strong vocational factor, including separate vocational schools. Dewey's opposition to separate vocational schools was both social and political, as well as educational:

> The kind of education which I am interested in is not one which will adapt workers to the existing industrial regime; I am not sufficiently in love with the regime for that. It seems to me that the business of all who would not be educational time servers is to strive for a kind of vocational education which will first alter the existing industrial system, and ultimately transform it.
>
> (Dewey, 1915: 42)

He believed that the right *occupation* was the key to human happiness (Dewey, 1916: 308), and that this was not something that one could be adapted to, or drafted into like a slave. Given that a person could find out 'what one was fitted to do', then (loc. cit.):

> Education *through* occupations consequently combines within itself more of the factors conducive to learning than any other method. It calls instincts and habits into play; it is a foe to passive receptivity. It has an end in view .... Hence it appeals to thought; it demands that an idea of an end in view be steadily maintained so that activity cannot be either routine or capricious ... the only adequate training *for* occupations is training *through* occupations.

If the most efficacious learning was to take place *in* occupations, then schools could not easily, at that time, provide the technology of the workplace. Dewey saw the most advanced technology as exemplifying the most advanced *problem solving* of the day, and that the young could be introduced to this technology without either *preparing* them for a future occupation or *adapting* them to the world of work. But how were the young to be 'introduced' to a workplace which they were meant to be able to transform?

At best, he believed, one can only have a sketch for use in future directions, or an outline of the field in which further growth is to be directed, as one cannot prepare in a determinate way for a future which can only be indeterminate. If a rigid education which hampers growth is to be avoided, preparations for vocations can only be *indirect*, Dewey argues. If not, people will be left: 'in a permanently subordinate position, executing the intelligence of others who have a calling which permits more flexible play and readjustment' (loc. cit.).

What can schools do? Here, as elsewhere in Dewey, problem solving and scientific method (Dewey, 1938) have much of the burden to carry. Dewey believed that technology had increased the intellectual and educational possibilities of industry, whilst at the same time the industrial conditions of work had narrowed the educative potential of the workplace (Dewey 1916: 314). The intellectual possibilities and educative potentiality of industry had been enhanced by technology which represented, for Dewey, problem solving at its most advanced intellectual state. Because the conditions of industrial work had been narrowed, the 'burden of realising the intellectual possibilities inherent in work is thus thrown back on the school' (loc. cit.). It was the school, then, that would have to provide, through the reconstruction of the educative experiences of the young in technology, the transformation(s) needed in the world of work.

For Dewey this required the gradual reconstruction of school methods and materials so as to utilise the best of modern technology and the problem-solving potential inherent in educational activities associated with that technology. This was not to make the schools an adjunct of industry and commerce and to acquiesce in the 'untransformed, unrationalised and unsocialised phases of our defective industrial regime', but to utilise the intellectual problem-solving potential inherent in modern technology, 'to make school life more active, more full of meaning, more connected with out of school experience' (loc.cit.).

This was not to give the young a mere technical proficiency which would promote technical efficiency in the carrying out of the plans of others, but rather a *competency* which extended insight into its social bearings and permitted an efficiency in formulating and carrying out one's own plans. The transformed industrial and social order would have been, for Dewey (1916: 316):

A society in which every person shall be occupied in something which makes the lives of others worth living, and which makes the ties which bind people together more perceptible .... It denotes a state of affairs in which the interest of each in his work is uncoerced and intelligent ...

Another concern of Dewey (1916: 318) was that a narrowly conceived approach to vocational education would perpetuate social divisions in a hardened form, for both the employers and the employees would be intellectually limited. This could leave the employer class confined to issues of profit and power, and the employee class concerned only with monetary return from their labour. This would involve a limitation of intelligence to 'technical and non-humane, non-liberal channels'.

Dewey's solution was to reject the dualism between the liberal-humane and the vocational. Properly conceived, the liberal-humane and the vocational merge through the rational problem solving of technology. The autonomous person must choose a form of vocational education, but a form in which rationality is writ large in the advanced problem-solving potential of modern technology. To put it another way, faced with a question similar to Wirth's question above – should I pursue a liberal arts curriculum or a vocational curriculum? – no answer can be given. There can only be one meaningful option – that of the vocational curriculum as envisaged by Dewey, where the canons of rationality are deeply embedded in the problem-solving and rational potential of the most advanced technology. Dewey's answer to Wirth's question is, therefore, that technology can be used for liberal-humane aims, but that this requires a certain approach to technology and the transformation of the industrial conditions of the world of work where technology is housed, so as to promote its educative potential. So the dualism is collapsed.

Globalisation

For better or worse it would seem that, according to Anthony Giddens (1999: Lecture 1), 'we are being propelled into a global order that no one fully understands, but which is making its effects felt upon us.' If the term 'globalisation' is neither elegant nor attractive, its widespread international use is some evidence for the kind of developments to which it seems to refer. Yet the term was not to be found a decade ago in *The Fontana Dictionary of Modern Thought* (1990). Nevertheless, as we saw in one of the documents of *Bright Futures* – MoRST 1999 – globalisation is said to be one of the major underlying causes of the move to the knowledge society. Presumably, therefore, if it is said to be driving the knowledge society then, within a decade, we have come to know what it is. Or perhaps the term is used for its emotive and rhetorical character?

Whether we understand globalisation at all is hotly disputed between what can be called the proponents (the radicals) and the protagonists (conservative sceptics). According to Giddens (1999: Lecture 1):

> The radicals argue that not only is globalisation very real, but that its consequences can be felt everywhere. The global market place, they say is much more developed than even two or three decades ago, and is indifferent to national borders. Nations have lost much of the sovereignty they once had, and politicians have lost much of their capability to influence events. It isn't surprising that no one respects politicians anymore, or has much interest in what they have to say. The era of the nation state is over. Nations…have become mere fictions.

On the other hand the sceptics, who tend to be on the political and old left, and who wish nations to remain autonomous and promote the welfare state, argue that (loc.cit.):

> Most countries … only gain a small amount of their income from external trade. Moreover, a great deal of economic exchange is between regions, rather than being world wide …. The notion of globalisation … is an ideology put about by free marketeers who wish to dismantle welfare systems and cut back on state expenditures. What has happened is at most a reversion to how the world was a century ago. In the late 19th century there was already an open global economy, with a great deal of trade, including trade in currencies.

Giddens supports the radicals and goes on to argue that many see globalisation in purely economic terms. This is a mistake, he says, for it should be seen in cultural, political and technological terms as well. This is because instant electronic communication also shapes us and our lives in certain ways (for a discussion of how this might happen see Marshall, 2000). Furthermore, globalisation is a complex set of processes which may be incompatible and have contradictory outcomes, and thus it doesn't simply 'denude' smaller and weaker economic states of language, culture, power and influence. Yet it may well do this with the homogenisation of computer language, causing the demise of minor languages and accompanying cultures. If this is a problem for Maori and Pacific Islands languages and culture, it may also be a problem in Europe, where already there are discussions on a 'Euro' language in response to globalisation issues.

In order to have international and wide-reaching homogenising effects such as a common language and culture, there would need also to be a reorganising of the underlying infrastructures in order to support such free-market globalisation tendencies. Education, as we have seen in *Bright Futures*, is a key 'player' in the knowledge society and we should look at some of the restructuring that has occurred there. Because not everything that has happened in the restructuring of education in New Zealand since 1988 can be covered, we will look at two features only – education policy and new public management strategies as applied to education. As we have covered education policy in the Introduction to this book, we will look briefly at that area first.

Education Policy and Globalisation

We noted in the Introduction that there has been a major international shift in how educational policy is to be conceived and articulated in policy documents. At one time education policy was domestic in that essentially it was conceived and articulated in, and resided in, local domains or nation states. To what extent the concerns of localised and indigenous groups were met was another matter – the history of education for Maori is, unfortunately, a good example of that problem.

Since the 1960s, arguably as a result of studies by comparative educators, a number of universalistic issues, dilemmas and policies, which transcend localised nations or areas, have emerged in the field of education. They appear to have the status of genuinely international issues, and have become of much concern in OECD countries as well as in developing countries. How these might have arisen is discussed above, but clearly these international definitions of issues and policies have become very important, especially for developing countries. To a certain extent these issues have become globalised, as all of these matters permit of a worldwide definition and a worldwide treatment.

With globalised definitions, problems, solutions and potential policies it becomes easier for agencies such as UNESCO to prioritise between countries/areas, as all would then be on a common, 'level' playing field. But just as the development of definitions and purported solutions have become globalised, in its applications to developing countries the education offered through the globalised policies will *itself* globalise what is on offer to the young, homogenising language and culture. And it will change the very selves of the young. As education is a key underlying element for the knowledge society, these young will also take part, as they later aspire to and accept positions in that knowledge society, in homogenising education, language and culture. It is not clear that this will happen, but the forces driving these issues seem difficult to oppose.

Jean-François Lyotard's (1984) notion of 'performativity', or the subsumption of education to the efficient functioning of the social system, explains in part how this is all happening, but it is not clear what the alternatives are. Certainly certain kinds of *governable* individuals are required. But the states will only survive if they not only ensure the security and economic well-being and power of the state, but also the welfare and well-being of the population. But if nation states do not survive, how is this to be assured?

New Managerialism and Globalisation

In the restructuring of New Zealand's education system (as in other state education systems) during the 1980s and 1990s there was a significant theoretical and practical shift from an emphasis on *administration and policy* to an emphasis on *management*. This *'new managerialism'* has drawn theoretically, on the one hand, on the model of corporate managerialism and private sector management styles and, on the other hand, on public choice theory and new institutional economics (most notably agency theory and transaction cost analysis). These theories and models have been used both as the legitimating basis and as the instrumental means for the redesigning of state educational bureaucracies, educational institutions and the public policy process.

In practice we can note a decentralisation of management control in schools away from the centre to the individual institution – often referred to as the doctrine of self-management – coupled with new accountability and funding structures. This very important shift has often been accompanied by a disaggregation of large state bureaucracies into autonomous agencies (the splitting up of the old Department of Education in 1988, for example), a clarification of organisational objectives (as in school charters, say), and a separation between policy advice and policy implementation functions (the Ministry of Education advises the Minister, and the Education Review Office evaluates school functioning against charters and policy).

Under this move towards managerialism we should also note a shift from input controls to quantifiable output measures and performance targets, along with an emphasis on short-term performance contracts, especially for CEOs and senior managers. In the interests of so-called productive efficiency, the provision of educational services (teacher aides, advice, etc.) has been made contestable; and, in the interests of so-called allocative efficiency, state education has been marketed (there are 30 plus institutions offering pre-service education for teachers in 2000, as opposed to 7 in 1988) and (partially) privatised (vastly increased fees, high fee-paying international students, etc.).

Despite important and unaddressed questions about the value of managerialism, its legitimating rhetoric and its role in governance, it was imposed by legislation as part of a more comprehensive package of reform. That the application of business practices to educational institutions was highly problematic was not seriously considered in the 1980s and 1990s by successive governments.

Whilst the individual is seen as a utility maximiser (*homo-economicus*), the ways in which managerialism functions as a technology of self-governance are not evident. Whilst managerialism can be seen and understood as part of a new institutional economics, it can also be seen as a mode of governance, underpinned by problematic economic theories. As a mode of governance it will produce selves who are autonomous choosers, committed by self-interest to forms of consumerism (see neo-liberalism section in the Introduction), but also selves who are governable so as to act within certain norms. Managerialism should therefore be characterised as a form of governance (see Foucault, 1979). This is particularly concerning, as managerialism has probably been pushed as far as anything else in the restructuring of government institutions including welfare, health and education. Davis (1997: 228) notes that in New Zealand, 'the logic of managerialism (was pushed) further and faster that any other nation'.

If globalisation is inevitable, then even whilst it is concerned with more than economic factors the application of managerialism to all sectors of New Zealand society opens up the possibility of rapid penetration by the sorts of world view that underlie at least the economic face of globalisation.

Conclusion

Bright futures? Certainly the knowledge economy and society are upon us but what they will bring is another matter. At best we might hope for some kind of compromise between the radical and sceptical positions outlined by Giddens above.

What we can be certain of is that the major restructuring of education that has happened in the last decade or so cannot easily be underdone. True, the Labour Government in 2000 has undone certain things in education: in relation to bulk funding (abolished) and employment contracts; in curtailing de-zoning and moving towards ameliorating the hardships caused by tertiary student fees. The government has also expressed concern at the enforced competition in a tertiary sector which must have limited resources. But there is little or no sign of restoring autonomy to tertiary education. This is because the knowledge society and globalisation demand the subsumption of education, in Lyotard's sense of performativity. Whether that will result in the liberated autonomous individual of traditional liberal education is another matter.

References

Access, 13(2), (1995), Special Edition on Constructivism.
Corson, D. (ed.) (1988), *Education for Work,* Palmerston North: Dunmore Press.
Coxon, E. *et al.* (1994), *The Politics of Learning and Teaching in Aotearoa–New Zealand,* Palmerston North: Dunmore Press.
Davis, G. (1997), 'Implications, Consequences and Futures', in G. Davis, B. Sullivan and A. Yeatman (eds.), *The New Contractualism?* Melbourne: Macmillan.
Dewey, J. (1915), 'Education vs Trade Training: Dr Dewey's reply', *The New Republic* 3,15 May, 42.

Dewey, J. (1916), *Democracy and Education,* New York: Macmillan.
Dewey, J. (1935), 'The Need for Orientation' in J. Dewey (1958), *Philosophy of Education,* New York: Littlefield Adams.
Dewey, J. (1938), *Logic: The Theory of Inquiry,* New York: Holt, Rinehart, Winston.
Fontana Dictionary of Modern Thought (1988), (eds), A. Bullock, O. Stallybrass & S. Tromley, London: Fontana.
Faucault, M. (1979), 'On Governmentality', *Ideology and Consciousness,* 6, 5-26.
Giddens, A. (1991), The Reith Lectures, London: BBC.
Hayek, F.C. (1978), 'Adam Smith's New Message in Today's Language' in *New Studies in Philosophy, Politics, Economics and the Study of Ideas,* London: Routledge & Kegan Paul.
Heidegger, M. (1977), *The Question Concerning Technology and Other Essays,* Transl. W. Lovitt, New York: Harper and Row (Original version of the essay in the title was delivered in 1950).
Hirst, P. H. (1983), *Education and the Foundational Disciplines,* London: Routledge & Kegan Paul.
Information Technology Advisory Group (1999), *What is the Knowledge Economy?* at <http://www.moc.govt.nz/pbt/infotech/knowledge_economy/knowledge_economy-04.html>
Lyotard, J-F. (1984), *The Postmodern Condition: A Report on Knowledge,* Transl. Geoff Bennington and Brian Massumi, Mineappolis: University of Minnesota Press.
Marshall, J. D. (1997a), 'Dewey and the 'New Vocationalism'', in S. Laird (ed.), *Philosophy of Education.,* Urbana, Il.: Philosophy of Education Society.
Marshall, J. D. (1997b), 'Problematising the Individual and Constituting 'the' Self', *Educational Philosophy and Theory,* 29(1), 32–49.
Marshall, J. D. (2000), 'Electronic Writing and the Wrapping of Language', *Journal of Philosophy of Education,* 34 (1), 135–149.
Marshall, J., Peters, M. and Smith, G. (1991), 'The Business Roundtable and the Privatisation of Education: Individualsm and the Attack on Maori', in L. Gordon and J. Codd (eds), *Education Policy and the Changing Role of the State,* Palmerston North: Massey University.
Ministry of Education (1993), *The New Zealand Curriculum Framework,* Wellington: Learning Media.

Ministry of Education (1995), *Technology in the New Zealand Curriculum*, Wellington: Learning Media.

Ministry of Research Science and Technology (1999), *The Knowledge Society*, at <http//www.MORST.govt.nz/bright/know_soc.htm>.

Peters, M., Marshall, J. and Massey, L. (1994), 'Recent Educational Reforms in Aotearoa' in E. Coxon *et al.*, *The Politics of Learning and Teaching in Aotearoa/New Zealand*, Palmerson North: Dunmore Press.

Peters R. S. (1966), *Ethics and Education*, London: George Allen and Unwin.

Poster, M. (1990), *The Mode of Information: Poststructuralism and Social Context*, Cambridge: Polity Press.

Russell, B. (1926), *On Education*, London: George Allen and Unwin.

Sexton, S. (1991), N*ew Zealand Schools: An Evaluation of Recent Reforms and Future Directions*, Wellington: Business Roundtable.

Shipley, J. (ed.) (1999), *Bright Future*, at <http://www.executive.govt.nz//brightfuture/shipley.htm>.

Strike, K.A. (1982), *Educational Policy and the Just Society*, Urbana, Ill.: University of Illinois Press.

Wirth, A. (1988), 'Issues in the Vocational-Liberal Studies Controversy (1900–1917): John Dewey vs the Social Efficiency Philosophers,' in D. Corson (ed.), *Education for Work*, Palmerston North: Dunmore Press.

The Authors

Eve Coxon began her career in education as a primary school teacher and later became a secondary school teacher. Her interest in Pacific education arose out of her experiences as a teacher of Pacific students in Auckland city secondary schools and her study of Pacific anthropology. Her M.A in anthropology included research in Tonga and her Ph.D. thesis focused on the development of education policy in Samoa. Now a senior lecturer in the School of Education, University of Auckland, Eve has undertaken research and/or consultancies in Fiji, Tonga, Samoa, the Cook Islands, the Solomon Islands and Vanuatu. A particular focus of this work is the critical examination of New Zealand's ongoing influence on education policy in Pacific countries.

Roger Dale, formerly of the Open University, has been a Professor of Education at the University of Auckland since 1989. His main interests are in sociology of education and education policy and he has published widely in these areas, particularly upon state theory.

Kuni Kaa Jenkins of Ngāti Porou descent lectures in Maori education at the University of Auckland. She is author, with Kay Morris-Matthews, of *Hukarere and the Politics of Maori Girls' Schooling 1875-1995* (Dunmore Press, 1995) and also of *Te Maranga o te Ihu o Hukarere: A Photographic History* (McMillin Craig Print, 1994). Her teaching career has been in primary schools in Wellington and Auckland, especially involving work with Maori pupils and Maori communities. She has been involved on advisory and educational working parties for Ministry of Education curriculum work and in-service teacher training. She has served on boards associated with the education of Maori girls.

Alison Jones teaches courses on feminist theory and gender in the School of Education at the University of Auckland. She is also Director of the Institute for Research on Gender at the University. She is an author and an editor of several books and articles on gender and feminist theory and pedagogy, including *Bitter Sweet: Indigenous Women in the Pacific,* with

Phyllis Herda and Tamasailau Suaalii, (Otago University Press, 2000), *Women and Education in Aotearoa*, with Sue Middleton (Bridget Williams Books,1992) as well as her still-popular *"At School I've got a Chance" Culture/Privilege: Pacific Islands and Pakeha Girls at School* (Dunmore Press, 1991). She is currently editing a book on teachers touching children.

Diane Mara is a Senior Lecturer in Education at the Wellington College of Education. She teaches professional studies in the primary graduate programme and sociology of education, Pacific Nations education and human development in the college's degree courses. Diane is proud of her Tahitian and English heritages as a first generation New Zealander. Her doctoral studies are focusing on Pacific women in tertiary education in New Zealand: issues of identity, ethnicity and gender.

James Marshall is Professor of Education (former Dean) at the University of Auckland. He was a secondary teacher and a teacher educator in Great Britain for eight years before returning to New Zealand in 1973. His present interests are in educational philosophy and French poststructuralism, especially Michel Foucault. He was a major co-author/editor of *Myths and Realities* (Dunmore Press, 1990 & 1995) and *Learning and Teaching in Aotearoa/New Zealand* (Dunmore Press, 1994).

More recently he is the author/editor of a number of books and monographs, including: *Michel Foucault: Personal Autonomy and Education* (Kluwer,1996), *Discipline and Punishment in New Zealand Education* (with son Dominique - Dunmore Press, 1997), *Wittgenstein: Philosophy, Postmodernism, Pedagogy* (Bergin & Garvey, 1999) and *Education Policy* (Edward Elgar,1999) (the last two with Michael Peters). A co-edited book on Nietzsche will be published in 2000. In addition he has contributed to a number of edited collections and has published widely in international journals in educational philosophy, education, social theory and policy.

Judith Simon is a former member of staff at the University of Auckland, where her last position was as a member of the Research Unit for Maori Education. She spent 20 years as a primary teacher, including eight years in the Maori Schools service and three years in Britain. Returning to university in the mid-1970s she majored in Education and Anthropology, and her doctoral thesis involved both historical and ethnographic research into the place of schooling in Maori-Pakeha relations. Her teaching and research interests are in the history of Maori education policy, sociology of education, and issues of race and ethnicity in education.